TRIAL BY FIRE

TRIAL

BY

FIRE

A Woman Correspondent's
Journey to the Frontline

KATHLEEN BARNES

THUNDER'S
MOUTH
PRESS

WB

Published by Thunder's Mouth Press

54 Greene Street, Suite 4S

New York, N.Y. 10013

First edition.

First printing, 1990

Library of Congress Cataloging-in-Publication Data:

Barnes, Kathleen, 1948–

    Trial By Fire : a woman correspondent's journey to the frontline / by Kathleen Barnes. — 1st ed.

      p.   cm.

    ISBN 1-56025-004-6 : $19.95

    I. Title.

PN4874.B325T75 1990

070'.92—dc20   90-10995

[B]   CIP

Text design by Loretta Li.

Manufactured in the United States of America

12/19/01

FOR CHRISTINE AND JOE —

You were the wind . . .

CONTENTS

PREFACE

THIS BOOK IS MY LIFE, my true colors laid open before you. This is an adventure story, a documentation of historical events, an intense personal journey.

Writing it was at times painful. I had to delve into sad memories, open half-healed wounds, confront old fears, re-examine old failures, and dredge up faces and places I would rather bury. The starving children of Negros, the frightened children of Belfast, the lives ended too soon by bullets from so many insane wars, all of those are engraved indelibly on my memory. But I knew that I couldn't take you along with me on this odessey unless I was totally honest.

I often wondered if it was presumptuous of me, at the ripe old age of forty-two, to write about my life. What could I have to say that you would want to read?

Yet, I answered myself, my experience is unique. Most people, let alone most women, don't throw away comfortable lives to live beyond the pale. Even today, I often feel my stomach lurch in fear. Can I make it on my own? Although I display a demeanor of confidence, I am often terribly unsure of myself. Despite the professional accolades I have received, I sometimes wonder if those who judge me with such warmth aren't making a mistake.

But I feed on the challenge, on the newness of each day, on the excitement of unfolding history. I realize my identity is intertwined with my career. I cannot imagine any other profession that would challenge and excite me the way journalism does. We journalists live on the edge, constantly searching out the next bit of excitement. I have been accused of being an adrenalin junkie. I plead guilty to this charge.

As a woman, I think I have brought a degree of sensitvity to my writing. My male colleagues are no less moved by what they witness, but some cultural mores make them rely on more than numbers. I think that you who read and watch my stories want to know about people, feelings, fears. I want to take you there—to not only experience the facts, but also delve below the surface and experience the feelings.

Successful women are often called bitches. I have had my share of that. But my ambition had always been very personal. I compete with myself and rarely with anyone else. If I have stepped on toes along the way, I humbly apologize. My success is based on a firm belief, insecurities notwithstanding, that whatever happens in my world is my own creation. I have had a lot of help along the way. But my successes and failures are my own responsibility. I program my life to win. I work hard for what I want, and most of the time, I have won.

For readers who are wishing for more in their lives, I hope this book will serve as a catalyst. For readers who want a good yarn, this is it. All of the events are true. Except where I have indicated, all of the characters are identified by their real names. Only a few people are protected for their own safety. There is no fiction. I believe reality is much more graphic than fiction.

KATHLEEN BARNES
Manila, January 1990

1

FULL CIRCLE: *Manila, June 1988*

I CRADLED THE .38 IN TWO HANDS, trying to sight down its stubby barrel despite my trembling hands. The target twenty yards away was shaped like a man. I was to aim for the heart.

"Go on! Pull the trigger!" my instructor urged.

Time froze. I was suspended in the moment, arms outstretched, finger on the trigger, reviewing the lifetime of violence I had experienced in the four years since I left the United States.

I thought of my shock while I watched a rotting mess that was the body of a young woman, a human rights worker, as it was exhumed from its temporary grave. The woman's mother wailed. We friends clutched each other and gagged and wept at the sight of an unrecognizable lump of meat that was once a vibrant and laughing woman. As the corpse was lifted, a tiny fetus dropped from its mother's body.

I thought of my helpless frustration at the moment I became convinced that I was about to die at the hands of abusive soldiers on a dark and frighteningly isolated rural road. Of how I wished I had a gun. And of how that wish was followed by the paralyzing fear and deep certainty that there was nothing I could do to fight them all off even if I had an arsenal at my disposal.

I wanted to weep when I remembered the three innocent men walking down a street, greeting passing soldiers with chants of "Cory! Cory!" and being mercilessly mowed down by dark-of-the-night soldiers who had chosen that tranquil moonlit night to attempt to overthrow the government.

I thought of my rage in a hospital emergency room when I held the hand of a friend who had been shot. In the same nanosecond, I thought of the face of a demonstrator captured on film. The woman's mute rage expressed so eloquently her agony over the death of her husband at the hands of soldiers of private armies who wanted to stop their protest.

I grieved as I remembered the bullet-riddled car that had been parked in my driveway only a few weeks before, still reeking of the blood and brains of a man who was nearly my brother. I had never fired a gun before. Yet an avalanche of events brought me to that instant in time when a life decision had become necessary. If I pulled that trigger, would I become part of that violence myself? I felt a gnawing pain in the pit of my stomach.

How could I throw away a lifetime of sincere belief that violence begets violence? All of those college days of peace marches and antiwar editorials? All of those nights spent drinking wine with friends and theorizing about how I would react if armed villains invaded my home? All of those hours of meditating on the mysteries of life and death that resulted in a deep personal belief that God is embodied in each human life? All of my highbrow soliloquies on the evolution of society beyond violence became compressed into that single instant, that single tiny motion of squeezing a trigger.

I swayed, on the verge of fainting.

Then I squeezed the trigger.

PAK!

I shuddered.

The bullet plunked into the target's shoulder.

"Wow!" whistled the colonel, a friend who had insisted on teaching me to shoot.

His fellow officers applauded. "Are you sure you have never fired a gun before?" one asked.

I fired again, with more confidence. Another hit, this time in the target's abdomen. If that paper and straw target were a man, he would be dead by now. My hand still trembled, my stomach still burned, my head was still light. But it seemed that my eye was steady.

PAK. PAK. PAK.

Two more in the target. One near miss.

The colonels began to make jokes about Deadeye Dick. They didn't know me. They didn't know what personal price I paid each time I pulled that trigger. I didn't feel at all like Superwoman, but my hand wasn't shaking anymore.

"Try this .45," one offered.

The .45 was heavier and had a bigger kick. I only hit the target three of five times.

I hated it, but I was achieving my objective of feeling comfortable with guns.

A couple of weeks before, I had returned to Manila from a long trip to the States. I had returned to an empty house that still echoed with the pain of the death I had recently suffered. The house reverberated with a very real threat to my life and the lives of those I loved.

My first night home, the phone rang. A sinister woman's voice hissed, over and over, "I'll kill you bitch."

I began to lie awake listening for sounds in the night.

Her calls became a daily burden. She would sometimes repeat her hate message into my answering machine a dozen times until it ended in a screeching crescendo of fury.

After nearly four years in Manila, I was feeling overwhelmed by the violence of the culture that surrounded me.

I was tired of the McDonald's security guards who brandished shotguns in some paranoid fear of Big Mac thieves. I was tired of the swaggering goons carrying clutch bags concealing handguns. I was tired of the need to stay completely on the alert for robbers, whether in a taxi, on a jeepney or walking down the street.

One night over drinks in a rowdy Australian bar, I had confided my fears to the colonel, who was strictly a professional source, but who would soon become a friend.

He demanded to know if I was living alone and if I had a gun. I answered "yes" to both.

"Do you know how to fire a gun?" he asked.

"Well, I guess you just pull the trigger," I hedged. I was terrified of guns. To me, they were like snakes waiting to strike. Yet there was a gun, a strangely placed gift of love, paradoxically nestling on my bedside table with a picture of the man I loved, an incense burner and a subliminal tape, the gift of a concerned friend, called "Getting Out of Anger."

"You come out to the range and I'll teach you how to shoot," the colonel insisted.

After several invitations that eventually became demands, I went to the shooting range one Saturday. My friend noticed I was lacking in enthusiasm.

He matter-of-factly cleaned the .38 while he explained its function to me. My mind refused to focus on his words. I simply stared mesmerized at the instrument of death in his hand. I wondered if it was the same type of gun that had killed the human rights worker, or that had blown out the brains of countless rebels, policemen, soldiers, Catholics, Protestants, Muslims and ordinary folk all over the world.

The colonel gave me some ear plugs and showed me how to cradle the gun to steady shaking hands.

I shot several dozen rounds that day. By that time I had become sufficiently at ease and confident of my capability to hit the target. I finally convinced myself the gun would not explode if I touched it. My colonels dubbed me a crack shooter.

I thought back to a bucolic summer day on the St. Lawrence River a bare five years before. I thought of how far I had traveled in those five years, in terms of physical distance and in even greater personal terms. I had turned all of my belief systems upside down in a search for the meaning of violence. I had lived in the heart of violence and I had not emerged unscathed.

My bizarre odyssey has led me to strange, confusing and frightening places. I have met the great; those the world thinks are great, and the humble. I have met the everyday people who have left indelible marks on my soul. I have been excited, scared out of my wits and always challenged.

My quest to understand the roots of violence left me on that Manila shooting range with a .38 in my hand, more confused than ever.

I doubt if I will ever be psychologically capable of shooting another human being. But then I think of my days of rage and I wonder.

2

CHRYSALIS: *August 1983–February 1984*

I AM THE CHILD OF MIDDLE AMERICA, a baby boomer who dallied with radical politics in the sixties, with inner consciousness in the seventies and restlessness in the eighties. I'm really no different from my comrades in this confused generation. Perhaps a little crazier, perhaps a little more adventurous.

In 1983 I was thirty-five years old. I had been a reporter for a small-town newspaper in upstate New York for eleven years and wife of a fellow journalist for thirteen years. I studied and taught yoga to give my life some meaning. The provincialism of Watertown, New York was suffocating.

I had never traveled outside the United States with the exception of brief forays into Canada and Mexico that didn't really count. Small-town American life was like a cocoon: safe, warm, secure, insulated from all the vagaries of a world gone mad.

It was also completely unexciting. I was in the midst of my mid-life crisis. I knew it was time for change. I wasn't unhappy, but I wasn't happy, either.

Summers in northern New York had their bucolic charm. My usual seven A.M. to three P.M. shift at the *Watertown Daily Times* left me free to while away the long summer afternoons in my beautiful little wooden boat, the *Dalliance*, on the St. Lawrence River. The *Dalliance* and the river were my escape from the increasing discontent of a dead-end job and a marriage that had lost its zest years before.

Everything began to move into perspective on one of those rare sultry summer days to which we clung so tightly along the Canadian border.

The breeze was cool, but the sun was uncharacteristically hot that day as I drifted aimlessly in the *Dalliance*, sharing a bottle of ice cold white wine with my dearest friend, Christine Burkard-Eggleston.

We sipped wine from plastic cups, attempting in vain to get some color into our pallid white bodies. It was hopeless. There simply isn't enough sustained sunshine in the Thousand Islands to get a serious tan. Northern New York bears a marked resemblance to the Arctic Circle for most of the year. I listened to the swells slapping the wooden bottom of the *Dalliance* and dreamed of Mediterranean beaches.

Although it was early August, the St. Lawrence was still bitter cold. Most of my friends were too squeamish to swim in the freezing and murky waters of the huge river, but I insisted on swimming frequently, even in May when a quick dive in the water would leave me with heart pounding, gasping for breath.

"What if . . ." Christine began, but her voice trailed off to watch a gaudy yellow seaplane flying fifty feet over our heads, a stunning contrast to the brilliant blue of the sky and the flaming red of a nearby boathouse.

She began again, "What would you do if you could do anything in the world?"

It was a familiar game.

I replied without hesitating, "I'd travel and write."

I stopped for a moment, surprised at myself.

I began to fantasize that I'd go to Beirut or Belfast or some bloody and violent place.

"Why bloody places?" Christine wanted to know. It was difficult for her to believe that her best friend could actually choose to live in the midst of violence.

"You, Barnes, a leftover hippie? I don't believe it!" Christine choked.

I was a radical college newspaper editor in the anti-Vietnam war days, thrown out of Purdue University for offending the stolid Indiana governor by playing "The Stars and Stripes Forever" on a kazoo during a peace demonstration in 1970. I was her foolish friend who nursed infant mice back to health after their nest was invaded by my horde of adopted street cats. I was the one who refused to enter a friend's house when I learned he kept guns.

It was beyond the scope of Christine's imagination that I would seek out violence.

I mentally cross-examined myself as I continued to sip my wine. I shudder as I look back on the ingenuousness of my answer, an appalling naivete for someone who had lived for thirty-five years.

It was precisely because I didn't understand violence that I had become fascinated with the idea of examining violence more closely. America has become so sanitized and insulated. We don't understand violence or why people engage in it. I had never seen a dead body. Death rarely happens in our midst. It is always at a distance. Maybe Americans have become too removed from the consequences of their actions and the actions of their government. Maybe violence has become too impersonal. Violence is something entertaining. Something on television and in movies, something that happens to someone else. I didn't crave the touch of violence for myself. I simply wanted to understand why religious and political differences so often resulted in death, and so often the deaths of innocents. It seemed a barbaric and ineffectual means of settling arguments.

I thought of writing about war and about other types of violence by telling the personal stories of the victims. I wanted to make the horror glaringly real.

It was complex, yet so simple at the same time.

Christine turned interrogator.

"Why don't you go?" she demanded.

With characteristic self-defeat, I ticked off the reasons why my fantasy was an impossible one. I couldn't leave a marriage of thirteen years, could I? What would I do about money? I had none to speak of. How could I leave a comfortable job for the uncertainty of travel in foreign lands?

Christine and I have always had a relationship of brutal frankness, and that summer day was her finest moment.

As she poured herself another cup of wine from the jug, she said, "I have watched you wither here. Face it, your marriage to Bert isn't all that exciting. Your talents are far beyond what the *Watertown Daily Times* deserves. And money, you know, there's a way, somehow. Why not think about how you can do it rather than why you can't?"

A week later, there was another languid afternoon on the St. Lawrence. I sat with several friends on the dock of the beautiful red boathouse while my husband, Bert Gault, played another of his endless rounds of golf.

That afternoon, a group of heavy-drinking friends idly gossiped about who was having an affair with whom, listing the latest divorces and speculating about who would run for sheriff in November.

Suddenly, with the same shock I would have received if I had dived into the freezing river, I realized that I could be sitting on the same dock in thirty years, drinking the same Bloody Marys and listening to the same people swapping the same pointless gossip. I was absolutely positive that I didn't want to spend my life that way. I felt choked with claustrophobia. I had built walls of security in my life that had trapped me in an existence I could no longer tolerate.

A couple of weeks later, there was another summer day, another body of water. This time Bert and I were on a vacation at a lovely lake in the Adirondacks. It was isolated and quiet. I had spent three days doing very little. I had polished the varnished hull of my humble little *Dalliance*, all fifteen antique feet of which was mine, paid for and maintained (very expensively) by me alone. But three days were enough. I had reached the limits of my tolerance for idleness. It was time to go into town for a news fix. I needed a *New York Times*.

The seven-mile boat ride was exhilarating. I recklessly opened the motor all the way, even though I wasn't familiar with the waters.

In town, I stopped at a little cafe, bought the *Times*, ready to sit down for a cup of coffee and a good read.

The three-deck headline in the upper right-hand corner stopped me before I got to a table: "Marcos Foe Slain As He Goes Home From Exile in US."

I didn't know anything about the Philippines except there was some sort of dictator named Marcos there. I had never heard of Aquino and, I confess, I would have been hard pressed to identify the Philippines on a map. But it was clear to me there was something seriously wrong there.

It was August 22, 1983. I would personally have summoned the little men in the white jackets if anyone had told me on that day that I would be living in the Philippines a year later.

It was as if that headline catalyzed me into a decision that had been lurking just under the surface of my consciousness since the day Christine and I floated down the river.

Dalliance and I returned to the cabin in the special golden glow of the late Adirondack afternoon and found Bert absorbed in a spy thriller I had left him with, his can of Bud at his elbow.

"Let's talk," I said.

For more than ten years, Bert and I had been reporters for the *Watertown Daily Times*, a regional paper with a circulation of 45,000 in a town of less than 30,000. It was a pleasant existence, but hardly challenging. I had covered the courts, murder trials, juicy lawsuits and, for the past two years, I had focused on the activities of white supremacists and neo-Nazis in the area. I felt I was one of the *Times's* best writers, but I was stagnant. I wasn't improving. I knew there was more.

Bert was and is a gem. But somehow, the romance had left our relationship. The love was still there, but it had evolved into a comfortable brother-sister co-existence. Where we had once shared almost every interest, we had few passions in common anymore. He was addicted to golf. I hated tramping around in the hot sun. I love the water and particularly my *Dalliance* and its predecessor, a very tipsy sunfish. Bert can barely swim. Bert reveled in small-town political battles. I suffocated in smoke-filled rooms. We had already had every possible political discussion and knew one another's arguments to the letter.

I explained how confined I was feeling. I told him I needed a change. That wasn't any surprise to Bert. He knew of the insatiable itch that had been nagging at me for years. We had both tried to find other jobs, but in those post-Watergate days when journalism was a much-glamorized profession, it was difficult to find one job, let alone two. Besides, I knew that Bert was very comfortable with his well-crafted political reporting for the *Watertown Times* and the ease of small-town life. He had found his home.

I reached for Bert's hand, hoping desperately I wouldn't see the pain in his eyes that I knew would be there. "I need to do something else. I need to leave Watertown," I whispered, unsure of my embryonic decision.

Without a sign of the pain I had expected, Bert said he was surprised it had taken me so long to make my decision.

"I love you. I'll always love you and I know you must go on to bigger and better things," he said, gripping my hand.

I felt a flood of gratitude and relief. I didn't deserve such unswerving support. Many of the failures in our marriage had been mine. I knew he would always be a beloved friend.

It was a beginning and an end. We talked and made plans late into the night.

The Philippines was in my thoughts only because of the Ninoy Aquino assassination. I gave no serious thought to going there. Not at that time, anyway. Maybe I subconsciously wanted my first foreign adventure to be, well, not too foreign. That's why we talked about Belfast that night and for many nights afterward.

Ireland had always drawn me, maybe because of some real and some imagined Irish roots. My father always called me, "Kathleen Mavourneen" (Gaelic for "my darling") when I was a child.

I saw Ireland as a land of shadows and light. The "Troubles" of the craggy North, the beauty of the rolling green hills of the South, the melancholic charm and sudden passions of its people.

Our big-hearted friends Mike and Jackie Schell had been hosts to a little girl from Belfast that summer. The unsubtle differences between Michelle Miles and the Schell's five rowdy girls made me even more curious to know about her country where people have been killing each other for generations, all in the name of some warped God. Michelle, a Protestant, was appalled the first time the Catholic Schells tried to take her to mass. She believed with the utter simplicity that only a nine-year-old can muster that God would strike her dead if she crossed the threshold of the Catholic church. I wondered if she would grow to a stunted womanhood, herself engulfed in the hatred that has crippled her land.

A few months in bloody Belfast seemed like a good beginning for me. Then I had nebulous ideas about traveling to the Middle East and perhaps South Africa. My ideas were ridiculously unformed.

It was Bert's suggestion that I ask my moderately well-off grandmother for financial help.

Grandma, at eighty-five, was fading in and out of the Alzheimer's disease that would trap her in helpless victimhood for four more years before releasing her to a welcome death. Grandma was very sharp the day I called. She was excited about my idea. I think she saw my plan as a fulfillment of the unfinished dreams she had as a girl before the conventions of marriage and post-Victorian society trapped her. During an uncharacteristically long stretch of lucidity, Grandma told me, "Go. Do it. Live your life now. I don't see any reason why you should wait for your inheritance until I die. I want to see your success."

I don't know if Grandma ever really understood my ABC broadcast tapes that my doting mother played for her or the occasional television appearances I made or the clippings of my stories sent from newspapers all over the world. I hope she somehow understood that she provided the means for me to reach for my dreams.

The last hurdle: my job. Could I really take the risk of resigning and having nothing to fall back on? The thought made me feel sick to my stomach.

John Johnson, Jr., the *Watertown Times*'s managing editor and I saw eye to eye on almost nothing. We had many city room shouting matches and many disagreements about news judgment. After ten years we had come to a grudging truce based on a wary mutual respect neither of us was willing to admit.

One day in September, I straightened my shoulders, took a deep breath and walked into his office, determined to eliminate that last obstacle.

"I want a year's leave of absence," I announced. "I want to travel and write and learn about the world."

Even to myself I sounded embarrassingly naive, like some cardboard character in a soap opera.

"OK," John agreed, barely hesitating to consider. "But there's one condition. You must stay away the entire year. You can't come back before January 1, 1985."

My stomach lurched. Those were big stakes. I would have to support myself outside the womb of the *Times* for at least a year. I didn't know if I could do it professionally, emotionally or financially.

I gulped down my panic and agreed.

The next few months were a frenzy of preparations.

I did not have a clue how to be a free-lancer. There seemed to be a conspiracy of silence among my colleagues. No one wanted to tell me how to find people who might be interested in my stories, how to transmit stories, how much I should be paid. I was not an initiate to their secret society, which does not share its mysteries. It was terribly frustrating.

I was well aware I wasn't doing this thing the conventional way. If I had done it the conventional way, I would have gotten a job with some larger and more respected newspaper than the *Watertown Times*. I would move up through the newsroom again, covering police and fires and city council meetings until, maybe, in five or ten years, with a lot of luck, I would get a foreign assignment. But I was finished with fires and school board meetings. I had paid my dues. I wasn't willing to wait anymore.

So I began to bombard newspapers, magazines and wire services with letters. Next, I would shamelessly namedrop to bull and cajole my way into the offices of bigwigs. I went to Washington twice and New York once attempting to gather clients and visas.

I still was thinking of making my way to Lebanon, but the Lebanese were particularly obstreperous. They wouldn't give me a visa as a journalist unless some media organization was willing to take responsibility for me. My explanation that I was self-employed had no effect whatever on the friendly Lebanese diplomats who smiled politely, nodded their heads and continued to insist chauvinistically that as a "little girl all alone," I needed a daddy to take care of me. That outraged me.

I finally gave up the Lebanese visa application in helpless frustration.

But I did manage to get a glimmer of hope from *Newsweek* and the Associated Press, who agreed to introduce me to their London bureaus.

A wonderful lady named Sandy Close runs Pacific News Service in San Francisco. Sandy is a leftover hippie a few years older than I am. She is very willing to support adventuresome journalists. She pays almost nothing, but she is willing, sight unseen, to provide invaluable letters of introduction that enabled me and many of my colleagues to obtain press credentials from foreign governments.

Armed with Sandy's credential, more than 100 batteries (I wasn't sure if I could buy them in the remote reaches of Northern Ireland), and a heart fluttering with apprehension, I set off.

On February 5, 1984, Bert saw me off at the Syracuse Airport. We sat silently holding hands in the departure area of the airport. I felt like I was waiting for an execution. There was so much to say, and at the same time nothing left to say.

It felt like an amputation. I had excised my entire past life and turned to face something unknown, at once fascinating and terrifying. It was my first venture into self-reliance. My fear and pain were almost paralyzing.

When my flight was called, I hugged Bert goodbye. Finally, some sort of self-anesthesia had taken effect. I was numb. Bert's forlorn face would come back to me at many difficult and lonely moments over the next few months. I fought off the last-minute urge to run back to him and say it was all a joke, that I never really intended to leave. He told me later he went out to the car and sat in the snow-covered parking lot and cried for an hour.

I'm glad I didn't see that. It was Bert's unwavering support and that of Christine and my family and numerous friends that gave me the courage to know I could face the world on my own.

My journey had begun.

Even at the darkest moments I never doubted the rightness of the decision that began that sunny day on the *Dalliance*.

3

LONDON AND BELFAST: *February 1984*

I WAS ASTONISHED AND DELIGHTED that London looked exactly like the travel posters. Double-decker buses, bobbies and taxi drivers who called me "Luv." I was unabashedly charmed. There were the earliest signs of English spring. A few daffodils poking their heads through the moist earth raised my spirits immensely. I felt like I had been let out of the prison of the interminable northern New York winter.

I always thought jet lag was a figment of the imagination, until I spent two days wanting to fall asleep at one o'clock in the afternoon fighting the urge to go jogging at one A.M.

Once my body recovered from the time shock, I spent a few days being a simple tourist, burying myself in the British Museum, the cheap seats at the theaters, the Tower of London, the pandas at the zoo. I indulged in shameless people-watching—the eccentrics in the underground, the punks in Picadilly Circus, the pubs and their rough clientele, even the old ladies feeding the squirrels in the parks. I had come alive. London was a kaleidoscope of sensory input after the colorlessness of Watertown. There was a bounce in my step and a smile on my face for even the most phlegmatic of Brits.

Then the time came to for me to learn the ropes of the free-lance business. I started by literally knocking on every door in town. AP, UPI, *Newsweek*, the *Guardian*, the *Times*. I knew of no other way than just to present myself and hope to convince them to buy stories from me. How could I convince them? I had never even been to Belfast. I knew nothing about it. I felt like I was being very bold and perhaps making a fool of myself by daring to knock on those hallowed doors. But I kept reminding myself, "If you don't knock, the door will never open."

After all these years, I have found that there is still no more effective method of getting editors interested in my work than legwork. I knock on doors, literally and by telephone and by mail. If you knock on a hundred doors, one or two people are bound to open up. But it is grueling work and not an occupation for the thin-skinned.

Of course, as in nearly every business, it helps if you know somebody. I didn't know a soul, but I had a few names given to me by people whose doors I had knocked on in New York.

I didn't have much success at the beginning. AP and UPI were polite but cool. After all, I was unknown. A pocketful of clippings of my *Watertown Daily Times* stories wasn't a big bargaining tool.

Some editors were rude. The London newspapers insisted chauvinistically that no one was interested in Northern Ireland anymore.

My self-confidence plummeted. The bubble of delight began to burst. I started to doubt my ability to convince anyone I had anything important to say.

I got a much better reception from Tony Clifton at *Newsweek*. Tony, who was phenomenally busy, found time to meet with an unknown and inexperienced free-lancer. He gave my sagging ego a boost at a time when loneliness and the terror of what I had left behind were starting to catch up with me. He made no promises, but he did it graciously. For that I will always be grateful.

I could see I needed more time to get used to the British way of doing things. Maybe it was that aloofness and dryness that was wounding my wide-open American psyche. I hadn't been in London for a day when I heard my first Irish joke, which is the rough equivalent in terms of ethnic slur to Polish jokes told in the States. I was offended. At second glance, the Brits weren't very endearing.

And I was lonely. I was so far away from friends, family, from anything familiar. I had chosen to go to London first because I thought it wouldn't be too unfamiliar. I laugh now to think of it, but I was in intense culture shock in those first few weeks. Maybe it was a shock because it was similar, but so different. I felt like Kurt Vonnegut's Billy Pilgrim who was always coming unstuck in time.

One day I ordered a ploughman's lunch in a crusty little pub. English food was predictable and bland, but I got a rude shock when I slathered some fiery hot mustard on my cheese. Tears gushed from my eyes. I found out what it meant to have my hair literally stand on end. My face flushed purple while everyone in the pub roared with laughter. It was the wrong timing. I was humiliated. My loneliness caught up with me. I couldn't stop the tears. I laid some bills on the table and stumbled into the street.

There were breaks in the loneliness. One was provided by an overzealous Italian who followed me from the theater and back to my hotel and then sent me flowers the next day along with his profession of undying love. It was flattering, but he quickly became a nuisance.

Pamela Carrington was a breath of fresh air in the growing darkness of my new world. Pamela was a friend of a friend in Watertown. She was warm and American and had been living in London and working in a publishing house for ten years. She knew the ropes and she understood. Pamela invited me and four other people to her postage-stamp-size apartment one night. She cooked an amazing gourmet dinner in the closet kitchen while climbing over everyone's legs. My strongest memory of that night was how all six of us had to stand and fold up the table in order for anyone to go into the bathroom. It was the kind of college days humble living that I had always found romantic.

After a week, I flew to Belfast, steeling myself for the worst.

Belfast is one of the ugliest cities in the world. It is crammed with factories, smokestacks, barbed wire fences and dreary houses. The entire downtown shopping district was surrounded by a high security fence. No cars were allowed inside the barricades because of the numerous car bombings. Pedestrians and bus passengers were carefully searched before they were allowed inside. The dismal rain and February cold didn't make Belfast any more pleasant. I desperately tried to be cheerful by grasping at the smallest delights—a single daffodil pathetically struggling for survival in someone's weedy front garden, even the grimy turn-of-the-century government buildings that are of only the barest interest. I sent tape-recorded journals home to my family in which I tried to present a cheery picture, but my voice betrayed my depression.

It was necessary for me to find a place to live, and quickly. The bed and breakfast in the quaint brownstone with the cabbage rose curtains was too expensive.

I copied several addresses from the notice board in the post office and spent an entire day in the freezing rain, trudging from one depressing flat to another. By nightfall my fingers were stiff. I wasn't sure, but I was afraid there were frozen tears on my numbed cheeks. It didn't matter anymore. I was totally miserable as I walked up the front walk of the last place on my list and rang the bell.

A young man answered. Without even asking who I was or what I wanted, he drew me inside and gave me a cup of hot, milky tea. I had found my home.

The brownstone on Malone Avenue wasn't fancy, but there were coal-burning fireplaces that gave off a bit of heat, and there was lots of warmth from the five people sharing the house. Jimmy, the young folk singer who won my heart that first night, was an architecture student and a Protestant, "a Prod," he laughed with a devilish look in his eye. After the cup of tea, Jimmy offered me a "spot of poteen," fiery Irish moonshine that can make you go blind. He brandished a match as he lit a teaspoonful to demonstrate that it was pure, a comforting guarantee against blindness.

Jimmy shared his room with Mickey, a moon-faced zoology student who happened to be a Catholic. Jimmy and Mickey were boyhood friends who had crossed sectarian barriers by attending the Quaker School in suburban Lisburn, the only haven of neutrality in a country mad with religious division. They constantly bantered about their religious differences, but I soon learned that most of their bickering was in jest, unlike that of their countrymen.

Then there was Geraldine, a thick-accented Catholic geographer turned nursing student, and her fiance, Peter, a philosophy graduate turned dog food salesman.

The last room was occupied by Paul, a mysterious bartender at a nearby pub who kept to himself and played his collection of two or three rock tapes dozens of times in the room next to mine until I thought I would lose my mind.

We were like the cast of one of those zany and incomprehensible British sitcoms.

I was to have the pink-flowered room at the top of the house. It was well lighted, but woefully unheated. After a few days when my fingers were so cold I couldn't type, I bought a pair of those little wool gloves without fingers. They did no good. I finally remedied the situation with the purchase of a second-hand gas heater that I could use during the day. I was terrified to leave the gas lit while I slept, so I made do with a thick comforter. It was really difficult to get out of bed and face the freezing mornings. I developed a twenty-five-yard dash, which entailed jumping out of bed, lighting the gas heater, sprinting down to the second floor, turning on the immersion heater so I could get an inch of tepid hot water in the icy bathtub, then fleeing back to the warmth of my bed to listen to the news on the BBC while I waited for the room to warm up and the bath water to heat. After a couple of weeks of practice, I could do it all in less than thirty seconds.

I soon learned that it was highly unusual for Protestants and Catholics to share the same house. I was to live right in the center of The Troubles. My flatmates were ordinary people. The Troubles did not have a great effect on our home life, although there were times when, in the midst of all the joking and banter among lifelong friends, there were raw nerves and reminders of deep-running divisions. I was at first puzzled that a bunch of twenty-year-olds would want a thirty-five-year-old woman living with them, but I think they were excited by the novelty of having a pet American in the house. They mocked my accent endlessly. All Irish have an appallingly bad John Wayne imitation of American accents. For my part, I frequently couldn't understand a word they were saying.

"Are we all speaking the same language?" I would inquire innocently.

Mickey delighted in holding up a pair of trousers and asking me if they were paaaaaaants, or a biscuit and asking me if it was a cooooooookie. I would tease them with my mental image of a "car park"—a field of automobiles with geraniums sprouting from the hoods, whoops, I mean bonnets. We got along famously.

If I was going to be a journalist in Belfast, I needed to have a telephone. There was a phone in the Malone Avenue house, but it had long since been disconnected. I was told it was easy to have it reconnected. A few journalists I met told me it was simply a matter of giving the telephone company time to install the bug. I thought they were joking.

A couple of weeks later, I came home to find a workman on the roof. I asked what he was doing and he mumbled something in such a thick accent I couldn't understand a word of it. I asked him to repeat his answer several times, but I still couldn't make any sense of what he was saying. The phone was connected later in the day. It wasn't long before there was evidence it was bugged. Cracks, pops, wheezes and echoes annoyingly punctuated every conversation. I learned to make sensitive calls from pay phones.

I began to make some contacts. Ordinary people on the bus would always talk to me when they heard my American accent. There aren't many tourists in Northern Ireland, so I was a novelty. I met John Trew, the somewhat shell-shocked editor of the Protestant *Belfast Telegraph* in a pub and he introduced me to his Jewish wife, Karen, a psychology professor at Queens University. Since no one could be neutral in the sectarian violence in Northern Ireland, Karen was considered a Protestant since she was married to one.

In general, the journalists were unhelpful, and finally hostile. I was puzzled until I learned too late that some of them felt threatened that I would take away jobs from them.

In time, I met the Peace People, winners of the 1983 Nobel Peace Prize, and I met Andy Tyrie of the Ulster Defense Association, a group of Protestant para-military thugs who were most definitely not candidates for the Nobel Peace Prize. Nor were their opposite numbers, Gerry Adams and Sinn Fein, the barely disguised political wing of the Irish Republic Army.

And I met John McCullough, a young Catholic teacher, only about a week after I arrived. John offered to take me on a walking tour of Belfast, so we set off one cloudy Saturday morning. I had my little pocket camera and was casually snapping photos here and there. In front of the courthouse, I took a photo of the statue of the lady with her scales of justice partly blocked by the barbed wire atop the courthouse fence. Within seconds, we were accosted by a squad of young Scottish soldiers, weapons pointing at us. They demanded I hand over my film.

I had been warned not to take photographs of any police stations or policemen or soldiers and I had complied. I couldn't understand why we were being treated this way. I told them so, but got no reply. They demanded my passport and John's identification papers. Then they started to ask far more questions than they had a right to ask. I was at first righteously indignant. I resisted, stalling for time in hope they would forget about my film. Once they had established that I was a journalist, the freckle-faced nineteen-year-old in charge began to ask some very insistent questions about what type of stories I was planning to write. I had already been clued in by the American consulate what was acceptable and what was not. I told them I wanted to speak with the consulate.

Freckle-face smirked and told me that since it was Saturday the consulate was closed.

"I can get in touch with them, don't you worry," I snapped back. I was furious that I could be treated this way. I insisted that Freckle-face either arrest us if we had committed a crime or let us go. This wasn't America, that was abundantly clear, but I made the mistake of believing that justice would prevail.

John wasn't at all sure of that. He was standing half a pace behind me, a grown man trembling in fear of these teenaged thugs in uniform. I was foolishly too angry to be frightened. Freckle-face seemed to be somewhat cowed by my churlish response. He eased off a little. But it was clear we weren't getting away from them until I turned over the film. I carefully wrote down the address of their regiment so I could retrieve it later. They told us we could go.

As we turned our backs on them. John walked briskly with a curious robotlike gait. He said he was waiting for them to shoot us in the back. I told him that was silly, they couldn't do such a thing. He looked at me with an expression of exasperation, "This sort of thing happens all the time. You had better get used to it. You will be stopped and questioned ten times a day. It doesn't help to get mad. We've all learned to just roll with the waves."

John was right. I realized, too late, that my abrasiveness had unnecessarily endangered him. It wasn't the last time that my insensitivity endangered others. That was a lesson long and painful in the learning.

I got the processed film back, along with an apology from the police. I joked with the police spokesman that I should just turn my film over to them any time I had some to be developed, since the processing was cheaper.

It was hard to get used to the saturation presence of police and soldiers. Often they would play cops-and-robbers games, skulking around corners and crouching in darkened doorways with their weapons ready. Many times I saw them take aim at the backsides of unsuspecting passersby, whether with purpose or for sport, I never discovered. Soldiers would patrol the streets in their Saracen armored personnel carriers, two facing opposite directions, weapons ready, in the turret was an antenna-like device extending a couple of feet over their heads. The antenna was designed to deflect nearly invisible wires stretched at neck level across the street by unfriendlies who dreamed of decapitating soldiers.

The soldiers would stop us. John was right. It didn't happen ten times a day, but interrogations once or twice a day became routine. "What is your name? Where do you live? Where are you going? Do you know anything about _____ incident?" That was all they were allowed to ask by law unless they had specific suspicions. They were usually polite, but not always. In a few weeks, I stopped being angry about the intrusions, and became bored like everyone else. I was quickly acclimatized.

People in Belfast had a defense mechanism I noticed almost immediately. They totally ignored the military presence. Even when they were being questioned, they would adopt the bland facial expressions of people talking to machines. It was classic avoidance. The Northern Irish lived by a simple credo—pretend all of those guys with high-powered weapons don't have them aimed at you. Just go on with your life and mind your own business. Stay alive.

Twenty-five years had passed since the most recent spate of the ancient Troubles had begun. A generation. And the Northern Irish had adapted in the best way they knew how: avoidance.

"It's the only way I can cope with the anger," said my roommate Mickey during a rare serious moment.

I met the family of ten-year-old Michelle Miles, the little Protestant girl who had come to Watertown the summer before. They were a warm, loving family who welcomed me like a sister. Michelle's father, John, had recently gotten a job as a bus driver after eighteen months of unemployment following the abortive Delorean Motors luxury-car adventure that dashed the hopes of so many Northern Irish. John's wife, Yvonne, was a cook in the cafeteria of a large company. They were struggling along and barely making ends meet in a tenement in the working-class Protestant section. Three short blocks away from the Miles's house was a twenty-foot-high corrugated iron fence, topped with barbed wire. It separated the Miles's Protestant section from a Catholic section. I thought it was terribly sad that children from those two areas would grow up, never meeting, never even seeing each other. No wonder kids like Michelle were afraid God would strike them dead if they crossed the threshold of a Catholic church.

A few weeks into my stay in Belfast, I was astonished to see the construction of new brick walls separating some sections; twenty feet high with barbed wire across the top. It saddened me. The corrugated iron fences were ugly, but they had a feeling of temporariness. The brick walls were depressingly permanent, like The Troubles.

One day when I was walking up the Falls Road, a Catholic ghetto with a 75 percent unemployment rate, I met a woman holding a three-day-old baby. I chucked the baby under the chin and we exchanged pleasantries. When I told her I was a journalist, the young mother confided her deepest fear to me: that her child would never have a job.

To grossly oversimplify a complex situation, Northern Ireland had been separated from Ireland a few years after the 1916 Easter uprising. It was a gerrymandered state, often called Ulster, made up of seven of the northernmost counties on the Irish island. It created an artificial Protestant majority, most of them Scots immigrants. There are roughly a million and a half citizens of Northern Ireland, two-thirds of them Protestants, a third Catholics. Many of the Protestants feel their British roots strongly, and are great supporters of whatever the "Brits" do there. Others feel they are "Ulstermen," a breed apart. They want autonomy and are therefore anti-British. Most Catholics feel oppressed. They identify themselves as Irish and the more extreme ones want reunification with Ireland. But the Irish aren't keen on that at all, because the poverty-stricken Catholics of Northern Ireland would create a huge public burden.

The Troubles had been with the Irish for more than 130 years. There seemed little possibility of a solution. Everyone I met wanted me to offer ideas for a solution to The Troubles. What could I say? If the Brits pulled out, there would unquestionably be a bloodbath. If they stayed, the bloodbath would continue. It was an Irish standoff: Protestants and Catholics seemed unwilling to sit down and talk about their differences. Each day the papers were filled with inflammatory rhetoric from both sides. It seemed hopeless to me.

Finally I sold a story. Derrick Ingram of Gemini News Service in London accepted a piece on the children of Belfast and their reaction to The Troubles. I got forty pounds, less than sixty dollars, for the story. It was a pitiful amount of money, but it was a milestone. I had survived a rite of passage. My self-esteem was restored. I felt that the first sale was a harbinger of success.

At a rather drunken party for the departing Belfast correspondent of the *Guardian*, I met Mark Ainsworth, a young English artist. Mark was appealing, gentle and very different from anyone I had ever known. I was fascinated by his aloof Englishness in the midst of all of this insane and passionate Irish conflict. The conflict in Northern Ireland was every bit as much Everybody versus The Brits as it was Catholics versus Protestants.

Mark was teaching art at Ulster Polytechnic University and painting abstracts that were totally incomprehensible to my uneducated eye. We went to art galleries, walked in the park and engaged in a short, sweet affair. The initial fascination was in our differences, but in a few weeks those differences lost their magic and things fell apart. One of the fascinations was seeing Northern Ireland through the eyes of an Englishman who was not particularly welcome there. As an American, nearly everyone I met saw me as an ally and friend. I was treated as everyone's special guest.

It was a different story for Mark. Bartenders became suddenly deaf when he ordered a pint in his limey accent. Shopkeepers turned away and refused to serve him. He was acceptable to no one. To the Protestants, he was a symbol of the British who had betrayed them. To the Catholics, he was an enemy plain and simple. It was devastating. If I felt so lonely in a basically friendly environment, Mark's loneliness was far deeper.

One night we were in a pub with a group of Mark's students when someone suggested we go to another pub in the Ardoyne, a Catholic enclave surrounded by Protestant working-class neighborhoods, to hear some traditional Irish music. There was an enthusiastic response from all but Mark. I asked why he had become so quiet.

"I can't go there," Mark answered patiently. "If I went there and there were the smallest bit of trouble, they would kill me because I am British."

He was right. His life was truly in danger.

I was where I wanted to be. Right in the midst of violence.

4 DUBLIN AND BEYOND: *March–June 1984*

In BELFAST, VIOLENCE WAS IN THE AIR. I could feel its weight everywhere. Each day the oppressive weight of that violence seemed to escalate. I was shocked by the ambush of Gerry Adams of Sinn Fein as he rode in his car through the noontime crowds in the center of downtown. It was rumored that Adams survived only because he was wearing a bulletproof vest under his ubiquitous tweed jacket. I was amazed that no one seemed concerned about the thousands of innocent townspeople, shoppers and office workers on their way to lunch, who could have been in the path of the bullets.

Adams's shooting ironically was a professional break for me. UPI in London wanted coverage, hourly coverage. At Malone Avenue the phone still wasn't operational, so every hour, late into the night, I went to the pay phone two blocks away to call the hospital and then file to UPI in London. Nobody ever said that journalism is always glamorous. In fact, it is hardly ever glamorous. Anyway, it was a start.

After three days of the hourly stint, Adams was out of danger and it was time for a break. Jack McCabe, an American friend, was passing through, and St. Patrick's Day was coming up. We decided to take a weekend jaunt.

Where would any phony Irish American with a Brit name like Barnes and a Scot like McCabe, or, for that matter, any member of the Boston Fire Department, want to be on St. Patrick's Day? It was only a two-hour train ride to Dublin.

Dublin was a world away, peaceful and gentle. There were no bag searches or barricades or soldiers in the street. I could breathe easier there.

Barnes, McCabe and the Boston Fire Department were ready to celebrate the birth of the saint who rid Ireland of snakes. The Irish had decided to sit this one out. St. Patrick's Day in Ireland is a religious holiday, not the drunken brawl it is in shanty-Irish towns like Boston, New York and Chicago. There was a bois-terous parade, but the paraders were mostly members of the Boston Fire Depart-ment who obviously had been swilling Guinness since dawn.

I was tired from the Gerry Adams vigil and wanted nothing to do with the news. I quite intentionally ignored the morning news broadcasts before I bundled up for the parade. When we went into a pub for lunch, I was obliviously waving my paper tricolor flag and thinking of sipping a nice cold pint.

The news brought the celebration to an abrupt end. The pub's radio was tuned to a BBC report that Irish police had captured Domenic McGlinchey, the chieftain of the notorious INLA, the Irish National Liberation Army. These guys made the IRA look like schoolboys with firecrackers. Further, the police wanted to deport McGlinchey to Northern Ireland, where there were warrants for his arrest on a you-name-it menu of charges. Irish police were afraid some of McGlinchey's boys would try to liberate him, so they wanted him off their hands as soon as possible.

I spent about five more minutes sipping my beer and wrestling with my conscience. Then I gave in to the journalist's compulsion. I called UPI in London. Did they know about McGlinchey's arrest?

UPI was overjoyed to hear from me. They couldn't find their regular Dublin correspondent. Would I cover it for them? This was definitely cause for fear and trepidation. I told them I had been in Dublin for only a few hours. I knew no one. I knew nothing about Ireland. What the hell?

I started making phone calls and filing reports to London from my hotel room. Jack disconsolately adjourned to a series of pubs. As the story unfolded, it was clear that the Irish government intended to bring McGlinchey into court, order his extradition and be rid of him before the day was done.

It didn't happen quite as efficiently as all that, but there was a late-night hearing in the Irish Supreme Court and McGlinchey was delivered to the Northern Irish border just after midnight. I hadn't gotten any rest, but I was on an adrenalin high from covering a good story. Jack was less than enthusiastic about being deserted, although he had connected with some Boston firemen, and none of them were feeling any pain.

After I got back to Belfast, Mickey and James made up a raft of jokes about my tricolor flag souvenir. They accused me of joining the IRA while I was in Dublin. The green, orange and white Irish tricolor flag is quite inflammatory in Northern Ireland. In fact, there was an unofficial ban on public display of the tricolor because it was viewed as a symbol of Irish nationalism, which translated to the IRA, and it often instigated sectarian violence. To me, it was just a cheap souvenir and I stuck the flag in an empty bottle on my desk and forgot about it.

The violence just wouldn't go away. One beautiful April Sunday, a month later, Mark Ainsworth and I spent the day walking in the park, reveling in the arrival of spring and avoiding even talking about politics or violence. I was overloaded with blood and guts. It seemed to follow me everywhere I went. Toward sunset we wandered home and found Malone Avenue full of soldiers. I asked a soldier what had happened. He told us a Catholic judge and his daughter had been shot that morning by the IRA at the church in the next street. They were searching houses for the killers.

Mark and I continued our stroll, but I was suddenly tight as a drum. When we got to the house, I calmly unlocked the door. Then I bolted up the three long flights of stairs to my room, snatched the paper tricolor flag souvenir from my desk and shoved it under my mattress.

Mickey and James were in hot pursuit. They stood wide-eyed in my doorway, panting from the sprint up the stairs.

"What the fuck are you doing?" Mickey demanded.

"If the soldiers search here, they will see my tricolor and they'll think I am an IRA sympathizer," I panted back.

Mickey and James both howled with laughter. Ten minutes after the shooting, soldiers had been to our house and searched it thoroughly. They knew an American lived there and they knew my name. They also thought I might be involved in the shooting because many Americans are known to be IRA sympathizers. They didn't care about the tricolor.

While I was chilled by the thought that a dossier already existed on me somewhere in the bowels of the Royal Ulster Constabulary, I was impressed with the efficiency of the soldiers. But I felt guilty that Mickey, James, Geraldine, Peter and Paul were all now the object of scrutiny merely because I was living in the same house. I was restricting their freedom to live peaceful lives, and it made me feel terrible. I was becoming afraid for them. I began to think that I might not stay in Belfast for very long. I also knew I wouldn't impose the danger I seemed to carry with me on any more roommates.

Easter Sunday is the day when the IRA and the INLA traditionally honor their dead from generations of warfare. The soldiers and police don't like it at all, but they are unable to stop the huge demonstration of Catholic solidarity that marks the anniversary of the 1916 Easter uprising in Dublin that eventually brought about Irish independence.

The IRA and the INLA marched quite openly up the Falls Road, through the Catholic ghetto, in battle dress, fully armed, to the cemetery at the end of the road, where many "revolutionary martyrs" are buried. Nervous soldiers stood on the hills outside the cemetery and trained their weapons on the crowd. Military helicopters hovered so low that no one could hear the endless political speeches (that was probably merciful!) and most of us were covered with droplets of oil sprayed from the helicopter blades.

At the main monument in the cemetery, we all stood for hours in the warm spring sun. I was standing very near the IRA and INLA honor guard. The IRA covered the lower halves of their faces with bandannas, but the INLA looked much more sinister in balaclavas. I remember watching one INLA man for a long time and realizing that he would be quite recognizable in another context because of his very light blond hair, beard and piercing blue eyes. Of course no one is supposed to know who these guys are, and I shuffled my feet and looked at the ground to avoid staring at him.

At the end of the festivities, the IRA and INLA fired off a volley in memory of their fallen comrades. In the pregnant silence that followed, the revolutionaries literally melted into the crowd. It was truly an amazing phenomenon. It happened right around me, I was looking for it because I had been warned it would happen, but I have no idea how it was done. The two dozen armed and uniformed soldiers were surrounded by the crowd. They obviously changed into civilian clothes and the uniforms were carried away, probably one piece at a time, by friends in the crowd. But even the M-16s disappeared. How could anyone simply stroll away with a three-foot-long firearm when there were literally hundreds of soldiers looking for just that?

Two days after Easter, I was on a bus indulging in my usual habit of scrutinizing my fellow passengers when I recognized my blond, bearded INLA man. He noticed me noticing him at the exact moment I realized who he was. The steady gaze of his brilliant blue eyes unnerved me. I tried hard not to react. It could be hazardous to my health to recognize these guys. I got off the bus at the next stop.

Just to see how the other side spent the holiday, I had accepted an invitation for Easter night from Andy Tyrie, the polyester leisure suit and gold chain–prone chairman of the Protestant paramilitary Ulster Defense Association.

We were going to the opening of a new UDA drinking club only about two miles from the IRA cemetery. The cheaply constructed barnlike building was complete with a Frank Sinatra genre singer, a 1940s-type band and a brilliantined night club comedian who told atrociously corny jokes. Northern Irish don't go in much for ambiance in their pubs, I guess, because they are serious about their drinking. The only decoration was a large painting of Queen Elizabeth on the north wall.

At 11 o'clock closing time (which he insisted was strictly observed), Andy urged me to my feet as everyone stood and faced the portrait on the north wall while the band played the traditional pub-closing song, "God Save the Queen."

Some, I noticed, clamped a hand over the heart and sang lustily. Others, like Andy, stood silently, hands at sides and eyes on the ground. I later asked Andy why. He explained that those who feel that Ulster is part of Britain salute the Queen. Others, like himself, who believe in self-determination for Northern Ireland and want the "Brits Out," as the IRA grafitti says, stand silent.

There is a war of grafitti in Northern Ireland, but the most violent grafitti was in the Protestant neighborhoods.

The Catholic grafitti was fairly uncreative, along the lines of "Brits Out," and "Down with Thatcher." The Protestant grafitti was far more personal: "Kill the Fenians" (a generic name for Catholics) and "Fuck the Pope." If you didn't already know, it was easy to tell whose neighborhood you were in by the grafitti on the walls.

A few days after the Easter evening jaunt, I interviewed Andy Tyrie with an eye toward doing profiles of the leaders of the various factions. After we had talked for a while, Andy invited me for a ride in his car. In hindsight, it was probably a pass that went completely over my head, but, at the time, I wondered if I was about to be murdered. These guys were supposed to be terrorists, weren't they? They seemed more like street hustlers to me, but what did I know about such things? Andy drove onto a country lane. For several miles, we followed a decrepit truck overloaded with sacks of fertilizer while Andy chatted about himself. Then he commented about the fertilizer, "There's a whole truckload of material for bombs."

I vaguely recalled that there was some way of making bombs from fertilizer. My paranoia was growing. Did he think I knew too much?

Stupidly, I surreptitiously pressed my fingertips against the window glass next to me, attempting to leave clear fingerprints. Tyrie noticed it and laughed. During a long walk on a dirty beach, Andy told me he wanted to be remembered as a peacemaker. Then he took me back to his office.

About this time another break came along when Tony Clifton of *Newsweek* accepted my proposal that we do a story on the obfuscated court system and how numerous people get caught in years-long imprisonment waiting for trial on political charges. The trial of twenty-six alleged IRA members was due to begin soon in Belfast, so there was a strong news peg for a good story. I was thrilled. It seemed unbelievable good fortune that I could sell a story to a magazine as prestigious as *Newsweek*.

Corymeela, an ecumenical retreat center on the wild northern coast, became an important part of my experience of Northern Ireland. In that stark wilderness, where the sea crashes against the shore with deadly vengeance, I finally discovered some people who were really working hard to change the hatred that had torn apart their country. I made several trips to Corymeela, and each was a personal discovery.

The Protestant and Catholic church people who ran Corymeela really loved to mix things up. The combinations were often explosive, but they worked. A fragile understanding was beginning to emerge, directly attributable to Corymeela's fearless insistence that Catholics and Protestants must communicate. For the first time since I arrived in Northern Ireland, I began to believe there was a glimmer of hope.

On my first trip to Corymeela, I was with a group of teenagers, a third of them black girls from a working-class section of London, a third of them boys from a Protestant school in Belfast, and a third girls from a Catholic school in Belfast. It immediately struck me that there would never be an opportunity in the real world for these kids to meet. They were separated by walls, oceans, ignorance and hatred.

By the end of that weekend retreat, I was amused to see that the inevitable had happened—several romances had budded among the teenagers. There was handholding and a little sneaking behind the bushes. I rode back to Belfast on the bus with them, and watched one couple holding hands and abstractedly doodling in the condensation on the bus window. The girl wrote, "IRA," the boy wrote, "UDF," then they laughed, erased their graffiti and kissed. It all seemed so idyllic. After just a weekend on the coast, those lifelong prejudices could be broken. But I was painfully aware that this was yet another romantic fantasy. That cute couple would probably never see each other again and certainly it would take long and painstaking follow-up to make any permanent changes in such attitudes ingrained by generations of hatred.

I spent another weekend at Corymeela with a group of women who had been victims of The Troubles. There was a Protestant woman whose husband had been a policeman, blown to hamburger by an IRA car bomb. A Catholic woman, who, with her husband, had peaceably run a small grocery store in a Protestant neighborhood for twenty years. She watched in horror as her husband was gunned down by Protestant paramilitaries who thought it was time for the Catholics to leave their neighborhood. Another attractive young woman lost her husband, an accountant in Belfast Jail and a Protestant, when the IRA arbitrarily decided to kill the occupant of the first car out of the prison that day at closing time. At the time of her husband's murder, Angeline McTier was eight months pregnant and already had two small sons. There was a Catholic woman, Moira Keily, whose son, an honor student in the university, had the ill fortune to be the first person to leave the church after mass one Sunday. He was shot by Protestant paramilitaries, the victim of tit-for-tat killers who so often target the innocent. Moira had started a group called Cross, that tried to cross the sectarian barriers and bridge the pain of these senseless deaths.

The stories of these women and their tragic faces were all engraved on my mind. Their courage was phenomenal. Even the act of attending the retreat at Corymeela opened them to criticism and possible retribution. I began to suspect there were forces in Northern Ireland that methodically worked against any solution to The Troubles. It seemed that Northern Ireland was plagued with some evil curse.

My last trip to Corymeela left yet another indelible memory. I was to join a group of engaged couples from different religious backgrounds, who would be counseled by already-married couples involved in mixed marriages, some of them for as long as twenty years.

Before I was even allowed to attend that retreat, I was sworn to absolute secrecy, not only about the identities of the participants, but against writing anything that might remotely hint at their identities, including their professions or where they lived. I reluctantly agreed to skew the story so that no one could be identified, although at the time, I thought the restrictions were rather melodramatic.

The day I was to leave for the Corymeela marriage retreat, a particularly brutal murder made the headlines. It underscored for me what mixed marriage was all about. A Catholic woman, mother of seven, was shot and killed, apparently by the IRA, as she watered the plants in her front garden. Her sin: marrying a Protestant.

During the retreat, no romantic pap was dished out. The married couples gave graphic descriptions of their lives to those planning to take the same step. Families had disowned them. Friends rejected them. Many had moved to other parts of the country where they were unknown. Often, one would convert to the religion of the other. Sometimes, they were killed. Some of the married couples even actively discouraged the engaged couples from marrying. It seemed amazing to me, in the modern world, that a marriage between two people of different religions could sign a death warrant.

Northern Ireland became more and more frightening. I felt the sickness of the place permeating my being. I felt horror and fascination at the same time. I was helpless in the face of constant requests from people there to offer them a solution to their sorrows. I knew it was time to leave.

I planned to move on to the Middle East. I had even booked a flight to Tel Aviv and made hotel reservations. In my quest for the roots of violence, I intended to jump right into the fire of the Middle East conflict.

There was a last story. Newsweek assigned me to cover Reagan's trip to Ireland in early June. It was a lot of sentimental crap about Reagan searching for his ancestral roots in a tiny Irish town called Ballyporeen. I was basically there on the death watch because no one expected any real news to come out of the trip. But it would be fun and I would get a chance to drive around Ireland and see the countryside.

A week before I was to leave for Galway, where Reagan started the trip, I locked myself out of the house. The only roommate I could find was Paul, so I went to the pub where he worked and waited for him to come on duty. While I sipped a beer and waited for an hour or so, a very good-looking man came and sat next to me. He introduced himself as Michael Cummings, an off-duty policeman, as we chatted and drank beer. I didn't think that was suspicious at the time.

I found Michael pleasant, so I accepted his dinner invitation. We spent a good deal of time together during the next week and fell easily into a rather torrid affair. It was easy for me to enter a relationship like the one with Michael, because I knew it was non-threatening. I knew I would be leaving Belfast in three weeks, so there was no danger of a sticky entanglement.

Michael aroused my journalistic instincts as well. He was a Catholic who worked as a detective penetrating the IRA cells. His work was exciting, glamorous and terrifying. I kept telling him he should find a nice peaceful job, a pretty girl and settle down in a little house with a white picket fence. He said he would find that as boring as I would.

There were moments of suspicion during that short affair, when I directly confronted Michael with questions about whether or not he had me under surveillance. He always strongly denied there was any professional reason for our relationship, so I let it pass.

I left for the Reagan trip glad for a week-long break and a chance to think about the mind-whirling affair with Michael.

The Reagan trip was cold and muddy. We spent hours and hours waiting in press tents only to get a momentary glimpse of The Man. We interviewed every living creature, including the dogs, in tiny Ballyporeen until the hapless residents would run at the sight of a notebook or a camera. The trip was a big nothing, but there were hours of idle time for me to talk to fellow journalists, correspondents far more experienced than I. I spent hours picking their brains about places to go and good stories. During those hours and the hours spent driving from one Reagan stopover to another, I had done a lot of thinking. Instinctively, I felt something was wrong with going to the Middle East. I couldn't pinpoint any logical reason; it just felt like the wrong time. Over my years as a journalist, my instincts and unexplained feelings have always served me well, so I was paying attention.

I began to get crazy ideas about going to the Philippines. There were no particular reasons except, again, my instincts were screaming that it was a good idea. At the time, two priests, one Irish and one Australian, were on trial for murder in the Philippines. That was a shocking idea to me. It was also strange that the two were interviewed on the telephone by the BBC from their prison cells almost every morning. What was going on in that country? I knew about the Ninoy Aquino assassination and I knew that there was a lunatic dictator named Marcos and that there was a churchman with the ludicrous name Cardinal Sin. The Philippines seemed like a strange and fascinating place.

In the meantime I drove through the rainy Irish springtime trying to keep up with the American president, who had it much easier. He was traveling by helicopter. Ireland didn't seem very big until I tried that mad-dash circuit. The highways are bizarre three-lane roads, one lane in each direction and a common lane for passing. It must lead to disaster sometimes.

The Reagan trip was becoming a drag. The Irish rain and cold brought on laryngitis by the time we got to Ballyporeen. It wasn't any help that Ballyporeen, a tiny town of two-hundred, couldn't possibly house the entire foreign press corps. So we doubled and trebled, etc., into whatever accomodations we could beg, borrow or steal. About ten of us wheedled a room in a bed-and-breakfast owned by a grandmotherly lady who seemed shocked that a pack of muddy journalists of both sexes would share the same room. I think she was a little concerned, and maybe just a little hopeful, that this batch of crazy foreigners would have an orgy. All we did was sleep and try to get clean the following morning in a bathtub containing an inch of freezing water. My colleagues sportingly recommended that I drink Irish coffee for my laryngitis while we waited for hours in the press tent in the middle of a muddy field in Ballyporeen. We were sufficiently anesthetized by the Irish coffee to howl with derision when copies of Reagan's sappy speech were distributed, but when The Man finally appeared, he pulled off the speech with such style that I was immensely impressed.

We raced off to Dublin, arriving just in time to see the presidential party take off for London. It was a relief it was over. I knew I had lots of thinking to do.

Some Irish journalists invited me to dinner to celebrate the end of the trip, but I decided to be alone for a few hours. I went to a Chinese restaurant and began writing a list of the advantages and drawbacks of going to the Middle East or the Philippines. Three hours later, I had made my decision: it would be Manila. I had to look it up in an atlas to find out how to spell "Phillipines"—or was it "Philippines?" I joined my Irish colleagues in a pub and we spent several more hours drinking to the Philippines, wherever it is and however you spell it.

I went back to Belfast for the final couple of weeks of preparation. I went to the library one day to get some material on the Philippines. The librarian enthusiastically handed me the library's entire Philippine inventory: a 1963 travel guide.

The affair with Michael resumed.

I was relieved at the prospect of leaving Belfast. The intensity of the conflict there was weighing heavily on me.

I was going to travel in Europe a bit and then I'd fly to Manila from Athens, where cheap plane tickets were available. In mid-June, Michael and I set off for London where we would spend a couple of days saying goodbye. Then I would take the trains and the ferry to Paris. I had all my worldly goods in one cumbersome suitcase and one carry-on.

Michael bid me a tearful farewell at the train station. I thought he was out of my life. But he wasn't, not quite yet.

5

THE EUROPEAN TOUR: *June–July 1984*

ANY OF MY FRIENDS HAD BUMMED around Europe years before, carrying backpacks and riding on Eurail when they were just out of college. The fact that my European trip didn't happen until a few years later in life didn't take away anything. At the age of thirty-five, I was still as excited as a kid in a candy store. There was an incredible wealth of things to see and do.

Paris was as romantic as I had expected. I exhumed my French from some dusty dungeon of my mind, and after a few days I could make myself understood. The Frenchmen thought I was "charmante." I thought my accent was excruciatingly bad.

I couldn't get over the excitement of actually being in the presence of all of those places that had been merely pictures in magazines and textbooks.

The Eiffel Tower (I climbed as far as I could and was disappointed to discover I would have to take an elevator to reach the top; that seemed like cheating), the Arc de Triomphe, the Louvre, Notre Dame and the dozens of famous churches. The sidewalk cafes, Parisians themselves—it was all a whirl of mental and emotional stimulation, I became like a junkie—the more I got, the more I wanted.

I was fascinated by the splendor of Notre Dame. Since it was near my hotel, I would stop there nearly every day, just to absorb the majesty of the rose windows and the glory of the place. After four or five of my daily pilgrimages to Notre Dame, I was approached by a pleasant-faced middle-aged man with a huge bunch of keys dangling from his belt.

He said he had noticed me in Notre Dame each day and wondered why I came there. I told him it was just because I found the place so overwhelmingly beautiful.

"Ah, that's what I thought," he said. "I am the caretaker of Notre Dame. I would like to show you some of the places tourists don't usually see."

Oh no, I thought. Quasimodo. At least this guy wasn't a hunchback. Was this a pass? A hype? I was suspicious since I had already naively fallen victim to a couple of minor con games, so I interrogated him rather roughly. He assured me that he simply liked people who liked his beloved Notre Dame and he wanted to share it with them.

He used a huge key from his ring to open a door at the base of a column to the left of the main altar.

We climbed a spider-web-infested spiral staircase. It didn't have torches lighting the way, but it should have. It was a scene straight out of *The Hunchback of Notre Dame*.

We came out on a mezzanine overlooking the main altar, where a mass was being celebrated by a dozen priests. They looked like little dolls way down there, performing their rituals. I exclaimed that it was lovely. Quasimodo tapped me on the shoulder.

"That's not all," he whispered, pointing behind me. I turned and was confronted with the enormity and the simultaneous delicacy of one of the rose windows, almost within touching distance. It took my breath away. I stood transfixed for several minutes. Then he silently took my hand and led me through a doorway. We were on Notre Dame's roof, elbow to elbow with the gargoyles, looking down the famous view of the bridges crossing the River Seine. I took a few snapshots that came out exactly like the postcards sold in every shop in Paris.

After a tour of the roof and a closeup acquaintance with the gargoyles, this gentle Quasimodo led me back down the circular staircase. He lit a candle for me at one of the many altars at the back of the church, gave me a quick kiss on the cheek and sent me on my way.

I took an overnight train south to Nice, arriving on a sunny Mediterranean morning. Nice was a relief from the bustle of the cities. I spent a peaceful week relaxing on beaches and meeting a couple of exciting Frenchmen with whom I could, by that time, actually communicate about something more significant than the weather.

One day I took a train to Monte Carlo to see the famous harbor, the yachts and the elegant casino. The casino looked exactly as I expected, but there were no tuxedoed men or bejeweled ladies gambling with detached gentility under its vaulted and gilded ceilings. Instead, there were hordes of tourists wearing T-shirts, shorts and sandals, having a rowdy good time playing the cheap tables. I found out later that the elegant had their own private salon to which we unwashed masses were not admitted.

At Monte Carlo a noisy bunch of American college boys adopted me and taught me how to play blackjack. I have always hated to lose money; probably some Scottish ancestor passed on his miserly genes. So I only staked myself for 200 francs, at that time less than twenty dollars. I decided I would quit if I lost that much, no matter what. I started winning a little, not much, because I was too cautious, when I noticed a handsome and mysterious Italian standing behind me. He knew not a word of English or French. He simply placed his bets on my cards and then nudged me as to whether or not I should take a card. I guess it was beginner's luck. He won several hundred francs on my cards, but I didn't know when to stop and, by 10:30, half an hour before the last train to Nice, I had lost all of my original 200 francs. True to my promise to myself, I quit when I had lost my stake. Mark, one of the American boys, was almost 2,000 francs ahead. The group was raucously cheering him on. Mark didn't want to leave to catch the train. He magnanimously promised to pay for a taxi for all of us so we wouldn't have to leave. At 10:57, Mark put his entire winnings on the table— and lost.

"Run!" he yelled.

We all piled on the last train as it was pulling out of the station. Although I have been in numerous casinos since then, gambling has never again carried the same excitement as that magical first night in Monte Carlo.

My next stop was in Rome and I made my way through the wonders of that city with childlike awe—the Colosseum, the Pantheon, the Vatican. The antiquity of Rome impressed me with its 2000-year-old catacombs and many-thousand-year-old buildings. And Athens, with its beautiful sculptures and the perfection of its ancient thousands-of-years-old architecture. I could see that America as a civilization is very young and brash, just out of infancy and perhaps thrust into power at a much earlier age than is healthy.

Corfu was paradise. I know that wasn't the place where the Sirens tempted Odysseus, but it might as well have been. The colors of Corfu are almost a caricature of themselves in their own intensity. Blue skies that pierced my brain with the purity of their color, the pristine white houses and the red, red geraniums were part of the magic that finally erased the horrors of Belfast from my battered psyche. I was lulled by the serenity and the beauty of the place. I was traveling with a bunch of Americans and Canadians encountered in various adventures. We stayed together in Paleokastritsa on the back side of the island, living decadent and lazy days. We rented little motor scooters and fancied ourselves some sort of suntan-oiled Hell's Angels as we zoomed up mountains and raced around hairpin turns each day, searching for yet another of Corfu's seemingly limitless supply of perfect beaches. We developed a ritual of riding up the mountain road above town every morning to a restaurant on the way for a coffee, while we allowed ourselves to be hypnotized by the blueness of the Mediterannean. The first day, and every day thereafter, we were accosted by an ancient leather-faced Greek man who sold almonds in paper cones. We always stopped to buy, but all he wanted from me for the almonds was a kiss on the cheek. One day we rented a paddleboat and rode it far out to sea, where we were mooned by a group of outrageous waterskiing Americans. Another day, I tried my hand at riding the giant multicolored kites towed behind motor boats. It was the closest I have ever come to flying.

All of my original companions eventually drifted on to other pursuits, but I stayed and stayed in Corfu. Ten days. Two weeks, I lost track. I had a great tan for the first time in my life. Since I was sixteen and started having after-school jobs, I had never had such a long vacation. Guilt began to nag at me and the brilliance began to wear off the colors of Corfu. So one night, with the salt of Corfu's sea still on my skin, I flew off to Athens.

If I felt part of history in Ireland, London, Paris and Rome, Athens was history personified. I could see the footprints of the ancients everywhere and feel the immensity of their culture. Somebody had given me the name of Phil Dopoulos, the Athens bureau chief for Associated Press, and he was more than gracious.

We went to the beach at Marathon (twenty-six miles from Athens, of course), ate barbecued octopus with some wrinkled old men playing the Greek version of backgammon and had dinners at those marvelous Greek restaurants that magically grow out of parking lots at six o'clock every evening. I never did discover where the kitchens were. Waiters always seemed to be carrying trays and dodging traffic.

One night, after dinner at the romantic harbor at Piraeus, Phil bought me a bunch of gardenias. I could have stayed there forever.

Sightseeing in Athens turned out to be a marvelous adventure. The Tourist Office was mobbed with throngs of people trying to scrounge scarce street maps. While I was doing battle with the mob, I noticed a meek and slightly dowdy-looking Australian woman who seemed to be progressing at about an equal pace. After a few exchanges of words, we agreed that whichever of us got to the front of her line first would get maps for both of us. Once the maps were procured, it seemed natural we would spend the day together.

Suzy was slim and pretty. But she seemed to be deliberately covering up her attractiveness. I hope my Australian friends will forgive me if I say Suzy looked like a typical Aussie tourist. She had long braids, big glasses through which she peered (looking slightly confused), a floppy hat, an ankle-length skirt, and dirty running shoes. She said she had just completed her master's degree in anthropology. She already had a degree in archeology. She seemed like the perfect partner for Athens. In the museums, Suzy was a wealth of information, bawdy as well as factual. She would often point to the sculptures of nude men and comment, "I knew one once who looked just like that." She was great fun. By late afternoon, we had wound our way up the twisting street that leads to the Acropolis. As we watched the sunset from a parapet overlooking the city, Suzy confided that she had put herself through school working as a call girl. I admit I was shocked at first, but why not? She was extremely practical about it. I had a hard time imagining this rather prim-looking Australian woman decked out in a black corset and heavy paint. She had dozens of stories to tell about the fun tricks and the violent ones. Suzy saw herself as a teacher with a sacred duty to teach her clients well how to please women. I liked her style.

My friend Phil was going to Amman, Jordan, on a short assignment and asked me if I'd like to come along. Although I was getting anxious to get to Manila, I couldn't pass up the opportunity for a glimpse of the Middle East with someone who knew it well.

At the airport Phil and I encountered Suzy. Small world, but somehow I wasn't surprised. She was going to Amman, too.

Jordan was an intense culture shock for me. I had been warned not to wear short-sleeved blouses or tight pants or any clothes that might inflame the apparently perpetually horny Arab men. Yet every time I walked on the street alone, I was followed by a pack of men who acted more like a pack of dogs. Although they didn't touch me, I felt as though I was being raped every minute. I hated it. I also realized I had made a wise decision not to work in the Middle East. As a single woman, I could see it would have been extremely difficult.

I made contacts with some of the Palestinian refugee authorities with the vague intention of writing a story about the refugee camps. They arranged a trip to Marka, a refugee camp just outside Amman that had been there since 1948, the year I was born. It was hard for me to imagine people who had been refugees for thirty-five years. At Marka I was jolted out of the reverie induced by my travels in Europe. I was deeply touched by the people I met in the camp. There were young children who sang bittersweet nationalist songs to a Palestine that doesn't exist on any map.

I had never seen poverty like this. Eight or ten people might live in a tiny two-room concrete block house. They cooked their food on a front terrace and hand-carried water from community taps a couple of hundred yards away. There was dysentery, cholera, malnutrition. For the first time I recognized a new type of violence. There was the blood-and-guts violence. There was the violence of a hopeless life of poverty. And now this. People had been robbed of their home-land by the Israelis, themselves displaced people seeking a homeland. No one seemed to see the paradox of it.

Not everyone was poor. My guide was a teacher who had chosen to build his house inside the camp. I was taken to a series of homes of community leaders where I heard the Palestinian tale of woe. In each house I visited, I was fed a cup of the supercharged mud-like Arabic coffee. By the end of the day, I had consumed at least a dozen cups. I was nearly in orbit from the caffeine.

The hotel had a package tour to Petra, an ancient city three hours south of Amman. 2000-year-old Petra seemed an essential part of my quest for an-cientness. Phil and I signed up for the tour, which was to include a horseback ride through the desert canyons. We couldn't believe the coincidence when we saw Suzy boarding our bus.

When we arrived in Amman, the tour guide announced that the Bedouins welcomed anyone who wanted to spend the night in their caves. Suzy jumped at the opportunity. Phil, not knowing Suzy's avocation, became alarmed and warned her that the Bedouins would just as soon rape a white woman as look at her.

Suzy replied, "Good," with a mischievous twinkle in her eye.

Off we went by horseback through exquisitely colored limestone canyons. Every few minutes a desert-clad teenager would flash past us in a madcap gallop to nowhere on a sleek Arabian horse.

Petra is an incredibly civilized and elegant series of thousands of caves. The caves have elaborate fluted columns and highly decorated architectural details. There was even an aqueduct system that carried water from a river a mile away. It worked until twenty years ago. No one knows how to fix it, although thousands of Bedouins still occupy the caves.

I bought a primitive little piece of clay shaped into a thumb-sized jug. The huckster told me the jug was 2,000 years old. It was probably more like twenty minutes old, but I liked the idea of it. He called it a mourning jug. Bereaved families would fill these jugs with their tears and, when they were full, the jug would be buried with the loved one. No more tears were allowed. Mourning was finished.

We somewhat uneasily left Suzy behind with the Bedouins. Phil had to chase away a group of sinister-looking foul-smelling men who wanted to watch me take a leak in a makeshift toilet in the rest house along the way.

Back in Amman, an unexpected complication arose. Suzy had left behind an enamored Jordanian tourist office functionary who had the bad sense to take her home to meet his mom. He was beside himself with anxiety over Suzy's decision to stay with the Bedouins. Sharif plagued us throughout the evening and all of the next day. He had worked himself into a frenzy by the time the tour bus returned from Petra the next afternoon and Suzy was not aboard. He was sure Suzy had been raped and/or murdered by the Bedouins, so he used his clout and sent the tourist police to Petra to find out if she was being held against her will. An irate Suzy sent the police away and lazed away a couple more days with the Bedouins, attending an interminable native wedding and drinking arak or what-ever potent stuff they were swilling. She appeared in Amman several days later, unrepentant. We said goodbye, but she still writes letters once a year or so.

Phil and I flew back to Athens the next day. I felt a little strange when I got on the plane. By the time we arrived at the madhouse that doubles as the arrival area of the Athens airport, I was dizzy and feverish. While we were waiting in the immigration line, I made several mad dashes to the bathroom where I was seized by violent diarrhea. I told Phil I thought I was going to faint. He warned me I couldn't faint because there was no room to fall down. We had been in the immigration line for two hours, I went out of my head. Phil recognized the sudden seriousness of the situation. He began to shout at he immigration officers that I was sick. I don't really remember how we got to the front of the line, but our passports were stamped and we fell into a taxi to the place where I was staying in Athens.

I don't remember anything of the next twenty-four hours, but there was a nagging awareness that I had to get on the plane for Manila the next night. Phil pronounced I had dysentery and got me some pills that knocked me out. Every time I would wake up, he would try to shove a few mouthfuls of yogurt down my throat.

When it was time to leave for the airport, I could barely scrape myself together. My knees were so weak they would hardly hold me. But I had a ticket that couldn't be changed.

In that pathetic state I was finally on my way to Manila.

6

MANILA: *July 1984*

FROM THE AIR MANILA LOOKS LIKE a neatly laid out patchwork quilt. I could identify vibrant green rice fields, fishpens that looked like arrowheads in the muddy waters of an inland lake and dollhouselike bamboo huts.

I was terrified. For the second time in five months, I had chosen to throw away an established life, to move halfway around the world, this time to an even more alien place. The move was additionally unnerving because my funds were getting low. I knew I would have to plant myself in Manila until I earned enough money to get out. The returns on my labors thus far had been less than encouraging.

I had once again embarked on a journey to a place where I knew no one. I was armed with a few names given to me by friendly colleagues along the way, but I was definitely on my own.

On the ground, Manila was a melange of sweltering early morning heat, snail-paced baggage handlers, Filipino tourists with enormous quantities of luggage, and hotel hustlers with an amazing level of aggression. I promptly got ripped off for twenty-five dollars a night, double the going rate, to stay at the moldering fleabag Palace Hotel on Mabini Street, in the heart of Ermita, only a stone's throw away from the whorehouses for which Manila is famous.

I was also cheerfully ripped off for a ride into town. A hotel tout told me I had to pay for a hotel car to take me to town, so I paid ten dollars for a Mercedes limo to deposit me incongruously at the door of the shabby Palace Hotel. I found out later the usual fare is about two dollars. Most tourists are the victims of far worse ripoffs. They say ignorance is bliss and, indeed, I thought the Filipinos were all very cheery, accomodating, friendly people. Over the years, I have become more cynical. Some Filipinos are often at their friendliest when they are ripping someone off. It's not fair that an entire nation is judged as thieves and prostitutes because a few victimize newcomers, but that is the unfortunate impression that most foreigners get.

At the Palace I was accosted by an army of cute snot-nosed four-year-old beggars, and a flotilla of money changers whispering and beckoning urgently as they lurked in darkened doorways, and a cacophony of gaudy jeepneys, their horns voicing constant complaint. I was still suffering from incredible stomach cramps caused by the dysentery, the muggy heat and the effects of a grueling twenty-six-hour trip. I fell gratefully into the not-too-clean bed and spent several hours in blissful unconsciousness.

I had grimly steeled myself for all sorts of hardships, so, at the beginning, I patiently submitted to all sorts of outrages. This was, after all, the Third World, wasn't it? I expected bad water, worse food, no phones, and the possibility I would live in a shanty. Secretly, when I first looked at the map and saw the massive Manila Bay, I harbored fantasies about a beachfront cottage decked with bougainvillea and perhaps a pet parrot and a chattering monkey thrown in to complete my tropical Eden. Those fantasies had evaporated on the limo ride in from the airport.

I woke up late in the afternoon, eager to take a walk and explore this new place. I left the hotel with a vague destination: the Associated Press office on Roxas Boulevard. Roxas turned out to be Manila's version of Lake Shore Drive, with towering coconut palms and surf crashing against the seawall. I was blindly enchanted with the friendly Filipinos and the glamor of a tropical country.

There were families camping there with cute little kids—they looked like something from one of those tacky paintings of the kids with enormous eyes. They were lounging under lean-tos constructed of pieces of plastic strung between trees. One family was napping in a crude wooden pushcart. They were cooking over campfires, the laundry flapping in the breeze. Since it was a Saturday, I thought perhaps these were the less affluent Filipinos taking advantage of the sea breezes—sort of like an urban vacation home, a charming weekend retreat. Later, I was shocked to learn the flimsy structures were their homes, all they had, and the children with the enormous eyes were starving.

There were aromatic little piles of garbage here and there, but my glamor-glazed eyes refused to register any ugliness so early in this new adventure.

I wandered for a mile or so up and down the boulevard, eventually stopping at the AP office. Phil Dopoulos had given me the name of Dave Briscoe, the very accomodating Manila bureau chief, and Dave had already received an urgently needed contact lens sent there to replace one lost in the Aegean during my stay in Athens.

I must have looked pretty bedraggled and probably a little glassy-eyed when I wandered into the AP office. I certainly brought out the earth mother in Coring, the AP office manager. She immediately took me under her wing and demanded to know where I was staying. Coring was shocked that a proper lady like me would stay in a whorehouse like the Palace Hotel, so she snatched a copy of the morning's paper and began to make phone calls about apartments. In about ten minutes, she had found what she considered a decent and inexpensive place where I could move in the next day. My head was reeling from the rapid passage of events and probably from the dysentery, too. But I was relieved I wouldn't have to spend more than one night in that moldy hotel.

My new apartment was clean and spacious, furnished in Howard Johnson modern. It was a mile down Mabini from the Palace Hotel, out of the worst of the red light district, but the neighborhood was far from wholesome. There always seemed to be a lot of people hanging around in the doorway of the building. My biggest problem with the Mabini apartment was the back door because it wasn't a door. It was only a screen covered with wrought iron grillwork. It seemed like it would be very easy for someone to slit the screen and slide a hand inside to unlock the door. The officious landlady, who was of an overly made-up and saccharine type I soon came to recognize as that of con artists, said not to worry about the back door, I was safe. I didn't feel safe at all.

Because the place was so sterile, I bought a few bright baskets and weavings to make myself feel better. It was still pretty grim. I placed my prized mourning jug from Petra in a prominent place. On rainy mornings, I wished I was anywhere else. The landlady had provided me with a tiny desk, and I had come prepared with my own copy of the *Editor and Publisher Yearbook*, a listing of all English-language newspapers in the world. Every night, after spending the day meeting people and familiarizing myself with my surroundings, I spent several hours writing letters to editors. I wrote over two hundred letters in those first weeks, each of them painstakingly individually typed out on my little electronic typewriter.

I was still suffering from the stomach cramps of the dysentery, but I couldn't take the Lomotil during the day because it made me so sleepy. I had staked out bathrooms all over town, some of them appallingly filthy. Virtually none had toilet paper, so I learned what every woman who has traveled in Asia must know—carry Kleenex. After three weeks, I was becoming weak and eating little but fruit. A helpful colleague recommended I go to a hospital. She said it didn't matter which one, so I went to Philippine General Hospital, because it was large and it was nearby. That was my introduction to the world of Philippine medicine.

The emergency room at PGH was dark and dirty and empty of anything immediately recognizable as medical equipment. Several patients lay on unpadded metal carts, their IV bottles suspended from rusty nails on the wall. Mangy cats wandered in and out. There was no door. On the floor just inside the doorway, there was a drying pool of blood. A dozen or more zombielike people sat on rusty folding chairs. I couldn't tell if they were patients or relatives of victims of some unspeakable disaster.

It was also my first experience with Filipino racial prejudice. Maybe I should call it cannibalism, because many Filipinos will fall all over themselves to be ingratiating to a foreigner while discriminating against their own people.

As I walked in the emergency room door, a young doctor waved away the man and woman she was talking with. I naively thought she was just chatting with them to pass the time until a real customer came along. Now I know that these poor people had probably waited hours to see a doctor, but by virtue of my white skin, I moved to the head of the line. I told the doctor my problem and she graciously wrote out a prescription for some rehydrating fluids. No charge.

July is the height of rainy season. It poured every day. My shoes dissolved. I was soaked through several times a day. My armpits were in danger of growing mold. No number of showers made me feel clean because the rain had no cooling effect in the sweltering heat. Manila was hot as hell. I began to have dreams about burning in hell.

My fellow journalists were nearly all male. Most of them were far more friendly than Belfast journalists. Several of them took special pains to help me get my feet on the ground. Guy Sacerdoti of the *Far Eastern Economic Review*, Mark Fineman of the *Philadelphia Inquirer* and Lin Neumann of NBC were the three musketeers who towed me along for a while. Unfortunately, while these three were accomodating to me in the extreme, they were obsessed with spending time in the red light district. I guess it is a disease endemic to the male community of foreign correspondents throughout the world.

I became one of the guys, and was therefore frequently invited along to outings on Mabini, as the tourists' honky-tonk heaven is called. I am no prude, but I found the flesh trade depressing and degrading to all parties. The clients, who were mostly foreigners (Filipinos have their own equivalents in other parts of town), seemed to be lonely men, some of them clearly losers, who could find love no other way than to pay for it. The girls were very young, often straight off the farm and very naive. Many of them were on drugs. The girls danced by the hour, lackadaisically waiting for some huge, hairy, sweaty foreigner to buy them for the night. It wasn't the prostitution itself that bothered me; it was the desperation on both sides.

Most of the girls were there because of the age-old reality that prostitution is the most lucrative profession available to an uneducated woman. On Mabini, an energetic young prostitute can make twenty, thirty, maybe even fifty dollars a night, which is ten times what she could earn in a department store. They sent the money home to help support swarms of brothers and sisters. All of the girls had the hope of catching a foreign husband, escaping from poverty and eventually bringing along the family. The closest most of them got to that dream was "catching" a foreigner's baby, since birth control is a no-no in this Catholic country, apparently even for prostitutes.

One night a group of us were drinking in the current journalists' current favorite bar, The Blackout. Next to me at the bar was Rusty Todd, a good-looking blond correspondent from the *Asian Wall Street Journal*, whom I had met an hour before. The bar girls were swarming around Rusty like bees around a flower. Three or four of them were being extremely persistent, although, to Rusty's credit, he was not expressing any particular interest. On my other side was Patti David, one of the few other women in the press corps. Patti leaned over and whispered to me that I should tell Rusty to be careful about VD. I really thought that was none of my business, but Patti was insistent, so I passed on the message.

A couple of minutes later, one of Rusty's "cuties" patted me on the arm and told me she hoped I was very happy.

I was a little perplexed until I noticed Rusty sitting alone on my right, head in hands. All the girls were gone.

"What did you tell them?" I demanded.

"I told them you were my wife," Rusty admitted sheepishly.

It wasn't the only time I got "married" on Mabini.

One night, I was with Sacerdoti, Neumann and a couple of other journalists in a small Mabini bar called The Spider's Web. Jean, one of the "girls" there, had a heavy crush on Guy and was not pleased when he slighted her, either in reality or in imagination. We were clustered around a piano bar and no one was paying particular attention to the Jean-and-Guy drama until I saw Jean pull out an ice pick. Quickly I announced that Guy and I had gotten married that afternoon. In the stunned silence that followed, I grabbed Guy's arm and we escaped through the door. Sacerdoti didn't go back to the Spider's Web for months.

I hated the bars and the sleazy life of the strip, but the journalists were my only friends in those early days. Without them I would have had little professional life and no social life in this bizarre city.

I was really lonely in the midst of so many people who were so willing to help me.

But nobody could help me with grief in those early days. A week after I arrived, I got a phone call from Bert with bad news. John Bastian, my old friend, the owner of the delightful little red boathouse on the St. Lawrence River, was dead. He had been electrocuted while he was working on the wiring at the cottage on the river. My friend Jack McCabe had found him a day later.

John's death really hit me hard. I was still suffering from the dysentery. I was depressed about the bar scene and generally feeling insecure about my ability to cope with this new situation. I was very far from home. When the news of John's death came, there had not been enough time for me to make friends who could really comfort me.

A week after I arrived in Manila, I was ready to pack it all in and go back to the States. Bert, as wonderful and as supportive as ever, told me gently that was a very dumb idea. As usual he was right.

At the American Express office, there were several letters from Michael, my

Irish cop. I wrote back and gave him my new phone number. One morning he called, full of pledges of undying love. He paused, and then asked if I had received his latest letter. I hadn't.

"Well," Michael stammered, "I wanted to let you know something because I have fallen in love with you. I was tailing you in Belfast for a couple of weeks before we met."

He paused. I was too stunned to say anything.

"Does this change our relationship?" he wanted to know.

My stomach lurched with disgust. This is how it must feel to be raped, I thought. I raged at him. I wept. I demanded to know why.

He said someone in Grosvenor Square (the American Embassy in London) asked for the tail because I was a little girl alone who was meeting some not-very-nice people in Belfast.

Why in hell did they think I went to Belfast? To write about the birds and the bees?

My fury was boundless. I felt violated in a way I had never before experienced.

Again Michael asked if it changed our relationship.

I said there was no relationship, since it had been based on a lie. I slammed down the phone and wrote Michael out of my life. I took a shower. And another shower. Yet I felt like I was still dirty. I still hear from him occasionally, but I have been unable to forgive that lie.

My lack of information about the Philippines was appalling. I was so incredibly naive. I didn't even know that Marcos was sick, much less any of the intricacies of the complex situation in the Philippines. I laugh now to think of myself in those earliest days. I wish I had known what I know now: that I understood as much in those first perplexing days as I would ever know. It is a constantly fluid political situation, based on rumor more often than fact and that completely defies logic and results in ever renewable wonder.

For nineteen years, Marcos had ruled the Philippines with an iron fist. He was elected in 1965 because he was a progressive who had been able to touch the hearts of the common people. The Philippines was growing economically stronger at the time of Marcos's election. By the end of his rule the country was an economic shambles. Marcos was enthusiastically re-elected in 1969 in the midst of a power struggle with the family of his vice-president, Fernando Lopez. It was during that campaign that Marcos had learned a lesson that affected his every action for the rest of his life and the lives of millions of his people: money is power. He began to steal, slowly at first, then frantically as his greedy wife, Imelda, got into the act. By 1972 it was clear that Marcos and Imelda had a wonderful boondoggle going, but they had to devise a way to circumvent the Philippines' constitutional prohibition against a president serving a third term.

He manufactured a series of events so that, coupled with some genuine unrest caused by a newly born communist insurgency, he declared martial law and promptly rewrote the constitution to his liking. Marcos stole billions during the nine years of martial law and took care of a host of cronies as well. The lifestyle he and Imelda adopted became legendary while his people became cruelly impoverished. He and Imelda created a conjugal dictatorship and a reign of corruption that has been unparalleled in modern history. No one knows how much they stole, but the estimates have run as high as fifteen billion dollars. The magnitude of their crime was so huge that a new word was coined to describe it: kleptocracy.

A vast quantity of information of varying quality was available every day in the Manila coffee shops. The oppositionists were at the Taza de Oro, a grubby little restaurant on Roxas Blvd., and the government types were at the 365 Club (which boasted it met 365 days a year) at the pricey Hotel Intercontinental. I could pick up the best of the current lies and get a direct line to Manila's rumor swamp at these coffee shops, although at risk of getting cancer of the pancreas from drinking gallons of coffee a day. I think there were some journalists who never did anything but go from one coffee shop to another to gather rumors. I always wondered when the coffee shop habituees ever went to work. They seemed to be in their favorite haunts at all hours of the day.

My letter writing barrage started to pay off. The *Toronto Star* was interested in a story or two. An old friend at the *Detroit News* would take some stories.

The big payoff came after I had been in the Philippines for almost three months. I was getting alarmed about money. I couldn't survive on a couple of hundred dollars a month, which was what was forthcoming from the *Toronto Star* and the *Detroit News*. I was feeling frustrated because there were so many stories and no market for me to sell them in.

At a party, I met Mark Litke, the ABC television correspondent for Asia. I was momentarily speechless when Mark asked if I would be interested in working for ABC Radio.

"Me? I don't know anything . . ." I choked.

"Never mind, I'll teach you. Come to my room at the Manila Hotel at nine tomorrow morning," he said reassuringly.

This was distinctly NOT a pass, although it would have been an original line, I must admit.

I went. Mark taught me how to hook up the alligator clips to the phone in the bathroom and gave me a few pointers on writing radio spots. I was a radio journalist! At fifty dollars a spot, I could survive, and possibly even prosper.

The folks at ABC Radio in New York were immeasurably patient with me in those early days. I was appallingly inept and frequently clumsy. Many times I cut the connection because I pushed the wrong buttons in my nervousness. Apparently they had decided I was worth the trouble, so they babied me along until I got the hang of it.

I was the only identifiably Western woman correspondent in Manila in those days, and that fact drew a great deal of attention to me. Whenever there was a press conference or a demonstration, local television crews would be sure to include me in their cutaways. I wish I could have charged a talent fee for the number of times I appeared unwillingly on local television news.

As I gradually distanced myself from the bar scene, I began to be the subject of gossip. Some of my colleagues were the worst gossips. They knew I wasn't sleeping with any of them, so they began to fantasize about who I must be sleeping with. The rumor mill was stoked up within a few weeks with lurid tales of my numerous affairs. I was annoyed. My colleagues were all on the rumor bandwagon and in fact fed one another's lust for gossip. If I had been sleeping with even a tenth of the people it was rumored I had invited into my bed, including several politicians, I would have been unable to walk, much less get any work done. I said that rather loudly and nastily when the subject of my sex life came up one night at a foreign correspondents' drinking brawl. That seemed to put a damper on the rumors, at least for a while.

Journalists who use sex as a door opener are of the lowest order. It hurt to think that I was being thrown into that garbage barrel.

The truth was that my love life was barren. I almost wished a couple of the rumors of my sexual escapades were true. The loneliness was starting to break me down.

7 A DEMONSTRATION A DAY: *Late 1984*

ALMOST A YEAR AFTER THE assassination of Benigno "Ninoy" Aquino, the streets of Manila had become the opposition's forum. For the members of what had become known as the "Parliament of the Streets," jobs, families, friendships had ceased to exist. All that mattered was the exhilarating headlong rush, toward nobody-knew-what. The air was electric with the collective certainty that something was happening, that change was coming. Nearly every afternoon there was a demonstration. The same unwavering stalwarts were always at the head of the march.

The Aquino moderates carried yellow banners, a takeoff on the "Tie A Yellow Ribbon" song, which was to have heralded the homecoming of Ninoy Aquino on August 21, 1983. Instead, yellow became Ninoy's death color when he was gunned down by Marcos's loyal military as he arrived at the Manila International Airport. The yellow rallyists came primarily from the middle and upper classes. Many were lawyers, businessmen, movers and shakers who were insulted by Marcos's claim that a communist gunman had somehow slipped through the airport security cordon of 1,199 men guarding Aquino's arrival and killed Marcos's number-one political opponent in a matter of seconds. The yellow crowd were angry. They sported yellow T-shirts carrying the various slogans of the opposition: "*Ninoy, Hindi Ka Nag-iisa*" (Ninoy, you are not alone) or a quote from Aquino, "The Filipino is worth dying for," or sometimes just an unlabeled but immediately recognizable and gruesome outline of Aquino's corpse dripping blood as it lay on the tarmac of the Manila International Airport. Some of the upper-class matrons turned the rallies into fashion shows, with each trying to outdo the next with outlandishly impractical yellow couturier ensembles totally unsuitable for the water cannons, tear gas, and the occasional bullets that had become increasingly common rally fare. Running from tear gas while wearing high heels had its hazards.

Cory Aquino was very much one of the players in those demonstrations, although she was rarely physically present. I don't think she ever got tear gassed. But Cory had evolved into a patron saint of the movement to bring down Marcos. She rarely gave speeches, and when she did her timing was off and her delivery was terrible. Yet her appearances always set off a tumultuous excitement. In private conversations Cory Aquino came off as mousy and reticent, as a housewife, as exactly what she claimed to be. In a February 1985 interview, Cory Aquino told me she was surprised that the protest movement had been sustained. She, like almost everyone else, thought it would last a month, like most Filipino crazes. I had the strong sense that Cory Aquino was being pushed into water over her head, but I didn't know who was doing the pushing.

From the high windows of the bank towers in Makati's financial district, demonstrators were bombarded with yellow confetti cut from the yellow pages of telephone books. Sometimes the confetti was several inches deep on Ayala Avenue, Makati's main drag. Enterprising scavengers swept up the confetti each night, packaged and resold it to the office workers so they could throw it again the next day.

The hard leftwing red-banner carriers were an entirely different breed. They were organized, disciplined and serious. They came mainly from the working classes, peasants and students. No cute yellow outfits here. Their uniform was jeans, T-shirts, rubber flip-flops and a bandanna to tie around the face when the tear gas came. The lucky ones had tennis shoes for easier running when the tear gas cannisters began to fall. They sat with incredible patience for endless hours at Mendiola Bridge on the approach to Malacanang Palace, listening to the dry rhetoric of the left.

Frequently the reds and the yellows would come together, like they did on August 21, 1984, the first anniversary of Aquino's death. Hordes of people, maybe a million altogether, gathered at the Luneta Park in central Manila, for the first huge demonstration of opposition to the Marcos government.

It was hot and sunny. I had only been in Manila for three weeks, but I had managed to get an assignment from Reuters for the day. I fought my way through the crowd to the grandstand. From that vantage point, I could see a vast sea of black heads and yellow and red banners stretching through the park and filling the surrounding streets.

I was happy, working the crowd, getting quotes and calling the Reuters office every couple of hours with reports. It had been a long dry spell without any real work. I was eager to plunge back into it.

I worked that day for Reuters, and helped tie up some details over the next two days. Graham Lovell, the Reuters bureau chief, promised there would be a check at the end of the month.

There was no check at the end of the month, so I went to the office and asked Lovell about it. He slapped his head with his hand and said, "Sorry, I forgot. I'll take care of it."

He left the room. When he returned, he silently handed me 180 pesos, less than ten dollars. I was so stunned I didn't even object. I had put in about eighteen hours of work for him, and that worked out to ten pesos or fifty cents an hour. That was what I earned baby-sitting when I was ten years old. I was insulted, completely humiliated and very close to tears. I didn't want to cry there in the Reuters bureau, so I made a quick exit. I felt that my professional integrity had reached an all-time low. I have never been very good at demanding just rewards for my work, but the Reuters episode was a particularly hard lesson since it was my first assignment in Manila.

I was on an emotional roller coaster in those first few months. One minute, I would believe I had really made it and the next minute the balloon would burst. Many times, I stayed awake late into the night wondering if I could hack this new life.

Tear gas hung heavy in the streets in those days. The pattern was almost always the same. The marchers gathered in mid-afternoon, often much later than announced. (I had learned about Filipino time, which always means an hour or two late.) Sometimes they would be allowed to march. Negotiations with police for space and time would begin at the point of destination. Sometimes, depending on the government's political agenda and mood of the day, the marchers would not be permitted to leave the assembly point. The negotiations always seemed to continue until late afternoon, when the police would set a dusk deadline for dispersal. I cynically thought that was because neither demonstrators nor police wanted to miss dinner. Every time there were the predictable speeches denouncing the "U.S.-Marcos dictatorship," followed by a little pushing, shoving, clubbing, rock throwing. Someone would toss a nail bomb and the police would fire back some tear gas cannisters. That would usually end it. Once in a while there was shooting with live ammunition. Then everyone would go home to dinner. It was becoming abundantly clear that the Parliament of the Streets was an embarrassment to Marcos, precisely because so many prominent citizens were part of it.

I wore my own distinctive "riot" wardrobe every day. This was no time for dresses or high heels. My mainstay was my khaki shooting vest with a dozen pockets, which I wore with jeans, a T-shirt and running shoes. In a back pocket, I always had a surgical mask, good for straining out the tear gas when soaked in water or perfume, and a pair of swimming goggles, perfect for keeping the tear gas out of my eyes, but not so great for focusing a camera.

The demonstrations seemed to blur together in a never-ending series. But I remember a few very clearly.

On a Sunday afternoon in late August, labor groups assembled on Taft Avenue underneath the new light-rail transit line, which was still under construction. That meant there was a lot of construction rubble for both sides to use as ammunition. The leaders lined up, arms intertwined, waiting for the water cannons to let loose. In my month in Manila, I had come to know some of them. Butz Aquino, a soap opera idol and brother of the slain Ninoy. Joker Arroyo, a human rights lawyer who defended the imprisoned communist party leaders. Rene Saguisag, another human rights lawyer who refused to shave his beard until the dictator was gone. Bobbit Sanchez, a sturdy labor lawyer. (Aquino and Saguisag are now senators and Arroyo served as Cory's executive secretary, the second most powerful position in the land, for two years. Sanchez served for a year as labor minister before he was hounded from office for his progressive views.) These guys weren't your usual type of street demonstrators. They were in their forties, experienced and well grounded in their ideas; some carried paunches from their soft lives as lawyers and businessmen. They were definitely not street fighters. Many of them had been in prison during martial law. Some of them would be again before this was over. I was impressed with their ideas and their courage. I knew that lining up in the street facing the water cannons and possibly the bullets was life and death stuff. This wasn't the college-kid adventure I had experienced in the American anti-war movement. There we had the protection of a democracy that, at least nominally, supported our right to protest. By contrast, the Parliament of the Streets was a direct threat to Marcos. There were no protectors at all.

The water cannons let loose. Rene, Joker, Butz, Bobbit and a thousand others stolidly held their ground against the torrent. Thirty seconds seemed like an eternity against the onslaught. Forty-five seconds, then Bobbit Sanchez was knocked off his feet. The others followed, swept away like leaves down a sewer. The ranks broke and rocks began to fly from the demonstrators and back again. We journalists, standing roughly in the middle, got the worst from both sides.

It was the first time I had experienced a "violent dispersal" of a demonstration. Everything happened so fast that I stood uncertainly, transfixed, at the edge of the street. A colleague grabbed me and pulled me to the ground behind a low wall. For the first time, I was frightened.

I peeked over the wall and saw Joe Cantrell, a photographer for Black Star, standing calmly in the middle of the fray, shutter clicking. A particularly well-aimed rock slammed into Joe's shutter finger and laid it open to the bone. The geiser of blood from the cut finger clogged the shutter mechanism and ruined his camera in a split second. As several of us struggled to our feet to go to Joe's aid, another rock, thrown with tremendous force, hit the thick webbed strap of his camera bag and severed it. The bag dropped to the ground as we dragged Joe and bag to safety. It was obvious that Joe had offended somebody out there.

On September 21, the anniversary of the imposition of martial law, a large crowd gathered at Mendiola Bridge, literally a stone's throw from Malacanang Palace. Marcos had announced that there would be no dispersal, so the demonstrators settled down to spend the night. I staked out a piece of pavement and made a mat of newspapers, like everyone else.

Sometime after midnight, I ran into Frank Chavez, a very angry young man and a very able lawyer. Frank and his companion, a man I didn't know, were dressed entirely in black. I asked what they were doing and they winked and answered, "Commando raids."

"What do you mean by that?" I asked.

They showed me a car they had parked on a side street. Clumsily pasted on the windshield was an expired Malacanang sticker. They were going to try to get inside Malacanang, just for the hell of it. It was an Abbie Hoffman "Yippie" tactic that appealed to my sense of fun. But I reminded myself again that this was no joke. They could be killed for this stunt. Malacanang is only a quarter of a mile away from Mendiola Bridge. Despite the presence of phalanxes of heavily armed police, the demonstrators had undoubtedly caused some apprehension among the palace guards. But Frank and friend claimed they were not even questioned by the guards. They drove through the gate, sometime after midnight and blithely made a lap of the palace grounds. They returned twenty minutes later, elated with their foolhardy prank. (Frank Chavez is now the government's able solicitor general, who wears trademark suspenders rather than black clothes. I have always thought that, had things gone slightly differently, Frank would have been in the mountains as a guerrilla fighter.)

Another group had bought a dozen pairs of wire cutters and some nuns were patiently snipping away at the complicated barbed wire barricades that separated demonstrators from police. The police were studiously ignoring the labors of the nuns, for fear that they would be forced to take action against the holy sisters.

As dawn approached, the police said the demonstrators must leave. The leaders pleaded for enough time to celebrate a mass, which turned out to be one of the longest masses in the history of the Philippines. A dozen priests stalled for time. For more than three hours they prayed for everything imaginable, even the cockroaches in the street. As the last prayer faded into the dawn silence, the cops swooped down with the clubs and the group scattered. Police even used their jeeps to chase some of the demonstrators down side streets. A picture that remains in my mind is of Don Chino Roces, then in his mid-seventies, who insisted on tottering feebly to every rally. Although he was the scion of a wealthy publishing family, Chino always wore a peasant's *buri* hat and rubber slippers. Chino was knocked to the ground and abandoned in the panic. The photographers gently helped the old man to his feet, unhurt this time.

There was another demonstration I can't forget. It was September 23, 1984, at the Welcome Rotunda on the northern edge of the city. I even remember the date for some strange reason. This day was different. There was palpable tension. Something was going to happen. There was none of the leisurely assembly or the cops lounging on their riot shields and smoking cigarettes. This time the cops were alert and ready for action. Many of them had pistols in their holsters and a few even had rifles. The marchers formed their ranks and placed one of the Philippines' most revered statesmen, eighty-five-year-old Senator Lorenzo Tanada, the grand old man of nationalist politics, in the front ranks. At "Tanny's" side was Don Chino Roces, as always wearing his *buri* hat and rubber slippers. I guess they thought the presence of the universally revered old men would moderate the tension radiating from the police.

It was 2:30 in the afternoon when the police faced off with the demonstrators and ruthlessly let the water cannons fly. Old man Tanada and Don Chino were mowed down like week-old rice shoots. Their security men picked them up and unceremoniously carried the bruised old men to safety as the cops madly chased the fleeing demonstrators. Journalists ran down side streets, as panicked as the demonstrators. I heard shots. I ducked behind a tree and stepped into a hole, twisting my ankle. A passing demonstrator jerked me to my feet and dragged me along with him.

I noticed Mark Fineman of the *Philadelphia Inquirer* was running beside me. We stopped for a breather in a gas station and snickered at a gaggle of well-dressed matrons who had taken refuge in a storage shed. Without warning, Mark shot out his hand and knocked me in the head, just in time to save me from being hit by a baseball-sized rock that would surely have brained me.

We ran down another side street and came across a group of frantic women led by TingTing Cojuangco, one of the fashion-plate demonstrators and sister-in-law of Cory Aquino. TingTing was calmly supervising the loading of a very bloody young man into a jeep. The young man had a bullet in his chest. Blood was pumping wildly from the wound. For a split second, which seemed like an eternity, I made eye contact with the boy. I couldn't tear myself away from his furious, anguished gaze. Somehow I just knew he would die. I felt I had looked into the eyes of death.

We went to the closest hospital in time to see another young man, only twenty years old, hooked to an EKG monitor displaying a flat line. I remember wondering why he had no shoes. I learned later they had been stolen by the hospital workers. He didn't need them anymore, anyway. He wasn't even a participant in the demonstration that day, just a bystander who had gone to his uncle's tailor shop near the rotunda to ask for a loan.

Upstairs we learned that the young man with TingTing Cojuangco was Fidel Nemenzo, the son of a respected left-wing university professor. The doctors said he would live. I was much relieved that my premonition of his death had been wrong.

Mark and I went back outside to find the police commander and demand an explanation. The fat colonel wearing a foolish Mexican sombrero denied that there had been anyone injured. When Mark and I insisted that we had seen victims of gunshot wounds and at least one dead body, the colonel, in typical Filipino fashion, jokingly denied it all and tried to change the subject by flirting with me. He even denied that any of his men were armed. In unison, Mark and I turned around and said to the colonel, "What's that?" pointing to a policeman walking ten feet behind us and carrying an M-16. The fat colonel smiled and shrugged.

At that moment, a local photographer snapped a shot of Mark and me, flanking the colonel as we walked down the street and looking at each other with expressions of absolute incredulity which fairly shouted, "Bullshit!" It was published on the front page of one of the Manila dailies the next day.

We drank beer far into that night, our clothes still soaked in fear-sweat, our faces still streaked with the city's soot. But we couldn't erase the day's images.

It was clear that the killings of September 23 were planned to allow the police to vent some of their accumulated rage from months of daily demonstrations.

I was seeing more and more raw anger each day. It bombarded me and assaulted my senses, but it still perplexed me. I had seen the poverty and the hopelessness of the people, but it still didn't seem to me that more violence would change that.

8 A MOUNTAIN OF GARBAGE: *November 1984*

EVERYONE HAS HEARD TALES of Manila's Smoky Mountain and the thousands of people living on that mountain of garbage. Now it is "the" story for visiting firemen to do, but in 1985, the horror of the place came to be a buzz among journalists.

One hot November day my Japanese photographer friend Toshi Matsumoto and I visited hell on earth for a few hours. We armed ourselves with cameras and lots of film and asked a taxi driver to take us to Smoky Mountain. The taxi driver pretended not to know the place, I guess because it shamed him, but we knew the general area, past the ports, merely a fifteen-minute drive from the elegant Manila Hotel. When we got close we literally followed our noses but I don't think anything could have prepared us for what we found there.

Smoky Mountain is the repository of a major portion of the garbage for a metropolis of eight million people. The place buzzes with millions of flies. They swarm over everyone, crawling into eyes, ears, every orifice. A few years later, an enterprising do-gooder offered bounties for the capture of flies in an effort to curb disease. Some of the Smoky Mountain kids rode on the boondoggle and made a good income for a few weeks until the largesse petered out.

The Smoky Mountain stench defies description. It is a combination of the sickeningly sweet scent of rotting flesh, the gaseous rotten-egg smell of bluish-gray sewer scum, and other things too horrifying to describe. The mountain is frequently on fire, hence its name.

People live there. They build their shanties in pathetic little clusters on the older, more compacted garbage. Some even plant straggly vegetable gardens. Children run barefoot among rusty cans and broken glass. There are no toilets, so human excrement is everywhere. There is no water, but water of questionable purity can be purchased from gougers on the street below. I guess people who live and eat on Smoky Mountain must have very strong constitutions to survive at all, so a few million bacteria in the water are of no consequence. Many of the children do not survive infancy.

Manila city garbage trucks queue up at designated points on the mountain all day long, waiting for their turn to discharge their odious contents: refuse to most of the city, treasures to the residents of hell.

Moments after we arrived, I tried to position myself to take a panoramic shot of the mountain. I felt something give way under my feet and I sank into the muck up to my knees. I was too horrifed to even consider what I had just stepped in. I knew I had two choices: I could either panic and insist on going home and starting over, which still meant sitting in the taxi with the abominable stuff all over me, or I could pretend that nothing happened and finish my work and get out of that hell forever. I chose the latter, although it was a struggle to suppress the hysteria that arose with every squishy sockless step in my tennis shoes. Eventually it dried and I forgot about it. Maybe the people of Smoky Mountain can only survive psychologically in the same way, by pretending nothing was happening. More likely, they are simply used to it.

About 20,000 people live on Smoky Mountain. Men, women and the smallest children spend their lives combing through the detritus of a city. They line up at the day's dump site and allow the garbage to be literally dumped on top of them. They scramble and claw for every scrap of recyclable plastic, glass or can. Best yet, they hope to find a scrap of food that is not too rotten. The children don't go to school, they trek the mountain, rake through the refuse with crude forklike tools and deposit their treasures in the baskets they carry on their backs.

I came across a small girl of eight or nine who was crouching in a little garbage valley, eating something unthinkable. She looked exactly like a starving animal protecting stolen food. I shot a picture. She looked up when she heard the sound of my shutter. Unlike 99 percent of her countrymen, even her compatriots there on Smoky Mountain who would smile and chant, "One Shot, Joe!" when they saw a camera, this pitiful little soul cringed in terror that I would take away the precious morsel she had discovered.

I talked at some length with Mang Manny, a picker who told me the logistics of working on the mountain. The people had worked out a communal and territorial system. Certain people raked through the fresh garbage, others sorted the type of garbage and others carted it down the mountain to the scrap dealers. The profits were shared among members of one team, which competed fiercely, sometimes violently, with other teams. Mang Manny had heavily tattooed legs and arms, a sure sign in this country that he had been in prison. I asked him what he did time for and he glossed over it quickly, "Robbery. Four years." He returned to Smoky Mountain in 1983, the only home he ever knew, only to discover that the Marcos government was forcing people to move away from Smoky Mountain to a "relocation" area down the coast in Cavite. Smoky Mountain was becoming an embarassment to the Marcos government because journalists had discovered it.

Mang Manny had gone to the new place, Dasmarinas, Cavite, but he came back after a few weeks. Dasmarinas was more than twenty miles from the city and there were no jobs there. In Smoky Mountain there was work, and on a good day Mang Manny could make a respectable forty pesos a day. That was just over two dollars then. Smoky Mountain was home.

Mang Manny was eating his breakfast while I talked to him. I asked what he was eating and he proudly waved a gnawed chicken leg.

"I found this yesterday. It was a good find," he beamed.

I had been queasy before. I felt queasier.

Mang Manny spoke to me in good English. He also spoke Tagalog, the predominant language of the main island of Luzon, and Bicol, his regional dialect. I wondered where else on earth I would find a man who could speak three languages sitting on a mountain of garbage, eating a half-rotten chicken leg.

There are few real treasures to be found on the garbage mountain, although there are occasional pieces of jewelry recovered. There is a mythical story about a gold bar accidentally discarded by the Central Bank. Although bank investigators spent several days at the mountain looking for it, wily mountain residents say they hid it from the government men until they gave up.

Toshi and I walked on and met a woman who beckoned us inside her house. I was curious to see how they lived, so I followed her. Inside, like some sort of freak show barker at a traveling circus, she displayed her son, who appeared to have no bones in his legs. She twined the little boy's legs around each other like pretzels and invited us to photograph him. Toshi said it was too dark inside, so the woman carried the pathetic boy outside. Toshi had no choice but to take pictures, but I pretended to be out of film. I was furious that the woman would attempt to exploit her child like that. I was reminded of beggar women on the streets who drug their babies to make them seem more pitiful so they will get more money. The woman offered us a drink of water, and although my mouth was parched from the heat, I declined because I could not honor her hospitality nor would I risk whatever disease the water might contain.

We had been at the mountain for nearly six hours and I had shot a dozen rolls of film. I knew I had some very good shots. I like to work with good photographers like Toshi because I always learn from them. Somehow their artistry seems to rub off on me. In fact, those Smoky Mountain pictures were the first I ever sold. They were published as a full-page photo essay in the *South China Morning Post* in December.

In September, I had succumbed to my fear of the screened back door on Mabini and moved into Sunset View Tower, a high-rise expats slum on Roxas Blvd. I jokingly referred to my new studio apartment as "The Beach," because the one room was dominated by an extremely tacky wall mural of a beach, complete with palm tree. But there was a nice pool, a real one.

Compared to Smoky Mountain, even the shabby one-roomer where I slept on

a mattress on the floor seemed like a palace. I felt a little guilty, but I also wanted to run away from that horrible memory. Toshi and I both wanted to escape to my pool, perhaps to psychically wash away the mountain.

But Toshi had no swim suit, so we asked the taxi driver to stop at a department store so we could buy one. Inside the department store Toshi quickly made his selection and we lined up to pay for it. I noticed several fastidious Filipinos wrinkling their noses at us. We didn't look all that dirty, but the stench of garbage had penetrated our clothes, our hair, even our skin. We had been at the mountain long enough that we had stopped noticing the stench. We began to giggle almost hysterically at the thought of two middle-class foreigners stinking of garbage in a swanky department store.

I think now that our hysteria was partly in relief that our six-hour-long torture was over. We had been to hell and escaped.

9 FIRST CHRISTMAS AWAY FROM HOME: *December 1984*

I<small>T WAS CHRISTMAS</small> in the Philippines, my first Christmas outside the States. Filipino Christmas goes on forever. I invariably hear my first Christmas carol in a department store sometime in September and, despite my unabashed romanticism and love for the gift-giving and fun of the holidays, by the time December 25 rolls around, I am pretty tired of all the hoopla. That first year I wasn't really homesick, just feeling blue and a little sorry for myself. It seemed especially strange that Christmas was approaching and it was still sweltering.

I perked up a bit in early December when I got a phone call from Jack McCabe, my persistent friend from the States and the disastrous St. Patrick's escapade in Dublin. Jack was inviting himself to Manila for Christmas.

Somewhere in the back of my mind was the hope that there could be some romance, but almost as soon as Jack arrived I realized that I had changed irrevocably. I was no longer the bored reporter from Watertown, nor was I the awestricken free-lancer who had timidly ventured to Belfast only ten months before. Jack is a retired U.S. Marine major and helicopter pilot who had spent several years since his retirement as a vagabond and party-lover. I was beginning to earn my stripes as a bona fide foreign correspondent. We just didn't have much in common anymore.

But we put a good face on it.

I had bought a Filipino Christmas tree—a unique little contraption made of sticks nailed to a central trunk to look like a pine tree, then painted white. This little two-foot wonder looked pretty bleak next to the gaudy mural of the beach. A group of colleagues had ingeniously suspended it from the ceiling and decorated it with dirty socks and toilet paper one night. But before Jack's arrival I redecorated it with some bits of red coral picked up on a beach somewhere and a few champagne corks from a collection of bottles drunk on special occasions.

We took a three-day trip to Boracay Island, with its snow-white-sand beaches and kaleidoscopic snorkeling reefs. I reveled in just relaxing for those brief days. They were the first days off I had taken since I arrived in July.

On Christmas Eve we ate a pleasant dinner at a Japanese restaurant. I didn't have much appetite, which is unusual for me. My skin felt strangely tender, as if I had a sunburn all over. The weight of my clothes was annoying.

Christmas morning Jack was already up when I awoke. He held out a glass of

champagne and my stomach lurched. That was also totally unlike me. I just felt rotten, but I couldn't pinpoint exactly what felt bad.

Bert phoned and it cheered me up a bit. I still missed him very much.

Jack and I were invited to a gourmet Christmas dinner at the home of John Bochen, an American friend in the airline catering business.

I still felt strangely detached, as if I were seeing things through the wrong end of a telescope. I declined all offers of alcohol. As we sat down to dinner I had the sensation I had drunk Alice in Wonderland's magic brew. The world suddenly became miniaturized. I was looking at a tableful of three-inch-tall people through a long tunnel. I didn't want to disrupt the beef Wellington and all the trimmings, so I pushed my food around on my plate and prayed not to faint before the meal ended.

The group was large, so no one had really noticed my silence. I was a bit frightened by my bizarre symptoms. But when the meal ended, I asked John if he could give me a ride to a taxi. Suddenly John and Jack galvanized into solicitous concern for me. I was whisked home and tucked into bed just as I began shaking from fever.

I guess my strange illness and our lack of rapport was too much for Jack. I certainly wasn't a party girl. He announced his plans to take a bus to Clark Air Base the day after Christmas. He had already put himself on the waiting list for a flight back to the States. I was very put out because he was abandoning me when I was so sick. I knew something was seriously wrong with me. But the next morning I dragged myself out of bed and saw him off on the bus. It was a relief not to have to feel like I should entertain him anymore.

As soon as Jack was gone I dragged myself back to The Beach and collapsed on my mattress on the floor, still shivering from fever. My skin was still so sensitive, I couldn't stand the weight of any clothing, yet I was cold. The inside of my mouth was covered with blisters and my chest was so congested that I couldn't breathe lying down. I was miserable and feeling very sorry for myself.

Later in the day a couple of friends looked in on me. One became alarmed at my condition and insisted on taking me to the hospital. I know I was incoherent in the hospital emergency room, but when a young intern insisted he wanted to admit me I was adamant that I would die if I was admitted to the hospital. Given what I know now about hospitals in the Philippines, I may have been right.

There was no positive diagnosis, but the doctor gave me an unappetizing smorgasbord of possibilities: malaria, typhoid, cholera, measles, dengue fever. He said we'd have to wait for more symptoms to develop.

I was so delirious that I must have frightened the intern. He even gave me his home phone number in case I developed any other symptoms. He said to call anytime of the day or night.

On the fourth night, I woke up at three A.M., drenched in sweat and clawing at my skin. I was covered with pimples! Every square inch of my body had big red pimples. They were even in my hair. I thought I would go mad with the itching. I remembered the young intern, so I called him and described my symptoms. I was infuriated when he laughed, but relieved when he told me it meant I only had the measles! I wasn't amused.

I couldn't remember ever having had the measles when I was a kid. My mother told me on the phone later that I had been given gamma globulin shots as a child to prevent me from getting the measles.

Measles at thirty-five is no joke. For a week I did nothing but lie on my mattress and bathe the itching blisters from a bucket in the shower. Friends and neighbors dropped in once a day to be sure I was still breathing. By New Year's Eve I felt better, but a trip in the elevator down to the lobby to retrieve my week's mail made me realize how weak I was. I put out of my mind any thought of attending a journalists' New Year's Eve party. I felt even sorrier for myself.

There's an old Chinese superstition that whatever you do on New Year's Eve, you will do for the rest of the year. I prayed it wasn't true. I had no intention of spending 1985 in a sickbed.

That New Year's Eve I stood on my balcony and tape recorded the war-zone sounds of the New Year's celebration to feed to ABC radio. There were exploding rockets, firecrackers, and a few lunatics firing guns into the air. Burning tires emitted fumes that scorched my lungs even from my eighteenth-floor balcony.

The folks on the radio desk in New York were thrilled. They said no one else ever filed New Year's Eve spots. I glumly replied it was because normal people went to parties on New Year's Eve.

My recuperation was maddeningly slow. I couldn't work a full day for a month.

In the meantime I had decided to move again. It would be my third move since my arrival in Manila four months before. I was fed up with The Beach and the mattress on the floor. The electricity in Sunset View Tower had become erratic and I frequently had to carry bags of groceries up the eighteen flights of stairs. The straw that broke the camel's back came during my illness when the water system broke down and I had not one drop of water in my apartment for two weeks. I couldn't wait to get out.

I mustered my feeble strength and found an apartment further up Roxas Boulevard in Legaspi Tower. It had lovely wood parquet floors, a stunning view of Manila Bay sunsets from the balcony and, wonder of wonders, a bedroom with a real bed! I thought I could afford the three-hundred dollars a month rent with the improving financial situation, thanks to ABC.

ABC seemed to be happy enough with my work. I was grateful for ABC's patience with my clumsiness and the willingness of the desk people to help me improve my performance. During my week of measles delirium, I had somehow cranked out my first effort at "Perspective," a ten-minute radio commentary that was a major endeavor for me. At my speaking pace, the ten-minute report was about 2,000 words long, the length of a magazine article. For several days, I sweated over writing it and then agonized over recording it until I was satisfied with the results.

I had no more thoughts of leaving Manila. I knew I was onto a good story and, though Grandma's funds were running out, I thought I could support myself.

All along the way from Belfast to Manila, I had sent stories to John Johnson at the *Watertown Daily Times*, with acompanying letters saying he was welcome to use any of them he wished, no charge. He never used one or had the courtesy to even reply to my letters. Maybe he thought a woman couldn't be a foreign correspondent with any credibility. I felt hurt. After eleven years of toil for the *Watertown Daily Times*, it was a slap in the face.

In early February my year's leave of absence was at an end. In that year I had gained confidence and improved my writing ability. I had, with a great deal of sweat, old-fashioned leg work, and grinding away as much as eighteen hours a day, established myself as a foreign correspondent. Editors were interested in what I wrote. There would still be struggles ahead, but I knew I had finally established my credentials. The end of my twelve-year association with the *Watertown Daily Times* was at hand; it was time to cut the umbilical cord.

Without regret, I wrote a curt letter to John Johnson:

Dear Mr. Johnson,

Please accept forthwith my resignation effective immediately.

Sincerely,
KATHLEEN BARNES

10 A NIGHT WITH THE COCKROACHES:
Bagong Barrio, February 1985

I HAD SEEN POVERTY in the countryside and, while it was jarring, it wasn't as desperate as in the cities. There was a certain dignity to the people who tilled the land and subsisted on rice and salt.

Urban poverty was something else. People lived in conditions worse than any zoo. They lived, literally, on top of one another, squatting on land owned by others, with no sanitation, no water, in tumbledown shanties built haphazardly of plywood, plastic, or whatever came to hand. The situation was made worse by the hundreds of thousands of migrants from the countryside, seeking the streets paved with gold, who found instead streets quite literally paved with shit.

In the countryside, throwing the garbage out the window causes no real problem: the pigs are natural scavengers. In the cities, ignorant barrio residents who throw garbage into the urban *esteros* (canals), and shit wherever they like, create an appalling health problem. Typhoid and cholera were and still are common. Children die daily from diarrhea, measles, and a horde of diseases that would not in themselves be life-threatening, but become deadly when coupled with chronic malnutrition.

There was no dignity for the hundreds of thousands of squatters in the city.

During the demonstrations on the first anniversary of Aquino's death, I met Rocky Divinagracia, a middle-class businessman who had a marginal business exporting fish and prawns. Rocky told me he lived in Tondo, Manila's largest slum, and invited me for a visit. A few weeks later Rocky picked me up in his Land Rover for a safari to the urban wilderness.

We turned off the main drag along the grubby waterfront just before Smoky Mountain and entered Tondo. The first thing I noticed was a row of cute little European-style townhouses with ceramic facades. There were dozens of horse-drawn carriages that seemed to be the taxis of the common people in Tondo. It was all rather quaint.

"This doesn't seem too bad," I observed.

Rocky laughed and explained that those cute little townhouses were merely facades, put up by Imelda Marcos for the visit of Pope John Paul II in February of 1981. It seemed that one of the Pope's stops would take him along this road and Imelda didn't want him to see the horrors of Tondo. Imelda had several cute little projects for cute little poor people, some of which included real houses built of sand stuck together with a nominal amount of concrete. Like most sand castles, many of them fell down. The projects had cute little names like "Bliss" and "Love."

As soon as we wove our way into the interior of Tondo, it was clear that this place was no bastion of "Bliss."

The "Love" part was a little more obvious: maybe there was a little too much love there. The streets were teeming with children—children hanging around candy stores, children playing basketball, children chasing one another in the street, children selling cigarettes, children pushing carts laden with jugs of water. Kids seemed to cover every square inch of sidewalk and street. It was difficult for Rocky to negotiate some streets because they were so crowded.

"What do you notice here?" demanded Rocky.

"Kids," I answered, somewhat stunned.

"That's right," he agreed with an angry shake of his head.

The core of poverty in the Philippines, Rocky believed, is overpopulation. "It's what keeps our people down. If we are ever going to climb out of this hole [of poverty], we've got to stop having so many kids."

We went to Rocky's humble house, a small concrete-block affair with squatter shanties huddled against the outer wall. He fixed a cup of coffee. Then I realized why Rocky had brought me to Tondo. He was a man with a mission. As a Protestant he was a man infuriated by his countrymen, who believe that they aren't virile if they don't have six or eight kids. Rocky was unique, a unicorn among Filipinos, a crusader against ignorance. He saw a problem and did what he could to solve it. Rocky ran a one-man family-planning program, dependent on no government or funding agency. Rocky Divinagracia had no Catholic hang-ups about birth control.

Rocky prowled the streets of Tondo, looking for pregnant women. He was becoming well enough known that his searches were becoming easier. He befriended the women and coaxed them to introduce him to their husbands. Then he would pop the question: "Do you want to have any more kids?"

The answer from these pathetically poor people was invariably a resounding "NO."

So Rocky would make his offer. When it was time for the baby to come, he would accompany the mother to the hospital and, as soon as the delivery was over, she would have a tubal ligation. Rocky paid the expenses. He guessed he had paid for a hundred or more.

"It's not much," he said modestly. "But I do what I can."

We took a walk around Rocky's neighborhood and it was clear he was a hero. I wish there were more heroes like Rocky.

Down the street in Tondo, Mother Teresa had a hospice and an orphanage. The Marcos government had ingratiated itself with Mother Theresa by giving

her land for the institutions, but there had later been some political disagreements, probably because the "Living Saint" wondered why the government did
nothing to truly alleviate the misery of its people.

In 1985 Mother Teresa paid a visit to the Philippines, but Imelda couldn't
seem to find a moment in her busy schedule to meet with the nun. There might
be too many difficult questions to answer.

During Mother Teresa's visit, I happened to be in the Manila Hotel one
morning when Imelda arrived for some shindig or other. As she swept through
the door, treading oh-so-gracefully on the red carpet, gorgeously coifed and
wearing an elegant designer evening gown, graciously accepting a huge bouquet
of orchids, I couldn't help but think that Tondo is only a ten-minute drive from
the Manila Hotel, but it is a world away.

Some Filipinos have even more desperate means of dealing with overpopulation. I once visited a fishing barrio a stone's throw from the massive American
navy base in Olongapo, where I met a woman who had sold her twin sons to a
childless Filipino couple for a package price of 600 pesos (thirty dollars). The
mother, at thirty, and her thirty-two-year-old husband, were the first adults I had
seen in the Philippines who were obviously suffering from severe malnutrition.
She had wispy gray hair, a deeply lined face, and only two or three teeth. His
skin, covered with sores, hung in folds on his skeletal frame. Baby selling is not
uncommon, but it was tremendously shocking to me.

I wanted to know more of barrio life in the city.

A community worker in Bagong Barrio on the northern edge of the city
happily accomodated me. I was invited to spend a night there with the family of a
labor organizer.

Bagong Barrio is even larger than Tondo. It sprawls on both sides of the
highway out of the city to the north. Practically no one in Bagong Barrio owns
the land upon which the shacks have squatted for fifty years or more. I walked
down narrow passageways, barely large enough to pass single file, and felt the
black stain of poverty everywhere. There are kids everywhere, just like in Tondo.
Many of them have big bellies and orange hair caused by severe malnutrition.
Many people there earn a living by washing used plastic items for recycling, most
of them found by Smoky Mountain scavengers. Tricycles and jeepneys thread
their way through the streets, skirting the clean plastic left in the sun to dry.
Others in the barrio work in the factories. They are lucky if they earn thirty pesos
($1.75) a day.

I was introduced to my hosts for the night, Joey and Malou and their two-year
old son Martin (not their real names). They were labor organizers affiliated with
the Catholic Church in the barrio.

As we walked toward their house, I found myself already feeling affection for

Malou, a plain-faced, intelligent and articulate woman. Joey spoke only broken English, so it was harder to get to know him.

We climbed to the second story of a very flimsy-looking plywood structure that was Joey and Malou's home. They had an eight-by-ten room at the end of a dark corridor. The room contained nothing but a single-burner hot plate, a sink with a jug of water for washing, a few utensils, a plastic basin for washing clothes, a plastic chamber pot, a small wooden-slat bed covered by a straw mat, a rickety table with two chairs, and a few items of drab clothing hanging from nails. A single unshaded bulb was suspended from the ceiling. These were the wordly goods of Malou and Joey. Malou confided they paid nearly two-thirds of their monthly income or about 600 pesos (about thirty dollars) for rent. They paid another thirty pesos for the electricity for the bare bulb.

Malou prepared a dinner of dried fish, rice and vegetables. It must have been three times the amount they would normally eat. I gave Joey 100 pesos (five dollars) to buy some beer, knowing that he could buy a case and a half of beer for that, but wanting to somehow help defray the cost of the elaborate meal without embarassing them. Joey returned with a few quart bottles and we drank beer far into the night.

Early in the evening there was a parade of people through the tiny room: fellow community workers, labor organizers, a nun, a priest, who all wanted to tell me about the problems of the people of the barrio. It was a bit of political indoctrination that had very heavy leftist overtones. I was more interested in the day-to-day struggle for survival.

When all of the visitors had left, Malou and Joey relaxed a bit. I asked how they had met. After they exchanged a significant glance, Malou whispered, "We met in our collective."

That confirmed what I had suspected. Malou and Joey were Communist Party members and part of a rather extensive underground network in Bagong Barrio. They were very committed to their task of organizing workers and helping them find a better life. But there was another agenda. Those organized workers would eventually become part of a civilian support group for the armed contingent that was already present in the barrio. They were *masa* or the masses who support the armed struggle. By being unarmed, yet politically very active, Malou and Joey put their lives on the line each day.

After drinking several glasses of beer, I was seriously in need of a toilet and then a bed. I hadn't noticed a bathroom anywhere and I was at first shy about asking. But I was desperately in need of a pee. Finally, I asked Malou, who was as embarassed as I when she told me there was no toilet. She told me to "just squat" on the bamboo slats of the second story porch.

Malou and Joey's place was typical of the barrio. There was absolutely no privacy. It was impossible to be more than a few feet from a dozen other human beings. Yet they were very modest in their lack of privacy. People bathed, fully clothed, at community water pumps. It is possible there are people who have never in their lives seen their own naked bodies. One friend described Bagong Barrio perfectly, "It's the kind of place where, if you fart, the entire neighborhood knows it."

I would never sleep if I didn't take a leak. But what if someone was walking underneath that bamboo slat porch? I didn't think I could do it in front of God and everybody. Even though it was dark, I knew that, as a foreigner, I was the object of intense interest. There were eyes watching in the dark. I squatted for what seemed like an hour, but my muscles just refused to let go. I finally gave up, my bladder still bursting.

It was after two A.M. when we finally went to bed, me in the bed, Malou, Joey and Martin on the floor. The bed was hard and mosquitos dive-bombed me relentlessly. I still needed to pee. And, worst of all, they had left the light on. I tossed and turned for what seemed like hours.

After I was sure everybody was asleep, I got up and used the plastic chamber pot in the corner. I guiltily emptied the contents on the leaky roof of the unfortunates who lived in the shack just under the window. I was relieved, but I still couldn't sleep. It was hot. No air moved through this congested place. The mosquitos began to have dog fights just over my face. I reminded myself that this was the ordinary way of life in the barrio. The light was in my eyes. Why the hell didn't they turn off the light? Malou told me why months later, when I knew her better: they left the light on to keep the monster three-inch cockroaches from attacking me in the night.

It was a short night, anyway. Before dawn, someone came banging on the door and said we were needed desperately. It was never clear if Malou and Joey were needed or if they wanted me because I was a foreigner. The entire barrio seemed to know I was there.

We made a hasty trip through Bagong Barrio's dusky alleys and sinister passageways, climbing over sleepers who did not even have the comfort of a shanty roof over their heads. Eventually, we came to a low hut with a door less than four feet high. We entered, but none of us could stand straight, so we stood heads bowed. It was almost as if we were making obeisance to the surreal scene that assaulted our still foggy senses. An ancient crone of a grandmother was sitting on the floor, weeping silently as she sewed the head back on the corpse of her sixteen-year-old grandson. All of us gasped in shock, even Malou and Joey who were much more accustomed to the struggle for survival there, and to the tragic results of losing that struggle.

The boy, Lito, and two friends had been scavenging in a nearby garbage dump, looking for bottles and cans they could sell. They wanted to raise a little money for a birthday celebration for Lito. They found a "plastic thing" that looked like a flashlight. Thinking it might have some resale value, they began to fiddle with it. They didn't know it was a grenade launcher, loaded with a live grenade that exploded during the boys' curious examination. The explosion decapitated Lito and blew a hole the size of a basketball in the chest of one of the other boys. The third boy miraculously survived. No one could explain why the grenade launcher was on the garbage heap.

Lito's family was grieving with an odd stoicism. I had noticed that Filipinos have a very personal, yet detached view of death. They weep, they mourn when anyone dies, particularly if it is a child. But they also take it in stride. Death is an everyday event for the poor.

As we left Lito's mourning family, the wake had begun and with it the traditional mahjong game. The gambling money and the rum bottle were on the table. The mahjong tiles clicked furiously as the roosters crowed. Yet another day of violence had dawned for the folk of Bagong Barrio.

11 STARVING CHILDREN: *April 1985*

THERE IS SOMETHING STRANGE and haunting about the barren and pain-wracked island of Negros that keeps drawing me back. The people are warm and accepting, perhaps too accepting of the tradition-bound *haciendero* system. The feudal sugar plantations, run by the *illustrados* and worked by the peasants, underscores the economic abyss between the wealthy *hacienderos* and their dependent and impoverished workers.

Each of my many visits to Negros has had one gleaming moment of stark reality that stays with me, but none more so than my back-to-back visits in April and May of 1985 when I went to Negros to write about the human effects of the failing world sugar market. The bottom had fallen out of the sugar market and the Negros economy, which was totally dependent on sugar, had literally gone to hell. Because the lifeblood of Negros is sugar, the island was swiftly bleeding to death.

One day I was riding through the streets of Bacolod in a yellow Mercedes belonging to a sugar planter friend. I felt guilty driving through those desolate streets flaunting such wealth, with so many ragged people looking on with such hopelessness. As my friend parked the car, she warned, "Don't slam the door too hard, I'm down to my last Mercedes."

I got out of the car and listened to the genteel "thunk" as the door closed. A little girl of four or five tugged at my shirt, reaching a filthy hand toward me in plea for a few coins. Her hair was orange-streaked, a sign of severe calcium deficiency, and her teeth were blackened and broken from sucking nutritionless sugar cane in vain effort to stave off the pain of hunger.

Workers, who earned as little as a dollar a day, were being laid off or borrowing from their bosses at exorbitant interest rates. If a child got sick, there was no money for medicine.

One humid afternoon, I interviewed four young renegade sugar planters in the Bacolod City home of a friend, Jane Benedicto. They were young planters with a social conscience. And they opposed Marcos, unlike many of their fellow aristocrats. The young planters detailed for me how Marcos had conspired to steal land from sugar planters who would not kowtow to him, and how payment for sugar crops had been withheld so the banks would foreclose on the land. The sugar industry was dying. Everyone but the Marcos cronies was panicked at the prospect of losing the land held by generations of Spanish mestizo families. The cronies knew they would walk away with the store as they always had.

The issues were much more basic for the workers. Without jobs, they had become desperate for any means of livelihood. Some sifted the riverbeds for gravel to sell to the construction companies, but that wasn't a very lucrative occupation, because there wasn't much construction going on. Others gleaned mussels from the river and still others combed the streets for stray scraps of paper, bottles, and cans they could sell. There was fierce competition for even the most menial task, the most fundamental commodity that might generate a peso or two.

As the afternoon sun faded, my sugar planter friends asked me to join them for dinner. I explained I had one more stop, the Bacolod Provincial Hospital, where I had planned to visit the malnutrition ward. They offered to take me there.

When we arrived at the hospital in yet another Mercedes, only Ed Alunan was brave enough to go inside with me.

A priest had told me about starving children and I thought a visit to the malnutrition ward might give the story a very human touch. I don't think any human being could have been prepared for what Ed and I encountered there.

We walked through the hospital's dingy and crowded hallways. Many patients lay on bare plastic mattresses in the hallways. There was one emaciated old man who fixed his listless gaze on a grease spot on the wall while flies crawled over open sores on his arms. There was a teenager who reeked of infection from a gunshot wound, a mere flesh wound in the left buttock, but there was no money for antibiotics. With a dollar's worth of medicine, his life would be saved. Without it, he would surely die needlessly.

The hospital administrators, doctors and nurses were more than happy to tell us about the plight of the children and to escort us into the children's ward. I got my tape recorder and camera ready, and the tape was rolling when we entered the waking nightmare that was the malnutrition ward.

I expected to hear children crying, but the ward was suspended in an eerie silence. These children were too weak to cry. There was only an occasional thin wail, a whimper, then silence. The little boy in the first bed had legs no thicker than a broomstick. His mother said he was four years old, but he looked like an infant. He clutched a soggy soda cracker to his pitifully sunken chest.

In another bed were year-old twins, Dawn and Moon, bright-eyed and alert. Their heads were completely bald, their tiny bellies swollen and their legs and arms not much bigger than my index finger. I touched Dawn's cheek with my finger and said without thinking that she was cute enough to take home. The child's anguished mother looked at me with pleading eyes.

"Would you take her, please, would you take her home with you?" she asked.

I could say nothing. I began to shoot photographs to distract myself from the tears that were already beginning to blur my vision.

Ed was crying.

He moaned, "They look like Ethiopian children, but they are my own people. How could this be happening here?"

He began to hand out 100-peso notes.

In the corner was Joel Abong, seven years old, one of seven children of an unemployed sugar worker. He weighed only eleven pounds. Joel's huge eyes looked like one of those cheap carnival paintings, but there was no life, not even pathos, in them. Every rib was visible through the tears in his ragged T-shirt. His legs were too thin to bear even the feather weight of his bloated body. It was obvious than Joel couldn't live long. His slightly more sturdy nine-year-old brother squatted helplessly next to the bed.

I shot a couple of rolls of film, feeling like an intruder in a private hell.

We left the hospital and drove to a rickety barbecue stand in the parking lot of a gas station. Jane said her cousin owned it. I was glad we weren't going anywhere ostentatious.

Ed and I gloomily drank far more beer than we had intended and ate almost nothing while we tried to talk about anything but the pain of what we had just seen at the hospital.

The next morning, I returned to the hospital to take some daylight photographs. The mothers greeted me like a sister. I looked around for the twins, Dawn and Moon, but Dawn was gone. "Where is she?" I asked.

The mothers looked at their feet in embarassment. One mother smiled. She said Dawn got better and went home. I knew that was impossible. Finally they admitted the awful truth. Dawn had died overnight. The image swelled gigantic in my mind's eye: those bright little eyes and the desperate mother who begged me to save her child.

Joel Abong was still in his corner, unmoving, unblinking, focused inward, perhaps meditating on his approaching death.

In outrage, I wrote about Joel during my short ferry ride to Iloilo later that day.

Back in Manila, I printed my photos. One particular shot of Joel was very moving, so I made several prints. When I was in Negros again two weeks later, I gave one to Ed Alunan. Ed and I had developed a bond because of the pain we shared that night at the malnutrition ward.

There was a farmers' rally that May day in Bacolod. Late in the hot afternoon, thousands of people had gathered in the town plaza. Ed approached me, a young woman trailing along behind him. He introduced her as a reporter for *Mr. and*

Ms. magazine, an opposition newsweekly that had emerged after the Aquino assassination. She had my photo of Joel in her hand. Would I give my permission for it to be published? she asked.

I hesitated. The photo was very raw. I had intended it as a memento for Ed. I hadn't thought of publishing it. I thought of all of the children. Of little Dawn, with the bright eyes, dead overnight. Of the children with the broken teeth. Of the man I met in Talisay holding his four-year-old son, blinded from starvation.

Then I thought of Joel, a shadow of a child to be sure, but still a human being with a right to privacy. Perhaps most of all to a right of privacy in his death. Would I be violating that last shred of Joel's dignity if I allowed the photo to be published?

I asked the reporter to let me think about it for a few minutes. There was no easy answer.

Ed sat down on a bench next to me.

"Maybe if it is published, it will save some others," he urged softly.

He was right. I gave permission.

The photo was published on the cover of *Mr. and Ms.* the following week. It caused a furor. The Marcos government attempted to disavow it. But how can you disavow a photo that speaks a million words? Years later, people tell me they still remember the photo and it still haunts them.

Many Filipinos were outraged to learn that such things were happening right in their own country. Filipinos like to brag that their land is so fertile that if you drop a seed, it will grow. So how could people be starving here?

Things began to move.

Popular folk singer Freddie Aguilar wrote a song to the children of Negros and donated all of the proceeds to feeding programs. Foreign governments were shocked to see a child who looked like a barely living skeleton. Aid money began to pour in.

That photo probably had more impact than any I have ever taken. The Filipinos were looking at the tragedy of their own people, foisted on them by the thievery of the Marcos government. Foreign governments began to be aware that the situation had become desperate. The photo was yet another exposure of Marcos, another chink in his armor of deception.

The Joel Abong photo is not the greatest photo in history. I am only a passable photographer. The photo was important because it showed stark and undeniable reality.

I still wonder if I did Joel Abong a disservice by robbing him of his privacy in those last agonized weeks of his life. Or if there was a greater cause in the children who lived. I am still torn by that inner conflict. When I travel to Negros even now, I still see children with orange streaks in their hair, broken and blackened teeth, and swollen bellies supported by wobbly matchstick legs. And I know that nothing has really changed despite the fact that sugar prices have doubled on the world market and sugar planters no longer complain about being down to their last Mercedes.

Joel Abong died in July of 1985. He will live forever in my memory.

12 IN THE MOUNTAINS WITH THE REBELS: *May 1985*

It HAD TAKEN NINE MONTHS of "getting acquainted" sessions before the rebel New People's Army (NPA) would agree to take me on a field trip. There had been endless "conscientization" sessions over countless cups of coffee in donut shops before I was judged sufficiently indoctrinated that I would not slam dunk the rebel's cause.

The NPA says it stands for justice for the oppressed and retribution for the oppressors and I couldn't argue with that. But in recent years, the lines have blurred and the NPA itself has sometimes itself become an oppressor. What then of justice?

The aggravatingly lengthy process of gaining access to the guerrilla zone had much less to do with indoctrination than it had to do with trust. Because I had arrived in the Philippines without making contacts with rebel support groups in the States or Europe and had no "recommendations," that trust was longer in coming.

Finally, in May of 1985, I had the unexpected opportunity to go into the guerrilla zone. It came, at least in part, because of my several trips to Negros and the contacts I had made there. Even more, it had to do with the furor aroused by the Joel Abong story. The "movement" decided I had earned my stripes.

On my third trip to Negros in a little over a month, I asked leftist contacts to help me look into "human rights violations." I was surprised to find myself climbing mountains with the rebels. Apparently I had unwittingly pushed the right button.

At midnight on a Saturday night, while I watched the cockroach races in the Sea Breeze Hotel in Bacolod, I got word that we would leave at six A.M. for the zone. I had been told I would be thrown together with some French television journalists who were staying in the same hotel, so three of us went off to the Bacolod City market in the dim hours before dawn to try to scrounge some canteens, flashlights, batteries, and whatever else seemed appropriate.

There was a bad omen from the beginning—the cameraman had diarrhea. I convinced the drug store to open early to sell me some of my staple for travelling in the countryside—Carbo-Guanacil, charcoal tablets that filter out the bad guys, but leave your intestines unpleasantly full of little lumps of charcoal. We gave the cameraman a quadruple dose of the little black pills. That brought the idea of climbing mountains just within the realm of possibility for him, something that would have been impossible an hour before.

It was typical of "Filipino time" that our six A.M. start dragged on until about ten, when we finally loaded what seemed like ten tons of TV gear into a car brought by a radical union organizer and drove to a Catholic *convento* about forty miles from Bacolod.

We were greeted by the sound of sweet childish voices singing Flores de Mayo (May Flowers) songs to the Virgin Mary. We were immediately whisked inside, but I was sure we had already attracted attention.

The radical priest told us we would have to stay inside until sunset because four white people with television cameras were much too visible in the tiny town.

We whiled away the afternoon, alternately dozing in the heat and listening to the priest tell us horror stories about the oppression of the peasants. I could see by their blackened and broken teeth that the children were sugar cane-suckers. Before the week was out, we shamefully well-fed foreigners would join them in sucking sugar cane to stave off the hunger pangs.

The priest fed us a feast of fish, vegetables and rice and a dish that I initially thought was some sort of spaghetti. It was actually pig intestines cooked in blood, a local delicacy I was told. I gingerly shoved it to one side of my plate.

At sunset our guide appeared. Pedro was young, swarthy, and wore a distinctive black *campesino* hat with a feather. Pedro fell on the ground laughing when he saw my disguise—a bandanna to cover my light hair and a pair of sunglasses to cover my blue eyes. Nothing could conceal my white skin. One of my companions was wearing leather dress shoes, bermuda shorts, and an Aussie slouch hat. The other two loaded the TV gear onto a tricycle—a motorcycle with a sidecar. With equipment dripping from all appurtenances of the tricycle, we four white people and a guide with a feather in his hat probably were the talk of the town for weeks. Certainly we were not inconspicuous.

We rode the tricycle on bumpy roads for an hour, gently climbing into the mountains through sugar cane fields, complaining about the rough ride. We would have been less inclined to complain if we had known that we would be walking for the better part of the next four days.

A child told us there were military patrols in the area, so we abandoned the tricycle and proceeded on a foot trail through a cane field. In a few minutes, we arrived at what appeared to be a vacant bamboo house in a small barrio of seven or eight houses. The entire population of the barrio (about fifty people, including some very noisy children) crowded in to watch us eat our supper of rice and the canned pork and beans we had brought from town. It is only in retrospect that I remember so clearly what we ate at what times, because we were to eat so little in the coming days.

Pedro and some of his barrio friends unearthed a guitar. They serenaded us for an hour or so while the barrio folk continued to observe us like animals in a zoo. I suppose they saw very few white people. I was trying not to be annoyed and to maintain my "solidarity with the people," but, in fact I was tired and grouchy. I didn't like the "zoo" routine at all.

Puritanical Filipino cultural mores and preferential treatment for women being what they are, I was assigned a sleeping room with a wooden bed covered with a straw mat. It was clear I was to sleep alone. I was not happy, because it was cold in the mountains, and I had no blanket. But it seemed there was no choice. My three companions huddled under our only weatherproof poncho in the adjacent room. Then the barrio settled down for the night to watch us sleep. That was too much for me. I was angry and tired of the constant observation, so I shooed them away like pesky flies.

In the morning I awoke, refreshed, to a glorious sunny day, made even more pristine by the muffled sounds of Pedro's guitar. Our guide and a newcomer were sitting in an abandoned truck with no wheels, picking out the tune of "The Internationale," singing the Tagalog version off key at the top of their lungs. I noticed with excitement that the newcomer was armed with an ancient rusty .38 caliber revolver.

The Frenchmen were pleased to have someone to take pictures of.

"Finally," I thought. "We are getting somewhere."

It took a very long time to get somewhere. The romance and novelty of climbing mountains with the rebels wore off fast. The next few days were a blur of walking up and down mountains under the blazing tropical sun, a desperate thirst that once forced me to drink water from a dirty jar which smelled of gasoline. Borderline heat exhaustion that got me a ride on an equally exhausted horse up one of what seemed like a hundred mountains. All of that was followed by intense thunderstorms while slogging shivering through mud and dense jungle undergrowth. And long periods of waiting, waiting, waiting. For what, we didn't know.

Pedro had turned back that first morning after he handed us over to the man with the .38 and his companion who had a weapon identical in make and decrepitude. When Pedro walked away, we lost touch with the English-speaking world. It seemed we lost a great deal of our connection with reality as well. When we would ask in pidgin English how far the camp was, we would get maddeningly vague answers, like "over there," with a shrug of the shoulders.

Late in the first afternoon, a downpour forced us to take refuge in a peasant hut. The six-by-ten-foot bamboo and thatch hut was home to a family of six. Our party of six could barely squeeze inside out of the rain while the children squatted underneath. I was shocked and filled with sadness when I realized that everything the family owned was on display in that tiny leaky hut. One ragged set of clothes on the back of each family member, a few dingy and torn T-shirts hanging on the line, a comb with several teeth missing, two skinny chickens scratching in the mud, one cooking pot, a wooden spoon and two glass jars for drinking. A few stalks of straggly corn clung precariously to a steep slope. I had never imagined such poverty.

The second night, we settled down in a large and well-built *nipa* (woven coconut frond) hut that was apparently an NPA safehouse. There, several comrades with M-16s joined us. It looked like we had penetrated the outer ring of defense. But we were told that military operations were being conducted nearby and we would need to be alert. We were fed a meager dinner of *camote* (cassava), which is what people eat when they are too poor to afford even rice. Then we insistently bedded down together, since it was a one-room house and I was eager for the warmth of other bodies. The four of us squeezed under the single poncho, which was showing its worth every minute as raincoat for the precious camera and blanket for us.

About two A.M. there was a commotion above the noise of a tremendous thunderstorm.

"Quick, wake up. We must go," whispered a cadre with a flair for the dramatic, brandishing an M-16 and dressed in black Viet Cong-type pajamas emblazoned with a red lightning bolt.

"Ka" (Comrade) Cobra hurriedly introduced himself and told us soldiers were very close by. The adrenalin rush caused by the fear of imminent attack by the military soon gave way to exhaustion and to the concentration necessary to keep up. As we struggled down one almost sheer mud-covered cliff and up another, grabbing stray vines to break what seemed like free fall and to pull ourselves up the next slope, I couldn't help but feel sorry for Patrick, the cameraman, who was desperately trying to keep from falling with the awkward weight of the camera.

Two hours of dead-of-the-night mountain climbing in the thunderstorm felt like a lifetime. Finally Ka Cobra directed us into a small hut in an isolated clearing. We left our sneakers, each weighing several pounds from the accumulated mud, outside the door. Once we were inside, Ka Cobra motioned with his M-16 that we were to lie down. "Sleep," he grunted.

We huddled together on the bare floor, shivering under the increasingly precious poncho, squirming to get comfortable and warm in our sodden and muddy jeans. Ka Cobra settled down at our feet, his back against the wall, cradled his weapon in his lap and lit a cigar.

By unspoken agreement, all four of us leaped up at the same moment. Ka Cobra jumped as if he thought we were going to attack him.

Instead, we peeled off our jeans in unison, dropped the sodden masses at Cobra's feet and huddled together again in our underwear. Perhaps our underwear wasn't as clean as Mom would have liked, but at least it wasn't as clammy as our jeans.

Poor Ka Cobra was so shocked, he lost his macho cool and turned his back on us, half in fear and half in hope he was about to be witness to a foreigners' orgy.

I have a good sense of direction. The next day I was sure we were going in circles, spiraling inward in some sort of evasive strategy. We continued to hear reports from local children that soldiers were nearby, but I never knew if those reports were real or for dramatic effect.

At lunchtime we stopped for plain rice at a farmer's house. The farm family had obviously shared the best they had with us. The poverty was becoming more wretched as we left the town further behind. While I was dozing in the shade, waiting for the sun to pass its zenith so we could continue the endless journey, I became aware of the sounds of a steady rhythmic pounding. I opened one eye and saw that two of our armed escorts had propped their guns against a tree and were pounding unmilled rice with mallets in a wooden trough. It was their way of paying the farmer for feeding us.

The third day we walked in a shallow river for the entire day. The fine gravel in the river bed got inside my sneakers and rubbed my feet to the consistency of raw hamburger. I sacrificed my handkerchief to tie up the foot that was bleeding the most and broke off a tree limb for a walking stick. By dusk we came to a small cluster of houses where we were left in the care of an incredibly wrinkled old crone. I had given up trying to figure out what would come next. It seemed as though I had become institutionalized and would do whatever my guides wanted: "Wait here." "Walk faster." "Lie in the grass."

I had been seeing black spots in front of my eyes and feeling nauseous all day and I knew that the dehydration and the diet of rice and *camote* coupled with the strenuous mountain climbing in the tropical sun were taking their toll. My French companions spent most of their time fantasizing about steak dinners and bottles of wine and chocolate souffle. I guess it is true that Frenchmen don't travel well. By sign language I was able to ask the old woman if we could have some of the *bukos* (young coconuts) growing on the dozens of coconut palms surrounding her house. She seemed surprised that anyone would think of eating them, but the children gladly knocked down a few *bukos* for us. I perked up quickly after a little shot of the glucose in the coconut water.

Sometime during the evening, a squad of ragtag comrades arrived, carrying their M-16s and dressed in everything from tattered shorts to faded jeans to usurped military clothing. One piece of apparel was universal: rubber thongs. No combat boots, not even sneakers. We had finally met "the people without shoes," as they were euphemistically called by the peasants.

We spent the evening hours talking to Commander Ricky, who spoke very articulate English. He was a university graduate in political science who had joined the rebels ten years before. The commander was what I later came to think of as a generic Marxist: almost pathetically thin-bodied with nondescript and totally forgettable facial features, thick wire-rimmed glasses, and a small black mustache. Over the years I have met dozens of party members and cadres who answer the same description.

Commander Ricky told us we would go into the camp when the moon rose. A few days before, I would have thought that was a bit of romantic drama designed to impress foreign journalists, but I had been sufficiently spooked by the reports of nearby military troops that I was ready to accept any precaution. For three nights, I had been having nightmares of helicopter squadrons right out of the old M.A.S.H. television series, storming us over the nearest ridge. I could almost hear the M.A.S.H. theme song.

At midnight we solemnly and silently began the last walk to the camp. After an hour's easy walk we were momentarily silhouetted against the moon along a high ridge, then we dropped into the dense undergrowth and were almost instantly inside the camp. We saw nothing that night except a lean-to constructed of new bamboo poles that had apparently been built for us that day.

It was almost like summer camp. A bugler woke us before dawn and, as the sun was coming over the ridge, the troops engaged in vigorous calisthenics with a pudgy stereotypical drill-sergeant as the nonparticipating taskmaster. While the television crew delighted itself with the opportunity for interesting shots, I wandered off to talk with some of the comrades in the camp. I learned that there were three squads in this company, one of them composed entirely of women.

I picked out a particularly sweet-looking woman in her early twenties, toting her M-16 as if it were a baby, and asked why she was a rebel. She introduced herself as Ka Viring told me she had been a college student when her family's home was torched by soldiers in a raid on their mountain village. She spoke matter of factly about her radicalization process that was escalated by the killings of two of her cousins whom the military accused incorrectly of sympathizing with the rebels. Finally she joined a communist-front organization at her college. Over a period of years, Ka Viring said, she had worked her way more deeply into the organization and her commitment had deepened. She met Ka Bobby through the NPA "matchmaking service" for those interested in romance with fellow cadres. The two became pen pals and later were permitted to meet. After undergoing the NPA's rigidly structured and puritanical courtship process, the two were finally allowed to marry. Ka Viring showed me a glimpse of herself as a blushing bride when she pointed out her new husband with a giggle. It was quite unusual that they were assigned to the same unit; many married couples saw each other only once or twice a year.

My fantasies about Ka Viring and Ka Bobby and white lace and M-16s were soon to be dispelled. We were to be witnesses to a unique occasion: an NPA wedding.

The company gathered together in a grove of towering bamboo trees, the afternoon light casting a light green glow on the wedding guests. The couple, Ka Manny and Ka Tess, looked anything but nervous. Both seemed to be hardened warriors in their thirties. The bride wore an elegant black T-shirt and the groom a plaid shirt and a Chairman Mao cap. The maid of honor and the best man draped a red hammer and sickle flag over their shoulders and began to tell the story of the couple's commitment to the revolutionary struggle.

The couple squatted while the commander extended his M-16 and placed a copy of the Red Book of Chairman Mao atop it. Then they swore their vow with their hands on top of the gun and book: they would give their lives for the revolution and only, secondarily, would they be committed to each other. Instead of wedding rings, Ka Manny and Ka Tess exchanged brass-jacketed M-16 bullets as keepsakes.

After the cadres sang a rousing chorus of "The Internationale," with weapons raised high over their heads, it was back to the business of warfare with a vigorous afternoon training exercise on the schedule. The ten-minute wedding break was over. No wedding cake. No champagne. Not even a lonely little bottle of beer. Certainly no honeymoon suite. During a break from running across a barren field and squirming on their bellies through the underbrush, someone brought out a guitar and the comrades dramatically shifted persona from fierce warriors to Filipino teenagers singing mushy love songs.

The next day, while we were hiking out of the zone, the reality of the revolution hit very close to home. A small boy dashed up to us as we passed a grove of banana trees and said that soldiers were in sight, just over the ridge. We literally dropped on our faces, too frightened to look up and see them. I could hear the soldiers walking by, they were that close.

That night we reached a sugar plantation and were warmly welcomed in the home of the caretaker. We were treated to an opulent dinner of rice and two bites of scrambled egg each. I was exhausted, my feet were bleeding from the river walk, and I was so grateful for that miserable scrambled egg that the food nearly left me in tears. My French companions, with whom my patience had evaporated, continued to talk about roast beef and coffee with cream. Then they asked our host if he would kill and cook a chicken for us for 100 pesos (five dollars). My tears of anger, frustration and embarassment for their insensitivity finally overwhelmed me. I felt sick to my stomach and said I was ill. I retreated to the caretaker's borrowed bedroom, the first solitude I had enjoyed since that first night as an animal in the zoo. This time I was glad for the privilege granted to me as a woman. Mercifully, everyone left me alone.

The next morning a broken-down horse arrived to carry me down to the town. I was still hobbling on my lacerated feet. Perhaps I overdid my expressions of gratitude as I sped off while my companions trudged glumly along behind.

Back in Bacolod, on the way to the airport, I met with the military commander to hear the government's views on the insurgency. By that time my feet were bandaged and my bag full of muddy clothes was in the custody of the colonel's men. I thought it was quite obvious where I had been, so I carefully concealed my notes and my film in my underwear. The colonel quelled my fears of helicopter squadrons and my nightmares of attack when he told me that his command, covering several hundred square miles of mountain, jungle and ocean, had only two helicopters.

I was not questioned at all, but when my French companions returned to Manila two days later, they told me the colonel had confronted them with every detail of our trip, including the name of the priest who had sheltered us in his convento until dark. Unfortunately they did not bother to deny what the military already knew and the priest was forced to move to another area.

I was beginning to understand why the common people were joining the revolution. What I saw on that trip convinced me that the vast number of people in the countryside had nothing to lose.

13 HOME AGAIN: *USA and London, June 1985*

AFTER SIXTEEN MONTHS ABROAD, it was time to take a trip back to the States to see my family, friends, and to try to generate some more business. I also wanted to find out if I had changed during those months away.

It was almost immediately apparent how different things were in the States, which underscored how much I had changed. The culture shock hit me practically the moment I touched down at the L.A. Airport. A friendly agriculture inspector winked and allowed me to bring in a bonsai I had bought for Mom during a three-day stopover in Tokyo. I almost wept at encountering a government official who obviously wasn't looking for a bribe.

Mom and I stopped at a supermarket. I felt like I had dropped in from another planet. Food that had once seemed so familiar had become a total novelty. There was bread in a hundred different shapes and sizes. There were cheese counters miles long. I could tell by looking that none of it would taste like plastic as it does in the Philippines. Cookie bars, salad bars, tender juicy steaks that were not made from worn out water buffalos. I bought cartloads. The food trip added several definitely unneeded pounds to my already zaftig frame.

There were no beggars on the street and there was no garbage stench in the air. And, wonder of wonders, when I dialed the phone, I was connected on the first try. I got an uncontrollable case of the giggles when the operator said, "Thanks for calling AT&T, Kathleen," instead of forcing me to spell my name six times.

When Mom suggested we might take a trip to Disneyland, I replied, without even missing a beat, "What do I need Disneyland for? I am already in Disneyland!"

For those first days, it felt good to be at home, but I wasn't entertaining any thoughts about staying.

I would tell Philippine stories to anyone who showed a glimmer of interest. Many Philippine idiosyncracies that had become commonplace to me were horrifying to my listeners. I began to realize how much I had changed.

I felt uncomfortable with everyday chitchat. I didn't want to talk about recipes or Johnny's report cards or the price of real estate. I wondered how people could be so superficial when the world was full of such horror. Coming straight from the NPA and Joel Abong, I was really wired. I knew I was too intense, but I didn't know how to turn it off. Nobody wanted to hear endless Philippine stories, but I didn't know how to talk about anything else.

My brief visit to see my Dad in Indianapolis left me feeling sad and very aware of mortality. Dad's wife had died a few months before and it was shocking to see how he had aged with grief. He was like a wounded child. I had heard from friends that there comes a time when the roles are reversed and the parent becomes the child. It was time for me to play parent to Dad. He was so desperately lonely and hurt, but I couldn't do anything but be there. I felt badly that I couldn't be there for long and that I hadn't been there when he needed me most. I felt helpless. My brothers and sisters take good care of Dad and he is far from being an invalid or a helpless old man. In fact, he is a handsome, healthy and dynamic man who still has a lot of romance left in him.

Dad drove me to Detroit, where we both had business to take care of.

Why are partings at train stations sadder than any others? Maybe it's because of all of those schmaltzy movies. When Dad hugged me goodbye as I got on the train for Toronto, I was painfully aware that it could be the last time I would see him.

Welcomes in train stations always seem so much warmer than in airports, perhaps because of the same old movies.

Bert met me at the train station in Kingston, Ontario, just across the river from Watertown. God, it was good to see his familiar bearded face and see him holding out his arms to me on the train platform! On the surface, everything seemed the same. Our easy companionship made me wonder if I shouldn't stick around and give our marriage another try. But after a day or two I became aware that our relationship had undergone a not-to-subtle change. I was observing it rather than really contributing. After I caught up on all of the local gossip, I started to get itchy feet. I knew it was time to let go of Bert and of Watertown. This was unquestionably the denouement of the incomplete farewell in February of 1984. Bert and I both knew that I would never return. I was enjoying some career success and there would never be a reason to try to turn back the clock. I knew I would always love Bert, but the form of that love had changed irrevocably.

Bert had been seeing Barbara Babcock, a teacher we had both known for several years. He said he wanted to go ahead with the divorce because he was thinking of marrying Barbara the following summer. With surprisingly little pain, I agreed to end our marriage of fifteen years.

Barbara is a very sweet and intelligent woman. She and I look so much alike that some people who don't know me well didn't even realize Bert had a new lady. Even my dear friend Christine Burkard-Eggleston found it difficult to be around them because Barbara and I share so many mannerisms. But there is one very fundamental difference. Barbara is from Watertown and has taught in a high school near there for twenty years. She won't leave Bert and go running around the world in search of crazy adventures like I did. Bert needs and deserves someone by his side.

I received the final divorce papers later that year, just before Christmas. It wasn't until years later, when I examined them more closely, that I realized that our divorce had been granted on November 27, 1985, our fifteenth wedding anniversary. I cried a few tears, mourning for fifteen years of my life. But I wouldn't have changed a moment of our life together. Those years with Bert's support gave me the courage to do what I had done.

I have always loved New York. The energy of the place is like no other place on earth. I was feeling really exhilarated and a little corny as I rode the taxi into the city and hummed to myself the tune "New York, New York."

Maybe I hadn't really made it yet, but this visit was a far cry from my departure sixteen months before. Before I set out for London, I had camped on the floor of an old college friend's fifth-floor walk-up. Now the ABC executives, who were high on me, had put me up in the Essex House. I had an elegant room with windows opening on Central Park. I was on top of the world!

At ABC, I was greeted like a visiting dignitary, with elaborate meals and great adulation from my boss, Mark Richards, whom I had already grown to love over the telephone. The top man, Peter Flannery, an old Notre Dame flim-flam boy full of Irish charm was alternately professional and flirtatious. The dynamic duo were real pros at making Little Miss Nobody feel important. I loved it!

I was speechless when the execs decided they wanted to include me in the team being sent to London in mid-July to cover Bob Geldof's Live-Aid concert to benefit the starving kids in Ethiopia. Why me? I was thirty-six years old. My tastes run more to soft music. Some friends have scornfully accused me of loving elevator music. That's not really fair, but I am no big fan of rock and roll. Yet didn't I go crazy over the Beatles in the sixties, like every other teenage girl? I wasn't going to argue if ABC wanted to give me a free trip to London. What the hell?

I barely had a chance to see a couple of old friends in New York before ABC shipped me off to Washington to get some American government viewpoints on the Philippines. Someone in the Washington bureau had set up a killer schedule that involved running from one end of Washington to the other, and ended with a screeching taxi ride to the airport with doors flying open and luggage flying out, just in time to catch the evening plane to London. ABC had booked me business class to London and Amsterdam and then back to Manila. I had never flown business class before and I was as excited as a kid in a candy store. I drank too much business-class champagne just to prove it.

Ah, those were the days when ABC spent money. That all ended much too soon when the glory train left the station and Capital Cities took over a couple of years later.

It was good to be back in London and to enjoy the only hot days of the English summer. I was terrified when I learned what was expected of me at Live-Aid. We would be broadcasting live. We would be heard by more than a billion people all over the world. I had never done anything live before. I was still stumbling my way through some of my recorded spots. So ABC's confidence in me was flattering, but I was really afraid it was ill-placed.

John Lyons, an affable gorilla of a man and an electronic wizard, was producing the extravaganza. He held my hand through the terror. I tried very hard to impress upon John and the team that I knew *nothing* about rock music. I pleaded with them not to ask me any hard questions while we were on the air or ask me to identify anyone. I might recognize Paul McCartney, but I wasn't even sure of that. John said it was OK. My assignment was to sit in the booth in what was essentially front row center on the football field at Wembley Stadium and do crowd color and interviews with people in the crowd. I thought I could handle that, just barely.

The idea of talking to a billion people live gave me butterflies in my stomach, but I remembered what Mark Litke had told me when I first started out: "It's just like talking to your Mom."

It was easy and it was fun. The day was bright and clear. The crowd was boisterous and friendly. The music was wonderful. After the first round on the air, all of my apprehension was gone and I was rolling. It was good old rock and roll. I didn't have to know anything about Sade or U2, but I knew Elton John, The Who, and Paul McCartney (yes, I did recognize him). Phil Collins and Sting also performed.

At one point, I said, "This is the day to tell your grandchildren about."

The only bad moment was when our anchor, Larry Jacobs, asked me during a live throwaround, "Who is that on the stage now, Kathleen?"

My mind raced. What could I say without sounding like an idiot in front of a billion people? "I don't know, Larry, the crowd is blocking my view," I answered lamely. I read him the riot act as soon as we were off the air and he was abjectly apologetic. That was the only hitch of the day.

The British Live-Aid crowd wasn't a political crowd. They were just there to listen to music. They had paid a hefty admission price (about fifty dollars a ticket), and they didn't want to think about politics. Every time the big screens up front flashed pictures of the starving Ethiopian kids, the crowd would figuratively turn its collective back and just keep on partying. But they weren't a mean or drunk or druggie crowd. They were well-behaved and fun, but they just weren't in the mood for anything heavy.

The twin concert in Philadelphia was being broadcast on Wembley Stadium's huge screens. Strangely, the fans were not much interested in the simulcasts. I guess it was too much like watching TV. They paid almost no attention to stars like Madonna and Bob Dylan. But when the Beach Boys came on, they went crazy. It seemed strangely incongruous to see an audience liberally sprinkled with punks wearing black leather, pink spikes in their hair, and spider earrings screaming, "I Wish They All Could Be California Girls."

For most of the day, I had been talking to a group of kids who had parked themselves around my little plywood broadcast booth. They gave me cokes when my little cooler ran dry.

As the day progressed, there were insistent and feverish rumors of a Beatles reunion with Julian Lennon standing in for his dead father. During a spell when I wasn't on the air, I told the kids closest to me about the Beatles' first US appearance on the Ed Sullivan show in 1964. I must have been really wrapped up in telling the story of how the crowd was screaming so loudly that you couldn't even hear the Beatles sing, because it wasn't until I was well into it that I noticed the blank stare I was getting from my youthful audience. I stopped.

"Oh my God, " I said, slapping my forehead with my palm. "I bet you weren't even born in 1964."

"I wasn't," one of them replied with all the awe of someone talking to a fossil.

We sat in the hot sun all day, having a fabulous time listening to the music. I was having so much fun that I refused to take a break when Lyons wanted to give me one. That turned out to be a mistake. Throughout the day, perhaps in response to the Beatles rumors, the crowd had surged forward. By mid-evening it was packed so tight that it was impossible to get out. After ten hours in the booth my bladder was about to burst. An early evening rainshower had cooled things off considerably and I started to shiver, which made my predicament even worse.

I was completely caught up in the energy of the crowd. An hour to go. Half an hour to go. Off the air, I told Lyons that if the Beatles reunion came about, I would wet my pants or cry or both. Lyons said wetting my pants was no problem. "It's radio, no one can see," he commented intelligently. As for crying, Lyons said, "Why not? It would be a nice emotional touch. As long as you can keep on talking."

There was no Beatles reunion and I didn't cry or wet my pants. The crowd filed out in a remarkably orderly fashion and I was thankful I could get out of there and to a bathroom within minutes after the concert ended.

All of us were exhausted, but we were unbelievably high and excited by the event we had just been a part of. We were already so high on the good vibes that we didn't even want to drink the champagne that Lyons had thoughtfully stocked in the broadcast booth's refrigerator.

With all that energy, there was no way any of us could sleep, so we spent a good part of the night dancing our brains out to more rock and roll in a London disco. It was truly a day we'd tell our grandchildren about.

Live-Aid was the perfect break from my Philippine-inspired intensity. I had finally relaxed.

After a stopover in Amsterdam to meet some Filipino communists in exile, I flew back to Manila. I was happy to be back where I felt I belonged.

14 DETAINED: *August 1985*

Bishop edmundo abaya of laoag, Ilocos Norte (Marcos's home province) and some human rights groups had invited me to join a fact-finding mission. Bishop Abaya, a joyful and fatherly man, was very concerned about recent alarming happenings in his diocese. One of his priests, Father Teodoro Remegio, was then in prison and on trial for subversion. The military had literally swooped down on him by helicopter in his mountain parish and arrested him one Sunday before the eyes of his stunned parishioners. Bishop Abaya's vigorous efforts to free him, even his personal pleas to Marcos, had failed.

Bishop Abaya was also concerned about Piddig, a small town an hour's drive from Laoag, where twenty young men had been arrested a month before on suspicion of being rebels. In an effort to force them to confess, the arresting soldiers had submerged some of them in a river for a terrifyingly long time while their families watched helplessly in fear they would drown.

In addition, a few days before our arrival, the government and the military had co-operated in a "mass surrender" of 465 "rebels" from Piddig. The government's propaganda machinery had become notorious for these phony surrenders, in which townspeople would be gathered on some false pretext. Firearms were stacked in front of them, photographs taken and the newspapers carried the "good news" that more rebels had surrendered. The government's propaganda machinery would always get screwed up, though. The military would release figures that there were 14,000 or 16,000 rebels and then the civilian government would release figures that 20,000 rebels had surrendered in a year. They never could get those numbers to make any sense.

Eight of us set out for Estancia, a tiny farming barrio that was part of Piddig town, early in the afternoon of August 12, crammed into Bishop Abaya's open jeep. My companions included Sister Joan Carroll, a silver-haired and slightly wacky American Maryknoll nun who had spent twenty years in the Philippines; Bobby Javier, a Filipino journalist; a couple of the bishop's church workers; the bishop's cook; a church worker from Manila; and Tina Remegio, the bishop's catechist in Piddig, the sister of the imprisoned Father Ted. Tina was to act as our guide and translator in Piddig to help us find out what had actually happened there. I suspected strongly that the diminutive and determined Tina was secretly a member of the underground National Democratic Front, the Communist

Party's political wing. There was something indefinable about her manner. Tina unquestionably had contacts with the rebels.

Bishop Abaya, concerned about our safety, extracted a solemn promise that we wouldn't do anything as silly as to try to spend the night in Piddig. He said the place was crawling with military and the rebels often passed through on their way across the mountains at night, so it was extremely dangerous. My feeling was that we would learn more if we spent the night in Piddig. I gave the bishop my promise with my fingers crossed behind my back.

Before we left the bishop's residence, someone gave me a small wooden cross to hang around my neck, joking that I might disguise myself as a nun if there was trouble. Everyone roared with laughter.

As soon as we arrived in Estancia, which was just a crossroads with a few houses and a lot of chickens, Tina recommended that we pay a courtesy call on the *barangay* captain, the village chief. The *barangay* captain told us he was firmly loyal to Marcos. That was no surprise. He wouldn't have held the office he held in Marcos's home province if he weren't in Marcos's pocket. During a twenty-minute chat, the *barangay* captain admitted he was concerned that Piddig was turning into a war zone. There were too many military, he said and well, yes, there were probably some rebels passing through from time to time. He, like everyone else we met in Piddig that day, was extremely uneasy in our presence. His eyes continuously darted around his little domain. He mindlessly plucked at his shirt, just like some mental patients I had seen. The strain must have been incredible in that place. He told us there was a six P.M. curfew and we must leave by then to avoid trouble with the military. Then, in the tone of the plea of a condemned man, the *barangay* captain asked us if we would make our presence known to the Scout Rangers (military elite anti-insurgency troops) camped on the hill above the town.

We didn't want to waste the time, but we humored the rattled *barangay* captain and trekked up the hill to the Scout Rangers.

On top of the small hill overlooking the Estancia crossroads, about ten Scout Rangers lounged in shorts and T-shirts. With typical Filipino hospitality, they offered us a cup of coffee, which gave us time for a casual and friendly chat. They never asked who we were or why we were there. Also in typical Filipino fashion, we did not answer questions we were not asked. I think they assumed we were all religious people because we were in the bishop's jeep, which was a well-known vehicle in the area.

Finally, we had completed the social and political niceties and we began moving among the shanties to talk to the people. Even though Tina knew the people of Estancia very well, they were obviously terrified to say anything. One man literally ran away when we approached. Another, whose son was among the twenty arrested a month before, turned down our offer of jeepney fare to Laoag to see his son and then a stop for lunch at the bishop's house for a more relaxed chat. The man firmly refused. He was too terrified, even though he hadn't seen his son since the arrest and he was frantic with worry about his safety.

An eighty-five-year-old woman told me she was one of the "rebel surrenderees" at the phony ceremony a few days before. She said the landless people of Piddig had been told they would be given titles to their land if they went to the municipal hall on a certain day. Hundreds, including the old lady, flocked there, only to find themselves marshalled into line by local military men for photographs with the obligatory weapons stacked in front of them. Then they were asked to raise their hands in an oath of loyalty to the government. Docilely, they did so. More photos were taken. Then they were shooed home, with no land titles. That scenario had become common around the country. What the government didn't seem to realize was that embittered "surrenderees," realizing they had again been hoodwinked by the government were likely to be more sympathetic to rebel overtures after the experience.

Someone whispered to us that the Scout Rangers on the hill, with whom we had shared a pleasant cup of coffee, were the same ones who had the month before held their prisoners under water in an attempt to extract confessions. It was hard to believe. They seemed so pleasant.

It had been pretty much a wasted afternoon. We had gathered very little information because the people were just too terrified to talk to us. But we dutifully piled into our jeep at ten minutes before six and headed out, mindful of the curfew. I had attempted a foolhardy last ditch proposal to Tina that she and I would ride out in the jeep and then hike back in through the mountains and spend the night in Estancia, in hopes that darkness would loosen tongues. After some consultation with the leaders, the idea was rejected as too dangerous.

Just after we passed the village crossroads, a hard-faced man in plain clothes, riding a motorcycle, carrying a .45 in his belt, stopped us and demanded to see our "pass." He identified himself as Sergeant Augustin of military intelligence. I knew that "intelligence" was usually a paradox in terms, so I mistakenly figured it would be easy to outsmart him. Sergeant Augustin seemed to be pickled in alcohol, and I made the initial mistake of thinking we could brush him off easily. We said we'd get the pass in town because we were having dinner with the provincial military commander. We breezily waved goodbye and I jabbed the driver with my elbow and told him to step on the gas. Sergeant Augustin obviously didn't buy that story. He pointed his gun at us. We drove just around a curve in the road, to a point where we could no longer see the houses of Estancia; where we encountered our "friends" the Scout Rangers, who had spread themselves across the road blocking our exit. The good guys we had been drinking coffee with an hour before were now in full battle dress and armed with automatic weapons. The driver stopped. I stuffed my notes and my press ID into my underwear. We got out slowly. Tina muttered to me we were in "deep trouble."

It was the beginning of a Kafkaesque nightmare. They would not tell us why we were being held, yet they wouldn't let us go. They asked no questions, not even our identities. Sister Joan, thinking possibly our obstreperous and drunken sergeant had been taught by nuns, tried a slightly abusive "stern nun" routine on him. Then she tried the "sweet sister" routine. Neither had any effect.

Darkness fell. We were out of sight of town with a cliff behind us and a rice field in front of us. No one was around, but we could hear some laughter and occasional gunshots coming from some drunken militiamen at the crossroads. My companions seemed to be paralyzed by fear. We didn't know what we were waiting for. One of the kinder Scout Rangers whispered to me that our problem was Tina Remegio, who was a "known communist."

All I could think of was the murder of an Italian missionary priest in southern Mindanao a few months before. Paramilitary religious fanatics had been arrested for the brutal broad daylight murder of Father Tulio Favali. Rumor had it that the military wanted to "get a couple of foreign nuns" to really scare the left-leaning missionaries. I knew they thought I was a nun, so I was afraid we might be the targets. I silently gave thanks for the little wooden cross around my neck. Things had gone far enough by that time that I knew if they discovered I was a journalist they might try something desperate to cover up their gaffe. I had never been asked to identify myself. I would not have lied if asked, but I was relieved I wasn't.

I had never experienced true terror before. For the first time in my life I came face to face with the prospect of death. My knees turned to water just like in a bad novel. I could clearly picture our bodies floating in the rice paddy next to the road, so I struggled to erase that horrid image from my mind.

The waiting was endless and nerve wracking. I am a typical American who grew up with the visits of "Officer Friendly" to my elementary school. I had the ingrained thought pattern that policemen are my friends, despite some minor incidents that proved otherwise in my earlier years. I had also seen too many movies where the cavalry always comes riding over the hill to save the day. My mind was doing cartwheels. Why doesn't someone call the police? I wondered. Then I realized: These ARE the police. There was little hope. There was even a desperate clutching and foolish idea that the NPA would come over the hill on white horses and save us. But, alas, there was no cavalry.

It was nine P.M. We had been hostages for three hours. Joan and I, in a whispered conversation, decided that it was our responsibility to move things off the stalemate we seemed to have reached, so we came up with a plan. Joan would pretend to have a heart attack. It was a risk, that, we figured, would force our obstinate Sergeant Augustin to make a decision, offer him a way to save face and end the standoff.

Joan started to fake chest pains, hacking and coughing and crying quite dramatically. It seemed like an eternity before the finally sobering sergeant made a decision. He took the bait for a face-saving way out and agreed to take us to the clinic in the population center of Piddig. Sergeant Augustin must have realized, as the alcohol bragadoccio faded, that it might be extremely embarrassing to have a dead American nun or two on his hands. As we climbed back into our jeep, with two armed escorts sitting on the roof to prevent us from trying to escape, someone handed me a rosary. I am not a Catholic and I don't know the prayers, but I earnestly prayed whatever came to mind. Among the prayers was one that no one would ask me to recite the rosary out loud.

We arrived at the clinic in town sometime after 8:30. Joan half-fell out of the jeep and our companions rushed to carry her. I stopped them. "Make the soldiers carry her," I whispered to Bobby Javier. We hadn't clued in the others to the drama, so their reactions were genuine. I remembered my college psychology. If the soldiers were forced to make physical contact with Joan and carry her into the clinic, they would have created a bond as her helpers. Maybe they would then be less likely to harm her.

I was relieved when we got inside the empty clinic, but I panicked again when I realized they planned to leave Joan and me and two guards at the clinic and take the Filipinos to the military outpost in Piddig. My brain was working overtime to figure how we could all get back together again. Filipinos are far more reckless with the lives of their own countrymen than with the lives of foreigners. I guess it has something to do with perceptions of justice and little faith in the justice system of their own country. I was frantic with fear they would imprison or even kill the others. I desperately clung to the idea that all would be well if we could get back to Laoag and to Bishop Abaya, who could help. I preferred not to think about the bishop's impotence against the military in the seizure of Father Ted Remegio. I also hoped that cooler heads would prevail if we worked our way higher into the military ranks and perhaps at provincial headquarters we could reason with someone.

A young doctor arrived. I knew we had no alternative but to take him into our confidence. It was a huge risk because the doctor might betray us, but we also knew that no doctor would ever believe Joan was having a heart attack, no matter how convincing her act might be to a lay observer. I was even becoming concerned that Joan's dramatic flair might bring on the real thing. I had a feeling that she was on the brink of hysteria. It was probably that knowledge that kept me from becoming hysterical myself. I felt strangely detached, although I was well aware that all of our lives might depend on what I did.

We confided in the doctor and told him how fearful we were for our companions.

I felt a tremendous weight fall off my shoulders when the young doctor, with kind eyes, said, "I understand. I am from Mindanao."

As if that explained everything. He meant that many people from war-torn militarized Mindanao would be sympathetic to the plight of someone in the iron clutches of the military.

"What do you want me to do?" he asked.

"Tell them she is seriously ill and must be treated at the hospital in Laoag, and that all of us must go there," I said with far more decisiveness than I felt.

It didn't take long for the young doctor to round up all of our group. There was a joyous reunion, even though we had only been separated for half an hour or so. We loaded ourselves into the jeep, half hoping that our military escort would send us on our way alone. No such luck.

Just as we were pulling away, Piddig's rotund mayor, Daisy Raquiza, appeared, outraged at the military's stupidity and intractability. She reminded Sergeant Augustin that there was no need for anyone to obtain a military pass to travel anywhere in her town. But she had no authority over our sergeant. So she squeezed her bulk into our jeep and rode along to Laoag.

Joan, the doctor, the driver, the mayor and I were dropped at the hospital with only one escort, but the six Filipinos were again taken away, this time to provincial headquarters. I had a sick feeling that they would keep Tina no matter what we did. Mayor Raquiza was torn between staying with us and raising hell at headquarters, so she commandeered a vehicle and shuttled back and forth.

Fortunately the bishop's residence is next door to the hospital. We immediately dispatched a little boy to run next door and plead for help. He came back a few minutes later with bad news. The bishop wasn't home. Other members of the fact-finding team were there, but they felt powerless to do anything.

Our doctor had now explained the situation to another doctor and they both looked to me as director of this bizarre drama. What should we do next? I asked if they could give Joan some sort of mild tranquilizer and order her to bed in the bishop's residence. They agreed. The tranquilizer was probably just what Joan needed at that point. As we were going out, not knowing if our military escort would continue to stick with us like glue, Mayor Raquiza came back and announced triumphantly that we were released, although the others were still detained. Our guard left, scratching his head.

We sped into the *convento* and collapsed with relief into the arms of the frantic fact-finding team members. Minutes later, Bishop Abaya arrived, fueled by fury. The news of our "arrest" had reached him at a dinner party. I told him briefly what had happened and the mild-mannered bishop roared off to storm the provincial headquarters with all the rage of an avenging angel.

Twenty minutes later, he was back with the rest of our companions, including a very shaken Tina. We all sat late into the night drinking the bishop's brandy to calm our nerves. Tina took refuge inside the *convento's* cloister. Joan and I decided it would be wise for us to leave by bus in the morning. I anticipated harassment if we went to Laoag's remote airport. We were reluctant to leave Tina behind, but we realized it would be more dangerous for her if she came with us. Things have a way of cooling off after a few days, and then perhaps she could move out safely.

It was over. I had never faced the possibility of my own death before, but I was convinced that night that I could die at any moment. For the first time, but not the last, I had personally become a victim of the violence that lies at the heart of this country.

In the early evening we arrived at Joan's home, the Maryknoll convent in Baguio. It felt safe and welcoming. I immediately called ABC and told them the story. The decision was made that we should go on the air with a first-person report about the experience. It was one way of putting the Marcos government on warning. But I wanted them to call my Mom first. Mom sleeps with the radio on and has the bad habit of waking up every hour to hear the news on ABC. I knew she would panic if she heard it first on the radio. They called Mom and assured her I was safe and well. Then the reports went on the air.

Over that weekend, I wrote a first person account of what had happened and then telexed it to every paper I worked for. I wrote that I had come to understand firsthand the fear in which many Filipinos live night and day. I said there were no human rights as I know them in the Philippines.

As soon as I returned to Manila, I went to Philippine Constabulary headquarters at Camp Crame to see Colonel Luis San Andres, the PR man of General Fidel Ramos, who was then acting military chief of staff. I handed him a copy of my story and said I was filing a complaint. I said I was willing to co-operate fully with any investigation. To his credit, Luis phoned Ramos while I was still in his office and Ramos instantly ordered an investigation. I was promised there would be a report within three days. Foolishly, I believed him. I should have known better. Investigations in the Philippines almost never come to anything.

Meanwhile, the radio reports had been aired on ABC and my stories had been published abroad. A couple of sensationalized reports were published in the local press.

Despite my repeated telephone calls to Luis San Andres, there was never an official report on the investigation. There was a one-paragraph item moved by the government-run Philippine News Agency wire three weeks later. It said the military had merely detained us for our own "protection" and "escorted" us from a dangerous rebel-infested zone. General Ramos was quoted as saying that I had been "hysterical."

Only years later, I found out that the much-feared Sergeant Augustin had been speedily transferred out of Piddig after the incident. That was a relief, because I was very concerned that the townspeople in Estancia might take even more abuse from Sergeant Augustin after the publicity about the incident.

That wasn't to be the end of the story. I had requested Philippine military clearance for a visit to the U.S. military bases a couple of weeks before the Piddig incident. Because of some sham facade, Clark and Subic are not American bases, but Philippine bases. Journalists are not permitted official access without the approval of the Philippine military high command. In more than a year in the Philippines, I had never visited the bases and I thought that was a situation which should be rectified, although I had no particular story in mind. Major Tom Boyd, the public information officer at Clark, had been quite helpful in arranging an introductory visit.

But one day, a few days before the scheduled visit, Tom called and asked whose feathers I had ruffled in the military. I asked why and he said there was a funny communication from General Ramos's office implying I might be a security risk.

I blew my stack. I phoned Colonel Reynaldo San Gabriel, Ramos's chief aide. In my most arrogant Ugly American tone, I demanded to know how San Gabriel and the Armed Forces of the Philippines *dared* represent me to the United States government as a security risk. I asked if the refusal of my clearance for Clark was related to my story about being detained. Colonel San Gabriel hinted it might be.

Filipinos almost universally deal with a sticky situation by avoidance. People will tell you Filipinos are nonconfrontational and that is absolutely true. Sometimes a forced confrontation produces results, sometimes they literally run away. To his credit, "Gabby" San Gabriel did not run. He suggested perhaps we should discuss this face to face and I was delighted.

A couple of days later, we met at the International Press Center. Vic Tuazon, the friendly and very nonconfrontational director of the government's press center, would clearly have preferred to have been on Mars than to be acting as a mediator in this little encounter. I was still outraged. I angrily rejected Vic's offer of a cup of coffee, which is an insult and was intended to be.

Since it was clear there would be no pleasantries, Colonel San Gabriel got down to business. He pulled out a copy of my story about Piddig, liberally marked with red ink. He claimed that a number of my allegations were untrue. I reminded him that I was present at the hostage taking and he was not. Point by point I countered San Gabriel's complaints. He was especially incensed by my allegation that there were no human rights as I know them in the Philippines.

I asked with deadly sweetness, "Then, do I understand it correctly, Colonel

San Gabriel, that I, as an American journalist, am being refused permission to visit a U.S. military base because of a story your government disagrees with?"

That was true, he conceded.

With even deadlier sweetness I began to gather my papers and deliberately and slowly put them in my bag. I said quietly, "Oh, that's fine then. In addition to your other violations of basic freedoms, you have no freedom of the press here either. I wasn't really all that interested in visiting Clark but I think you have given me a much better story about press freedom. Thank you very much."

San Gabriel's face turned purple, but he held his temper.

"Let's not be too hasty," he choked, man enough to admit he had been bested.

I got my clearance and no more problems.

San Gabriel and I emerged from the confrontation bloodied and bruised, but with a grudging respect for each other. I admired his willingness to face the issue and to cut his losses when they were becoming too great. I knew no one else in the military with that same spunk. Months later we met again at one of General Ramos's press conferences. Ramos clasped me by the shoulder and San Gabriel by his shoulder, like children who have been quarreling.

"I understand you two are fighting," he said.

We glared at each other.

"Why don't you shake hands and make up?" General Ramos asked.

We shook hands. Then we laughed. We've been friends ever since.

15

THE SPARROW I KNEW AND LOVED:
September 1985

M Y FEW GLIMPSES OF MINDANAO from the air had whetted my appetite to see more of the most beautiful part of the Philippines. There were wild uncharted wildernesses, green and brown velvet mountains piercing skies of improbable blue and millions of coconut trees, silver in the sunlight, ebony against spectacular sunsets. The sea was azure blue and achingly clear. I had seen tiny fishing barrios nestled under the palms, brawny-backed men hauling their catch, cone-hatted peasants planting rice, and brightly clad Muslims. I wanted to see more.

I planned a three-week bus trip around Mindanao, scheduled to begin after an international conference of leftwing supporters of the communist party. I frankly got bored and left the conference early for a visit to Kidapawan, North Cotabato, with Father Peter Geremia. Kidapawan was the home diocese of Father Tulio Favali, the Italian priest who had been murdered near Kidapawan the previous April. During the bus trip from Davao to Kidapawan, we endured the stench from a crate of *durian*, the huge ugly jackfruit much beloved of Mindanao people that "smells like hell, tastes like heaven." The smell is a horrible combination of burning tires, rotten fish and three-day old sweat. I confess they do taste good.

Our bus was stopped half a dozen times at military checkpoints. I guess the soldiers were looking for guns or bus-riding rebels. I think they wanted mainly to remind people menacingly of their presence and create a general nuisance. The women were required to stay in the bus while the men got down and were searched. Then the luggage was searched. Women were generally not subjected to body searches. The military inspections doubled the duration of what was normally a two-hour trip. At each checkpoint the soldiers made a point of leeringly greeting the easily recognizable American priest. Father Peter was convinced that he was the real target of Father Tulio's murderer and that the military still planned to kill him. The soldiers along the bus route were clearly baiting the priest.

In that brief visit, I began to think of Kidapawan as the sewer of the Philippines, where all of the blackest evil seemed to have accumulated. There were diabolical landlords; religious fanatics like the ones who killed Father Tulio and pocketed his brains; soldiers popping up like dandelions at every turn in the road;

NPAs who kept mostly to the highlands, but occasionally did battle with the military, with the religious fanatic cults, and with members of two Muslim rebel factions who were vying with them and with each other for territory. It seemed unreal. The people of Kidapawan lived in a war zone of amazing complexity.

It was a mess. I was glad, after a couple of days in the Kidapawan sewer, to return to Davao for a martial law anniversary demonstration, yet another in the never-ending series of swelling protests against Marcos. In Davao I was scheduled to meet my guide and continue my trip through Mindanao.

Gerry Santos (not his real name), who had been my guide on a couple of previous trips to Davao and held a medium-level position in the Communist Party of the Philippines, met me at the slightly grubby, but homey, Apo View Hotel in Davao. He explained that there was a great deal of paranoia in the communist undergound movement due to the discovery two days before of military infiltrators (called deep penetration agents or DPAs) in the highest ranks of the regional party committee. Many leaders had fled to the underground, to the hills, anywhere where they felt safe. Everyone was under suspicion. Gerry himself didn't know how long he would be able to stay above ground.

I was quite fond of Gerry. He was a former seminarian who had joined "the movement" when he was fourteen years old. We had spent endless hours together, talking while he performed his assigned tasks of continuing my political education and introducing me to the proper people at the proper times. I admired his commitment to his cause and enjoyed his humor. It didn't hurt that he was, as he liked to joke, "short, dark and handsome." We both saw the potential for our relationship to move beyond friendship, but there was just too much tension in September of 1985.

The martial law marches were usually massive, but the 1985 demonstrations in Davao, one of the most heavily communist-influenced cities, were thinly attended and lackluster. The underground apparatus that organized and funded the demonstrations had failed because of the panic over the DPA incident.

A transportation strike was scheduled to begin the following day in Iligan, in the north central part of Mindanao. I needed to move out if I didn't want to get stuck in Davao for several more days. With no ceremony, Gerry introduced me to my guide, Jun Sy (not his real name), a shy, stocky young man of Chinese extraction. Gerry kissed me on the cheek and we were on our way.

Jun and I flew to Cagayan de Oro to escape what had been described to me as "nine hours of boring and bumpy bus riding through uninteresting country." I've since learned to disallow some of the Filipino nonchalance about the beauty of their own country.

From Cagayan de Oro, we immediately boarded a bus for Iligan in order to make it before the anticipated strike. The public transport drivers in Mindanao were among the most highly organized labor unions in the country, so if a strike tooked place I had little doubt it would bring all movement to a halt all over the island.

Iligan is a small, prosperous city on the northern coast. Steel mills and a large flour mill a discreet distance away give Iliganons decent jobs and keep the specter of poverty further away from its people than most places I had seen. I knew that Gerry had instructed my guide that nothing was to happen to me, but I didn't realize how heavily he had put the fear of God into Jun. When we checked in at a modest rooming house, the shamefaced and retiring Jun insisted we would share the same room! I insisted we would not, as did the rather shocked middle-aged concierge. Jun was definitely outranked and had to agree to take the room next to mine.

None of the anticipated crowds were gathering in Iligan for the three-day strike as we had been led to expect they would. A little bit of poking around produced an answer: there had been more than five thousand people camped on the lawn of one of the churches the night before, but the organizers had sent them home. That didn't make sense, but Jun, who was a low-ranking cadre and not privy to the turmoil in Davao, ferreted out an answer that made sense to me even if it didn't make sense to him. The strike organizers had failed to appear with the money for food for the strikers. The strike could not go on. It was clear that the paranoia engendered by the DPA scare had spread like wildfire in only a handful of days. All legal and illegal activities had been shelved for the time being.

Jun appeared at dinner time with a friend in tow. Manny de la Cruz (not his real name) was a zany, sweet-faced, slightly bug-eyed young man of twenty-eight. We liked each other immediately. We were scheduled to spend a couple of days "seeing the sights" in Iligan, as Manny called it. We visited one of those idyllic fishing villages not far from the city where six young fishermen were training to be party cadres had been killed by vigilantes the week before. The local armed city partisans (rebel hit squads commonly called Sparrows) retaliated by killing two of the vigilantes in the market place two days later, but the vigilantes took out one of the Sparrows. The death toll for one barrio of 200 souls: nine in less than a week.

We went to find Cesar (not his real name), the sole survivor of the raid on the fishing village and finally found him hiding in the heart of another large barrio. Nineteen-year-old Cesar was being protected by the residents while he recuperated from stab wounds received in the massacre. He had survived only because the bodies of the other men, including his own brother, had fallen on top of him and spared him the bullets and the knives. Cesar related a heart-rending story of how they were herded into the jungle in the middle of the night by eight men reeking of the telltale sweet sacramental oil of the Tadtads, a religious fanatic cult. The attackers first annointed the youngest of the barrio cadres with oil, then submerged his head in the stream, "as an experiment to see if the oil would protect him from drowning." It didn't. Then they annointed their remaining victims with oil, fired their weapons and plunged their knives into the huddled group "to see if they would die." Cesar survived by playing dead under the pile of bodies. He said he now had no choice but to "go to the hills" (join the rebels) since the vigilantes would certainly hunt him like an animal if he stayed in the area.

Afterward we went to see the body of the sixteen-year-old Sparrow, one of the boys killed in the retaliatory marketplace shootout. In his coffin he looked like a fresh-faced schoolboy. I couldn't imagine that a face which had never known the touch of a razor could belong to a trained assassin. Although the bullet wounds were clearly visible on his neck, the grieving family firmly insisted they did not know how or why the boy died. Manny, who knew the family well, said they could speak freely with me, but they still refused to discuss their dead son's political activities.

What a waste of young lives! I felt sickened and saddened. It seemed that no cause was worth that price.

We took a quick trip up to Marawi to see the Muslim country and to visit some people I had met in Manila. During the thirty-kilometer ride from Iligan to Marawi, we encountered thirty military checkpoints, one for each kilometer. The NPA was active in the Christian areas and the Muslim-rebel Moro National Liberation Front (MNLF) was active in the Muslim areas. The two rebel groups had been known to join forces to fight against the military on occasion.

There was a clear border between Christian country and Muslim country. The Coca Cola signs in English were transformed into Arabic exactly at the dividing line where we started seeing people in colorful Muslim *malongs* (sarongs) and the women with head coverings. We arrived at sunset, and, as the imams called the faithful to prayer, my host shoved a long dress and a head scarf into my hands and begged me to shed my jeans for Muslim dress. I was relieved to be less conspicuous in an area noted for kidnappings.

I talked to some MNLF leaders in Marawi about their cause and made plans for a future visit to their guerilla camps. I was surprised that the MNLF leaders operated openly and with very little security. It was because, unlike the NPA which never knows who is trustworthy, Muslims have sufficient cohesiveness that the rebels were supported thoroughly against the common enemy, the Marcos government, by their community, so there was no need for secrecy.

Marawi is a dirty, muddy place on the shores of breathtakingly beautiful Lake Lanao. Filipinos sometimes call Marawi "Marumi," a Tagalog word that means "dirty." We slept in the home of a "wealthy" family among chickens stalking through the living room and ragged children sleeping in the corners.

The next day Manny asked me if he could accompany me on the rest of my trip, since Jun had other tasks to attend to. I was more than willing. Manny was pleasant, fun, and a good companion. We had aleady consumed half the beer in Iligan together and developed an easy camaraderie. The stuffy Jun seemed relieved to turn over his charge to Manny, although he had thankfully given up Gerry Santos's melodramatic order not to let me out of his sight.

Manny and I set off by bus early the next morning, laughing and singing along the way, telling each other jokes and generally scandalizing our fellow passengers. I loved Manny's sense of humor and his lack of an ideological bent. Although he openly acknowledged to me that he was a member of the Communist Party, he didn't proselytize or even talk much about politics. Instead, he tried to lighten the horror we were seeing each day along the way. It was enough that we were being hit at each stop by grisly stories. We needed to laugh in between to keep from cracking up.

In one place a woman told us how her husband's head had been cut off by members of a religious fanatic sect because he had not purchased his quota of "magic oil" from the cult leader, who also happened to be the local police chief.

At another stop an entire barrio slept in an open field because crazed religious fanatics supported by the local military raked the houses with gunfire each night.

In the house of a priest with a heavy Irish brogue, we reversed translating roles when I translated the priest's heavy Gaelic accent into American English that Manny could understand.

On another night he gently applied acupressure therapy taught to rebel doctors when I got a crippling migraine.

Manny began to tell everyone I was his sister. We laughed at their puzzled reactions and explained that we had the same father, but obviously, we had different mothers.

By the third day I needed to know more about Manny. There had been a hundred subtle hints. His contacts with the partisans in Iligan were a strong indicator. Manny was more than he was letting on. We were staying in the convento in the parish where the man had been decapitated. Between interviews I whispered to him, "When everyone goes to sleep tonight, I want to stay up and talk."

"About what?" he asked innocently.

"About what you really are," I answered.

After a long sing-a-long session in which Manny played the guitar and the Irish priest and I both got misty eyed over a haunting version of "Danny Boy," the house finally settled down. Manny and I sat at a crude wooden table with only the moonlight for illumination.

"OK, tell me who you really are," I demanded.

He looked at me for a long time before he answered.

"I was a Sparrow. Now I am only guiding you and doing propaganda work," he confessed. "I have killed six men," he added quietly.

I said nothing. My heart pounded, first with some animal fear in the presence of a killer, then with huge confusion, with a sense of betrayal I couldn't explain.

Slowly, through that long night, Manny's story was laid on the table before us like a diseased thing. I struggled to conquer my racing emotions.

Manny belongs to a family of thirteen, all of whom, including his mother and father, were part of the revolutionary movement. Several brothers and sisters were with NPA units in the mountains. One brother had been killed. Manny had been chosen for training as an assassin.

I had guessed it, but I didn't want to believe it. This sweet-faced young man, this laughing soul, the man I had begun to think of as a brother, how could he be a killer? I looked at his artist's hands and tried to imagine them holding a gun, pulling the trigger. I couldn't.

We sat in silence for some time after Manny's "confession." Then in a soft voice, Manny began to tell me of the travails of his poverty-stricken family and of the atrocities that had visited them. I cannot even tell them all now because it might identify them. To this day, the de la Cruz family is still in danger.

He detailed to me how he helped plan and carry out the executions of corrupt public officials and soldiers. He told me about the long hours of surveillance when he stalked his victims and learned their habits. He spoke of the butterflies in his stomach and the feeling that a band was tightening around his head when he pulled the trigger. He told me about the relief when it was over. He told me about the deep inner certainty he would never be caught. Manny killed one man in front of his screaming wife.

Finally, as the golden Mindanao sun was rising, Manny talked about his guilt. The only thing that saved him from being swallowed by guilt was his belief that he was accomplishing justice.

I searched Manny's face for hardness or cruelty, but I just couldn't find it. He was still the impish little brother I had grown to love. Nothing had changed despite his horrifying confession.

Throughout that dark night, I had grappled with revulsion. Finally I found some way to accept Manny for what he was.

I asked Manny if he was carrying a weapon on this trip. It was important. With all of the checkpoints we had been encountering, it could endanger both of us. He assured me he was unarmed. Then he dumped the contents of his backpack on the floor and insisted I search them and him.

We continued our travels, perhaps closer than ever for having shared the burden of knowing. In retrospect I know that trip was a turning point for me. It was a time when I began to understand the deep-rooted reasons behind the violence that has torn apart the Philippines.

Manny took me to visit his family in the small town where they live. He told his mother quite earnestly that he had adopted me as a sister. This is quite a serious matter in Philippine culture. I was most likely the only white person Manny's mom had ever met, but she welcomed me to the family's bamboo hut as if I were her own daughter. I still go to see her when I am in the area and she still greets me like a daughter. She's always wearing a little ABC lapel pin I sent her for her birthday.

Manny and I travelled on, always moving westward and southward, dipping here and there into the horror of life for ordinary people in the Philippines. The violence they faced every day was overwhelming; I really began to wonder why there wasn't more insanity. Many times we heard tales that seemed too gruesome to be true. If we hadn't been in the company of priests when some of those tales were told, I wouldn't have believed them.

The time had come for the bus ride to end. I had become accustomed to traveling to a new place every day, to the ocean breezes, to Manny's cheery company and the gentle suffering faces along the way. It seemed as though I had never done anything else and that I would continue traveling that way forever. I would miss the buses, the palm trees and the soft voices. And I would miss Manny. He hugged me goodbye at the pier, entrusting me to the care of a young priest on our journey to Cebu.

I always wondered if we had been deliberately assigned to travel together by the party so that I would discover his background and attach a more human face to the horror of the Sparrow killings. If that was the case, it succeeded in the sense of making the "struggle" human. I wondered if they had decided to appeal to me on an emotional level, while they might have approached a male journalist more intellectually. I didn't mind the thought. Emotions give greater depth to my stories. But I still could not condone the killing. I don't know how I would have felt if Manny had told me he was still working as a Sparrow.

I still see Manny once in a while. He has left the revolutionary movement to pursue a career as a photographer. I admit that relieves me. But I know we both still carry his burden. No sense of justice accomplished could ever erase those six moments when Manny pulled the trigger.

16

SNAP ELECTIONS: *October 1985–February 1986*

I'VE ALWAYS HAD INTUITIONS and premonitions, a sort of psychic antenna. I try to listen to those unexplained "feelings" carefully, almost superstitiously. It is definitely unscientific, and some of my more analytical colleagues might say it is even unprofessional, but these inexplicable feelings have guided many of my judgments throughout my career. I have made vital life decisions based on nothing but hunches. So far those hunches have never led me in the wrong direction.

I had one of those premonitions in late October of 1985. I was scheduled to go into the Cordilleras, the rugged mountains in the north, to an NPA camp. But I found myself dawdling when the time came to leave. I put off the trip for a day, then two days, and then I called my contact to say I was canceling the trip. There was no concrete reason. It just didn't seem like a time to leave Manila. I felt it in my bones somehow. I also felt a little silly about it. Fortunately Filipinos are very mystical. They believe in this sort of thing.

Paul Laxalt, the American senator and close confidant of President Reagan, had been in Manila on a mysterious mission. The rumor mill said that Laxalt was applying heavy pressure on Marcos to call early elections.

ABC-TV had scheduled a live interview with Marcos on the David Brinkley show on November 3, a few days after Laxalt left. When the crew arrived at the palace to set up, Information Minister Gregorio Cendana was chatting with Bill Thomas, our ABC producer. He told Thomas that the show that night would make international news. Not knowing of any special event forthcoming, Thomas inquired, "In what area?"

"Elections," Cendana tossed over his shoulder as he walked away.

Thomas grabbed a phone to be sure that the panel in Washington would ask Marcos about elections. When the question was asked, Marcos handled it brilliantly. He allowed himself to be badgered and made it appear that those insistent foreign journalists had forced him into a corner. Then Marcos finally appeared to be convinced. He would have elections sometime after the first of the year, more than a year and a half ahead of schedule. It was a convincing performance. Marcos had chosen his forum. He had manipulated the players and won sympathy. He looked good.

The opposition was ecstatic that it had won its long-standing demand for an early election. But within days the euphoria dimmed and the scramble for political supremacy was on. Everybody wanted to be the candidate. Everybody, that is, except the coy and reluctant Cory Aquino.

There was general agreement that, to have any chance of success, there must be only one opposition candidate. In response to Cory Aquino's comment that she would run only if a million people insisted, the ancient and venerable Don Chino Roces began a signature-gathering campaign that accumulated more than a million signatures in just under a month. Cory was drafted, but not before Doy Laurel was called on the carpet by a stern Cardinal Sin. The Roman Catholic prelate treated the future vice-president like a bad boy in school. Doy was instructed to suppress his ambitions for the good of his people. Like a good little Catholic boy, Doy gave in and agreed to be Cory's running mate. For good measure he handed over his UNIDO party machinery to Cory, who had no political party.

Gerry Santos from Davao had invited me to spend Christmas with his family in Mindanao. Christmas in the province was lovely; the weather was mild, the food was plentiful and good. The warm family companionship and the raucous Christmas carolers every night helped me over a·heavy bout of homesickness, the first I had experienced in nearly two years away from the States. Romance was blossoming. I was happy.

Gerry was caught up in the romance, too, but he was definitely not happy. He had been a victim of the DPA paranoia that had engulfed the Communist Party in Mindanao. He had been put on "trial" and, like thousands of his comrades, he had been purged. As a moderately high-ranking cadre who had devoted his life to the party for sixteen years, the purge was devastating for Gerry. He was like a lost child. I invited him to come to Manila and look for a new life there.

The Aquino election campaign was barely distinguishable from the yellow confetti anti-dictatorship rallies on Ayala Avenue, but this time there were no riot police to break them up. There was still an exciting sense of adventure and a vaguely bold illegality about those campaign rallies, but they were all peaceful. Everyone wore yellow, except the petulant Doy Laurel, who insisted on his own signature color, kelly green. Freddie Aguilar, the long-haired, Indian-faced Bob Dylan of the Philippines, led the crowds in endless emotional renditions of "Bayan Ko," the opposition national anthem about letting the caged birds fly. Some listeners even raised clenched fists in the air. But Cory and Doy, the cute team, demurely raised their fingers in the "L" for "Laban" (fight) sign.

The crowds at the Cory rallies were boisterous and happy. Based on crowd noise levels alone, it was clear that Cory would win hands down. It was also clear that these were not rent-a-crowds. There were no parking lots full of hired buses. People arrived on foot, by bicycle, in all sorts of disorganized manners. They just wanted to see her. Cory was taking on the aura of the Virgin Mary. There was an electric feeling of impending change coupled with heartbreaking naivete.

Nearly a year before the election, a group of military officers had formed a group called "Reform the Armed Forces," or RAM.

One of the RAM leaders was Navy Captain Rex Robles, an articulate and friendly young officer who had apparently been instructed to befriend the foreign correspondents. One October night, Rex threw a birthday party for himself. We drank brandy into the wee hours and gradually the other guests faded away. As we absent-mindedly slapped mosquitos on Rex's patio, we talked of the military grievances, of his personal feelings about Marcos, and of the eventual plans of RAM.

I couldn't get Rex to say anything definite, although I was certain the RAM boys were up to something more serious than holding prayer meetings. We had by that time consumed almost an entire bottle of brandy between the two of us, but the slippery Rex refused to be pinned down.

At three A.M. Rex drove me out of Camp Aguinaldo to EDSA highway where I could get a taxi. We were totally alone in his car. After a moment of silence, Rex turned to me and made eye contact. It has always made me uncomfortable when someone driving a car insists on making eye contact. I was convinced of Rex's sincerity.

"You don't really think, do you, that we would tell foreign correspondents if we were planning a coup?" he asked with an uncharacteristic air of pomposity.

I had never used the word "coup" in our hours of conversation. Rex was laying down some heavy hints. I stayed awake the entire night wondering what was afoot.

In January, when RAM announced a series of "prayer meetings for clean elections" at military camps across the country, I was sure they were up to something.

There was a sense of excitement in the air. People were aware that they had won a victory, even if it would only be an election and six more years of Marcos.

No one honestly believed that Marcos and his corrupt machine would ever allow Cory to win.

The Marcos rallies were vintage Philippine politics. Hired crowds, movie stars, Imelda singing her horrible off-key love songs and crying crocodile tears, Marcos, Da Apo, wearing his signature red shirt. It was a carnival.

I flew to Davao for a Marcos rally. There had been a heavy out-of-season rain. The rally was held on an athletic field knee-deep in mud. Everyone there was mired. A couple of journalists lost shoes. I was straining desperately just to stay upright. I was seriously concerned I would drown in the mud if I fell. Yet somehow Imelda daintily picked her way along the red carpet laid for her with nary a spot of mud on her satin pumps. There were obvious scatalogical analogies—Imelda and Marcos were immaculate while the rest of us were buried in shit.

Marcos was clearly very ill. At one rally he had a bandage on his right hand. He lamely claimed that someone had scratched him while shaking hands. I thought he looked heavily drugged. At a rally at the Rizal Stadium in Manila he stopped in mid-speech. He was like a wind-up doll whose spring had wound down, practically in mid-word. He looked around in confusion, unable to comprehend where he was or what he was doing. Imelda and some aides clustered around him, held the dazed dictator erect, and began chanting frantically "Marcos, Marcos." I dashed out a gate to the field to where his limousine was parked and saw his aides carry him from the stadium and load him into the car like a sack of rice.

The Marcos campaign had a bad smell about it. There was sleaze everywhere. Some of the politicians just oozed corruption right down to their diamond pinkie rings. By contrast, the Aquino campaign seemed so wholesome and sanitary. And poor.

In December Imelda visited her hometown of Tacloban, Leyte, dressed for the part of the returning queen, resplendent in jewels worth more than any of the people in her audiences would ever earn in a lifetime of labor. At a rally where a bunch of peasants had been dragged in for the day, she exhorted them to aspire to the highest, as she had.

Imelda told them she had been born a poor barrio girl, like many of them. She grew up without electricity or indoor plumbing, but she had always strived for the best and she got the best.

"Look at me, now," she said, spreading her chiffon-covered arms like angel's wings, "I live in Malacanang and in Malacanang even the toilets have chandeliers."

Marcos's people bragged they could never lose as long as they had the three G's—Guns, Goons and Gold. The Cory people idealistically insisted they had their own three G's—God, Guts and Glory.

The communists and even most of the legal left had made an ill-advised decision to boycott the elections. That made it clear how far out of touch they were with the desires of the people for change.

Long before the election was announced, Dad had planned a family vacation in Hawaii. I agonized over whether I should leave the Philippines for a holiday, but Mark Richards at ABC talked me into going.

"What will you miss?" he asked, "A couple of dozen campaign rallies?"

He continued prophetically, "It might be your last chance for a vacation for a while."

Hawaii was lovely. I fulfilled one longtime dream of learning to scuba dive. And it was great fun to roam around the Big Island with my brother and sisters on our rented motor scooters.

I got back in time for the home stretch and endless days of car caravans running around the city incessantly honking the Marcos or Cory codes— "Marcos Pa Rin" and "Coree, Coree." Despite my recent vacation, I wished it would hurry up and be over.

ABC had sent in Terri Taylor from London to help me. We had worked together at Live-Aid and we got along well.

On February 2, Election Day, Gerry Santos arrived on my doorstep, suitcase in hand. I let him in, handed him the spare key, gave him a quick kiss on the cheek and dashed off. I didn't see him or my apartment again for several days.

I shouldn't have been surprised that the election was a ripoff, but the blatancy of it astonished me. On election day, I went south to Quezon province. There were soldiers everywhere, terrorizing voters with their weapons even though they were supposed to be confined to the military camps and disarmed on election day. The voting lists were hopelessly mixed up. Many people who had lived all their lives in a single voting district had mysteriously been dropped from the lists. Not surprisingly, most of those who had been dropped were Cory supporters. The government's election officials were drinking rum in their offices and refusing to deal with voter protests. Several polling places in suburban Makati had been smashed up by goons and one voter was reported killed in the melee. It was a mess. Obviously there was a massive fraud under way.

The usual vote buying was going on. Marcos hacks were giving away "sandwiches," two campaign handbills with a fifty-peso note slid between in exchange for a carbon copy proving the voter had made the "correct" choices. But vote buying is such a routine part of Philippine politics that no one really pays much attention to it.

Terri had a more exciting and terrifying experience in Tarlac, Cory's home province. She was traveling with a flying squad of opposition lawyers who were monitoring the voting. They were stopped by a jeepload of armed soldiers on a lonely road not far from a polling place in Ninoy's hometown of Concepcion, and held at gunpoint for an hour while another bunch of soldiers stole the ballot boxes from the terrified schoolteachers who served as election inspectors.

The first signs of People Power manifested themselves on election night at the Pasay City Hall in suburban Manila, where thousands of people gathered to attempt to stop the ballot boxes from being broken open and ballots being stolen. I asked one very confused teacher why she was carrying an unlocked and empty ballot box into the collection point at city hall. She said she didn't know.

Later that night, yellow-jacketed NAMFREL (National Movement for Free

Elections) volunteers had mustered their supporters in many areas. Thousands of people surrounded the Makati City Hall for several days and nights to prevent ballot boxes from being moved.

Ever so slowly, the count began coming in. Two days after the election, there were no definitive results. Why was it so slow? No one at the Commission on Elections had any answers. The quick count center set up by the government had turned out to be the slow-count center. NAMFREL's own quick-count center showed Cory far ahead in early returns, but the rat was already beginning to stink. It had always been clear that Marcos would never allow himself to lose.

Senator Richard Lugar, sent to the Philippines as part of an international observer team, underwent a fascinating metamorphosis as he got his baptism in Philippine politics. When Lugar arrived in Manila, he said he was confident the elections would be fair and honest. In unison, the jaded press corps snorted derisively. Election Day, Lugar explained away the anomalies as if he didn't want to believe what he was seeing. A couple of days later Lugar was obviously incensed by Marcos's insult to his intelligence and that of the entire Filipino people.

Then Marcos's machine began to show some signs of wear and tear. Four days into the count, we got word that something was about to happen at the government's tabulation center. I went rushing over just in time to see the computer operators walking out in disgust. They were claiming the computers had been jiggered with a not-very-sophisticated "one for you, two for me" program.

The mob of journalists encircled them as we rushed out the door. I knew this was the beginning of the end for Marcos. His indestructible machine had cracked.

A van was parked outside. The frightened and crying computer operators jumped in. Someone pulled me inside, too, just before the door slammed shut. There was pandemonium inside the van. Obviously they had not planned this thing far in advance or planned what they would do after they walked out. Some wanted to go to the American embassy. Others wanted to go the Baclaran Church to seek refuge. The Baclaran Church faction yelled louder, so the driver took off to the south.

The next day I tracked them down at the home of their leader in a house at Camp Aguinaldo, just across the street from the home of Captain Rex Robles, of all places. They were still trembling. The computer operators' leader was the wife of a colonel very active in the RAM movement. The puzzle pieces were beginning to fall into place.

In spite of a tearful midnight plea from Imelda, the Catholic bishops issued a letter condemning the rotten elections. They stopped only a word short of excommunicating the Marcos family.

A few days later Marcos's puppet legislature proclaimed him the winner in a televised charade of "canvassing" the official election returns. While a handful of oppositionists in the legislature cried "Foul," Marcos was declared the winner by a landslide.

The handwriting was on the wall. Marcos must go. Even the American government was disgusted with him. But no one knew how or when or who would take the initiative. I was beginning to have some vague suspicions about the answers to those questions.

17 REVOLUTION—DAY ONE: *Saturday, February, 22, 1986*

THE DAY WAS A DECEPTIVELY QUIET ONE, but I felt uneasy. I had lived in Manila long enough to sense the rhythm of the city, the "vibes" of the place. That day the vibes just weren't right, but I couldn't put my finger on what was wrong.

At the foreign correspondents' weekly cocktails at the Hyatt Hotel the night before, several of us had discussed this strange discomfort, but no one was able to pinpoint exactly what was out of place.

That week had been an eventful one.

Marcos had announced he would not, as promised, retire the much-feared and despised General Fabian Ver as Armed Forces Chief of Staff to make way for his vice-chief of staff, Gen. Fidel Ramos, who was much better liked. I had a feeling this would cause trouble.

The previous Sunday, Cory held a massive rally at the Luneta Park in downtown Manila. She announced a boycott of products of Marcos-crony-owned companies, including newspapers, banks, and—horror of horrors!— Coca Cola and San Miguel beer. The Philippines is fueled by Coke and San Miguel. The boycott would truly be a difficult test of loyalty to Cory's cause. In the ensuing few days, I felt unpatriotic when I drank a San Miguel. Some people pawned off their private stores of San Miguel with the explanation it was "pre-boycott vintage."

The rumor cauldron was on high boil. One rumor I gave an eight on a ten-point credibility scale was that Marcos would declare martial law immediately after his inauguration on Tuesday. Another, more paranoiac rumor said that Marcos intended to arrest 900 opposition leaders, including Cory Aquino, and have them interned on an island at the mouth of Manila Bay.

Diplomatic missions had not sent Marcos the customary congratulations on his election. The ambassadors of key countries, including the American and British ambassadors, would conveniently be ill or out of the country the following week and therefore unable to accept Marcos's invitation to his inauguration. Foreign support for Marcos was eroding fast. This seemed to be a not very subtle message to the opposition that there might be foreign acceptance, even support, available for another government.

Philip Habib, President Reagan's confidential adviser and troubleshooter, was scheduled to leave early Saturday afternoon after a two-day confidential, but not so confidential, visit to Manila. He had met with Marcos, with military people, and some opposition leaders. Scuttlebutt had it that Habib had given Marcos a message from President Reagan that he had better clean up his act, or else. No one seemed to know specifically what "or else" meant.

Cory had gone on a provincial swing to Cebu and Davao, purportedly to thank the people for their support.

Chito Roque, an old friend who had served as Cory's security chief during the campaign, phoned me early in the week and asked if I would mind arranging a meeting over drinks for him and a British diplomat who was a friend of mine. He said he wanted to discuss a very sensitive matter, a matter so sensitive he could not arrange the meeting himself. I had questioned Chito why he wasn't accompanying Cory to Cebu and Davao. He said he was tired and so he was leaving it in someone else's hands this one time. The meeting over drinks was scheduled for Sunday evening, the twenty-third, at my apartment. But on Friday, the twenty-first, Chito's secretary called to cancel the meeting, without explanation. I thought that was strange because Chito had been so insistent.

It was clear that some kind of trouble was brewing, but it seemed like it would be long-term trouble. My guess was that it would take several months of increasingly violent demonstrations in which the left-wing groups would have increasingly greater control. Yet I was certain that the fall of Marcos had become inevitable.

On Thursday, ABC and the other networks had pulled out their extra crews. Many of the "big boys" from the print media left, as well. Terri Taylor left on Thursday. I was sorry to see her go because she had jumped into the fray with such great enthusiasm and such grasp of the story.

Everyone seemed to agree that Cory's movement would eventually lead somewhere, perhaps a bloody somewhere, but that it would take several months. Media organizations weren't willing to pay the bill for people to camp out in Manila waiting for that something to happen. They were sorry only two days later. In fairness, though, no one could have predicted how soon the proverbial shit would hit the fan.

Saturday morning I hung around the apartment alone. I couldn't seem to sit still and relax as I had planned. I sent a couple of radio spots about the unease in the military over the aborted promotion of Ramos. It was the longest time I had spent at home since the campaign began. I even cleaned some of the unrecognizable moldy leftovers from my refrigerator just to pass the time.

Habib flew out at one P.M. A U.S. embassy source who was with Habib at the airport later told me that as soon as Habib's plane was airborne Ambassador Stephen Bosworth turned to the senior embassy staff members and told them, "Go home, eat lunch and pack your things, and then come back to the embassy prepared to spend several days."

Bosworth, presumably Habib and, by translation, the entire American government, knew something was up.

At two P.M., I got a phone call from Roy Golez, Marcos's postmaster general. Golez was Marcos's fair-haired boy, the whiz kid. He was young, brilliant, good-looking, West Point-educated, a former Navy captain who cleaned up the corruption-riddled Marcos-era post office, making things work without apparent effort. There had never been a breath of scandal attached to Golez until the presidential election campaign, when allegations had surfaced that he had used his postal employees to help scramble the voters lists and disenfranchise hundreds of thousands of Aquino voters. I had felt sad when I saw Roy being interviewed by Marcos's robots on government television that week, defending Marcos and the election results. Roy had been my best source in the Marcos government. He was close to The Man and The Woman, but he was reasonable. We had drunk endless cups of coffee together and discussed the successes and shortcomings of the Marcos government. I liked and respected Roy, but it was a strictly professional relationship. He had never been to my apartment. I wouldn't say we were friends.

But Roy's Saturday afternoon phone call changed all of that. He asked if he could come over to my apartment. Puzzled, I said, "Yes." As he was about to hang up, he asked, "Do you have any Scotch?" and announced he was on his way.

Roy arrived an hour later in an obviously agitated state. He paced around the apartment and quickly tossed off two Scotches with water. Finally he turned to me, pulled a folded piece of paper from his pocket and handed it to me. In a voice breaking with tension he asked: "What do you think of this?"

It was a letter of resignation addressed to Marcos which said simply that Golez could no longer serve in a corrupt government.

"I just can't do it anymore," he said. His eyes were strangely glittery.

Instantly our relationship escalated to friendship. I felt a stab of fear. I knew what Marcos might do to him. Marcos had so routinely killed those he perceived as his enemies.

"Are you sure?" I asked. "You know this could be very dangerous for you and your family."

He was sure. Golez is a devout Catholic. He had discussed his attack of conscience with Cardinal Sin on Tuesday. The cardinal had urged him to stay in the government because "honest men like you are needed so badly."

Golez said the cardinal's encouragement didn't salve his guilty conscience. By Thursday, he knew he must resign. He talked it over with his wife, Naty. She understood the dangers and was willing to face them with Roy.

As a friend, I was genuinely concerned about Roy. I knew how many people had disappeared, their bodies never found. As a journalist, I knew his resignation would be a major blow, perhaps a killing blow, to Marcos. All of the hackneyed metaphors went through my mind: another chink in the armor, another nail in the coffin, another crack in the machine.

I told Roy I was behind him and would do what I could for him. But I knew there wasn't really much I could do. Then I convinced him to go on camera for ABC the next morning after he handed the letter to Marcos.

When he left, I felt a strange sense of foreboding as I closed the door behind him.

It was a helluva story, as those old city editors would say. I picked up the phone to tell the bureau the news. But they had other news for me.

Al Croghan, the sour-faced American Embassy spokesman, had been on the phone a few minutes before. He wanted to alert us that Defense Minister Juan Ponce Enrile and General Ramos were calling a press conference at defense headquarters. It seemed they thought General Ver was preparing to arrest them.

I forgot all about Roy Golez as I alerted New York and then ran for a taxi to take me to Camp Aguinaldo.

When I arrived at the military headquarters it was almost dark.

The corridors inside the Ministry of National Defense Building were ghostly in the shadows of the February twilight. Filtered light came from a few offices and the occasional match as a nervous soldier lit a cigarette. The dim hallways were lined with soldiers in full combat gear. I almost laughed. They looked like something straight out of Rambo. One had two Uzis and was festooned with ammunition belts and grenades.

In the conference room, Johnny Enrile and Eddie Ramos were seated behind a table, facing a battery of cameras. I rushed my microphone into place just in time to pick up: " . . . and so we have broken with the Marcos government."

Enrile said he believed Corazon Aquino was the rightfully elected president of the Philippines.

A military uprising! I felt a surge of adrenalin and a stab of apprehension as I raced for a phone. I got through to New York. A few minutes later, as everyone was milling around asking more questions, I found myself standing behind Enrile and staring almost clinically at the back of his head. I had a fleeting premonition that the back of Enrile's head would be blown off before the night was over. Fortunately my premonition was wrong. When I came out of the MND building I nearly stumbled over three nuns praying the rosary as they knelt in the driveway. I paused to put a few of my jumbled thoughts on tape for an ROSR (Radio on Scene Recording).

Next door to the MND building is the camp's chapel. Inside, as if nothing was happening outside, a children's choir was having its usual Saturday night rehearsal for the next morning's church service. My mike picked up their sweet childish voices singing hymns. I looked at the nuns and several dozen combat-clad soldiers and spoke into my microphone, "If this isn't a coup, I don't know what it is."

Back in the bureau, everything was chaos. The bathroom telephone was the only place for me to hook up my equipment. The operations people in New York who received my radio feeds, joked that I sounded exactly as if I was coming live from the bathroom at the beautiful Manila Hotel. Reality Radio, I called it.

I rounded up a couple of very confused hotel roomboys and had them dump several blankets on the floor of the marble bathroom to soften the echoes. I balanced cardboard boxes on the bidet and the toilet to deaden the room more, then I spent an hour or so filing radio spots while I sat on the floor.

This was the biggest story of my life and I was filing it from a bathroom! It's too bad there were no still photographers around to record the elegance of my accomodations.

The New York editors were, of course, very excited. We decided to open a telephone line to New York because dialing had become extremely difficult. That line was not to be closed for a week. I never found out the exact cost of that very long collect phone call, but it must have been in the neighborhood of $20,000.

We also anticipated this story could be a long time unfolding so we began to talk about getting me some help. Terri Taylor had just arrived in London, wasn't even unpacked, but was willing to turn around and get a plane due to leave for Manila in four hours. The bosses in New York hesitated. The airport closed the next day, so Terri couldn't get in. That hesitation meant that I got no help and no sleep for the next four days.

About nine P.M., Marcos came on television with a bizarre tale that he had discovered a coup plot led by Enrile and Ramos. He displayed a pasty-faced colonel he said was in charge of the plot to storm the palace and kidnap or even kill himself and Imelda.

The giddy staff in the bureau hissed, booed, hooted with laughter and threw paper balls at the television set. It was a typical Marcos trick. Later it became clear that for once in his life Marcos was telling the truth, but no one believed him.

Marcos said he had surrounded Camp Aguinaldo with tanks. He said he was prepared to attack at any moment. Enrile and Ramos and the dozens of journalists around them appeared to be very vulnerable.

I wondered, why did Marcos hesitate? Why didn't he attack? I knew Marcos and his bragadoccio and machismo. It didn't make sense to me because it was so out of character.

Cardinal Sin and Butz Aquino had gone on church-owned Radio Veritas to ask people to go to Camp Aguinaldo and provide support for the troops. People Power was born.

In one of the television reports I saw Roy Golez standing behind Enrile. In light of his afternoon visit to my apartment, I wasn't surprised he had joined the military rebels but I was worried about him. I was sure he had no idea in advance what Enrile was planning. It seemed like the afternoon with Golez drinking scotch in my apartment was a lifetime in the past.

I decided to go back to Aguinaldo to get a sense of what was happening.

At midnight a few hundred people were gathered outside the locked main gates at the camp. Their spirit of camaraderie touched me as I watched people hoist sacks of rice and bags of food over the fence to the soldiers cloistered inside. These were the soldiers who were their enemies, the same soldiers who had water-cannoned them, tear-gassed them, jailed them, maybe even executed their relatives. Unlikely circumstances had made these old enemies into allies.

Several people boosted me over the twenty-foot-high gate. Inside it was very dark and very quiet.

In the MND there was a sense of siege. Everyone seemed to be whispering. A hundred journalists were camping there. The floor was littered with McDonald's bags, chicken bones, and empty cups. Enrile and Ramos were moving in and out of the offices, talking quietly with aides and journalists like they were in church or at a wake.

I recognized several of the soldiers closest to Enrile. They were RAM members. There was no sign, however, of my friend Captain Rex Robles. I remembered he had told me that he is a coward. He likes to plan operations, but when it is time to carry out the plans he disappears. Certainly my suspicions about RAM's plans for a coup were confirmed.

It seemed to me that everyone inside the war room was waiting for the inevitable attack. Again I wondered what Marcos was waiting for.

The ruthless Marcos could do nothing but attack, could he?

Outside the camp, a hundred or so drunks were dancing in the middle of the EDSA superhighway. I recognized one of them, the playboy son of a courageous opposition mayor assassinated a year before. He announced gleefully that Marcos was gone.

I told him that Marcos was far from gone and the situation was still extremely serious. I told him that Marcos said his tanks were pointing their guns at him at that very moment. He seemed to sober up a bit.

Marcos was tough, very tough. I knew this would be a hard battle. Enrile and Ramos were quite likely to lose the war.

In the taxi on the way back to the bureau at three A.M., ten hours into the so-called revolution, I finally had a quiet moment to reflect. It was only then I realized that the press had been alerted to the start of the festivities by the American Embassy. That was completely out of character. Why should the American embassy care if Enrile and Ramos were having a press conference?

Then I knew. The Americans were in this thing up to their eyeballs. The journalists had been used as the buffer to keep Marcos from attacking Enrile and Ramos. There had been no display of arms or any rebellious statements or seditious acts until Enrile and Ramos were surrounded by journalists.

It explained in a flash of insight why Marcos hadn't attacked Aguinaldo. As part of the press corps, I had literally been too close to see the forest for the trees, too close to realize my personal danger.

The Americans had deliberately placed us in danger, gambling with our lives that Marcos would never dare kill the assembled foreign and local journalists. We were pawns with no choice in the matter, although given the choice we would have been there anyway. It was a great story. There were no American diplomats inside Camp Aguinaldo that night. I know the Americans weren't entirely sure when they gambled with our lives that Marcos would not attack in a desperate moment, but they were willing to compromise the lives of hundreds of American and other journalists.

My jaws clenched as I got that familiar feeling of being raped, of being used against my will.

It was a helpless and bitter anger.

Throughout the four-day "revolution," and until now, the Americans have denied they had foreknowledge of Enrile's and Ramos's plans. I know that is a lie.

18 REVOLUTION—DAY TWO:
Sunday, February 23, 1986

M ARCOS HAD CALLED A NOON PRESS conference. It had been a sleepless night for everybody. Not much had happened after my middle-of-the-night jaunt to EDSA; I was just holding my breath to see what would happen next. There had been no sign of Marcos's threatened tanks. It was a wonderfully exciting story.

Marcos called the Sunday morning press conference, so I bribed a taxi driver an outrageous amount to take me to the palace. Everyone was afraid of bombs falling and God knows what.

Malacanang seemed unreal. The silence was eerie on that pristine springlike day. The birds were singing. I could smell the blossoms of the *kalachuchi* (plumeria) trees that line the walk. It was the picture of tranquility; but the familiarity of Malacanang was somehow subtly changed. It seemed like a stage set. There were a few tanks scattered here and there inside the palace grounds, like forgotten child's toys. Only a handful of sleepy soldiers were hanging around; there was no extra security on the gate. The only sound that broke the silence was the sound of the hammers of a couple of workmen unenthusiastically constructing a grandstand for the Marcos inauguration ceremony on Tuesday. It all seemed absurd in view of the events outside and the hundreds of thousands of people who had started to gather at EDSA, about six miles away.

I sat with several dozen other journalists on the ornate gilt chairs in Marcos's vast red-velvet audience room overlooking the smelly and polluted Pasig. It was the first time in memory that we were allowed into the palace in jeans and sneakers. The relaxation of the rigid palace dress code, more than anything visible, betrayed the crisis Marcos was trying to minimize.

Marcos made a brave attempt to appear relaxed. His manner was characteristically cool, conveying a man in command of the situation. But his face was puffy and his eyes moved constantly, betraying the fears of a man who was slowly being entrapped. Several generals and colonels, including the infamous chief of staff General Fabian Ver, sat behind him in a demonstration of loyalty.

Despite the crisis, Marcos was, as always, masterful in conveying his astonishment that anyone would accuse him of wrongdoing.

Marcos said he was "surprised" and "saddened" that some officers had attempted a coup d'etat and that some of the participants were even part of his elite Presidential Security Command. He pointed to the "traitors": two terrified-looking majors and a colonel perching stiffly on the edges of their chairs.

He repeated his ludicrous coup-plot story of the night before. I mentally snickered again and then stopped short. On a table in front of me was a paper package, torn open to show several hundred Philippine flags cheaply printed on scraps of cotton. With shock, I recognized them from the night before. They were the countersigns pinned to the uniforms of Enrile's men for easy identification. For once, I realized, Marcos had told the truth. I immediately thought of Rex Robles and the RAM boys and their shadowy plotting. This was a wide and well-planned operation.

Marcos began to detail the plot: the participants, their backgrounds, and their plans. Marcos's intelligence network, which had failed at the outset, seemed to have been able to supply him with the information, probably extracted forcibly from the culprits being displayed.

Marcos pledged to end the confrontation without bloodshed. He said that Crame and Aguinaldo were surrounded. Then he purred that he would not allow his loyal soldiers to shoot. No bloodshed.

Then, as if nothing was happening outside, he turned to mundane matters. He planned to take up economic policy issues with his cabinet that day. But no one believed that.

The man had more balls than anyone I ever saw. The words just came come out as smooth as honey. I had to admire his style even though all of my nerve endings were screaming "Bullshit!"

I wondered if Marcos planned to deal with the Enrile-Ramos defection as if it didn't exist. It was a simple tactic that could work.

It was the last time I saw Marcos in the Philippines.

My feeling of unreality persisted as I walked out of the palace and got a taxi back to the Manila Hotel. Everything seemed so ordinary. The streets were quiet, even for a Sunday. I had a strange feeling that the events of the night before were a dream, or that the drama at Aguinaldo had already ended and somehow it had passed me by.

Back in the hubbub of the bureau, reality returned. I did a few radio spots, but I quickly began to feel trapped in the office. I had gotten a room just down the hall from the bureau and set up my equipment there. It gave me a sense of stability in the midst of the crisis to have a place for my things and to know they would still be there when I returned. The quality of the radio feeds from my room was unquestionably better than those broadcast from the bathroom.

In mid-afternoon, I headed for Camp Crame, the Philippine Constabulary headquarters across EDSA from Camp Aguinaldo, where Enrile and Ramos had moved in the early morning to consolidate their forces.

People Power was in full flower. The crowd was massive. The traffic snarls were monumental. The radio said there were a million people there. How could anyone tell? They were packed solid for miles. It took two hours to get there and I had to walk the last mile because no vehicle could penetrate the human wall that surrounded the camp. By the time I got there, I was already worried about having been gone from the bureau for so long, leaving the radio desk hanging.

Rumors were spreading quickly: tanks were on their way from Fort Bonifacio, a few miles south on EDSA. The crowd seemed to sway as the news traveled visibly through it. But the people held their ground.

As soon as I arrived at the headquarters I saw Colonel Luis Andres, Ramos's friendly public relations man. I asked how things were going and he said abruptly, "Just follow that woman."

I had no idea who they were, but I followed a middle-aged woman in a flowered dress accompanied by two teenagers in sneakers and jeans. We all went inside the headquarters building. The woman greeted me like a long-lost relative, although I was fairly sure I had never met her. In those desperate moments, any foreigner seemed to be an anchor in the storm to terrified Filipinos. The building was laden with smells of soldiers, weapons, half-eaten meals, and fear sweat. We climbed the stairs and entered a small anteroom, no more than twenty feet square, where at least fifty Rambo types were lounging and trying to look casual and alert at the same time. I remember one soldier had two bandoliers of bullets crossed on his chest, an Uzi on his back and an M-16 dangling from each shoulder. I wondered which he would use if someone attacked or if he would somehow grow a third arm and fire all three at once. I wasn't sure he could move loaded down with all that ordnance. Anyway, he looked impressive.

Inside a larger room was a very haggard-looking Johnny Enrile. Impossibly, he seemed thinner than he had the night before. The marks of the tension were deeply etched in his face. As Enrile quickly crossed the room and embraced the woman in the flowered dress, I saw that he had a rosary in his hand. I whispered a question to one of the dozen or so soldiers in the room. He whispered back, "She's his sister."

The sister, her children, and Enrile huddled together for a few minutes, heads bowed and praying silently. This was obviously a very emotional family farewell. If the tanks penetrated the crowd and the guns aimed at him at that moment from a ridge on the Aguinaldo golf course were fired, Enrile would soon be a dead man. I felt very awkward witnessing the intimate family scene, but after the intensity of the moment passed Enrile greeted me warmly. I knew I should ask him a question or two, but there was just no question that seemed worth asking right then.

I turned to leave. One of the soldiers was circling his upper right arm with ordinary masking tape. I asked him what it was for. He shushed me with a finger to his lips and said it was a secret. Then he whispered conspiratorially that it was a new and very secret countersign. I realized with a shock just how marginal this little revolution really was.

I wanted to get a look at the crowd, so I walked to the EDSA gate and was hauled to the top of the wall by a jovial group of teenage boys who were having a party, drinking Cokes and flirting with the girls. As far as I could see the eight lanes of EDSA had become an endless sea of black heads dotted with yellow ribbons, signifying their allegiance to Cory. It was a Sunday picnic. Everyone was eating: sharing food, laughing and buying peanuts, boiled corn, ice cream, and all sorts of junk from the sidewalk vendors who have some sixth sense and show up wherever there is a crowd. Some of the well-dressed matrons had brought picnic baskets, babies, and even lounge chairs. A few women were passing bags of cooked food over the gate to the soldiers. A young girl was passing out yellow chrysanthemums.

I had started to call it a revolution by that time, although the People Power festivities were far from a revolution. "Revolution" had become more of a code word, a sort of journalist's shorthand. Coup or "civilian-backed military uprising" was closer to the truth, but for journalists, and particularly for radio, those were just too many words. Maybe I was among those guilty of spreading the idea that what was happening in Manila was a genuine revolution. It was not, for many reasons: the participants were almost exclusively from Manila; the participants had no real ideology or objective for the future aside from removing Marcos from power. Most of them were members of the middle and upper-middle classes. More important, the price they were paying for their "revolution" was cheap. Although they might not have known it, there was little danger. There were few deaths. Unquestionably there were people at EDSA who exhibited raw courage and conviction. But for the most part, at the risk of sounding sacrilegious, the revolution was a massive picnic. What started out as a military coup developed into a coup by the middle class that was eventually co-opted by the elite class. But that is getting ahead of my story.

I kept thinking about these tanks rumored to be on their way. The rumor had gained solidity by that time. Some people said they could see the tanks at the intersection of Ortigas and EDSA about a mile away. Nobody could really see anything from the gate where we were sitting, but the rumor once again caused the crowd to sway like wheat in the wind. Nevertheless, no one packed up the picnic lunches or removed the babies.

I recognized a woman perched on the wall near me. She was a low ranking CPP cadre I had met on one of those countless coffee drinking sessions with the "legal left." She said she was "just sightseeing." We sat on the wall for half an hour chatting about the election, the communists' ill-advised boycott stand during the elections and what would happen next. Absurdly, she talked about how the rebels might seize some weapons from Crame's armory during the current confusion. She, like her Communist Party, had no inkling that the center of power was changing hands. They could have been running the country, or at least coalition partners if they hadn't made some stupid political errors; but they missed the boat entirely while they thought about how to seize a few trifling rifles.

I felt a chill go up my spine and tears blur my eyes when I later watched the video of the tank confrontation. Nuns knelt in urgent prayer in the path of the tanks. They were joined by hundreds of Filipinos who actually ran toward the danger, placed their soft bodies under the hard steel of military might, and won. Even the hatchet-faced Marines weren't tough enough for that. The tanks backed off. This was the Filipinos' finest moment.

By that time I was on the air almost constantly. Things seemed to be moving very fast. I would do several spots and bulletins an hour. Since I had no help, it was clear that I could not go back out on the streets—it just took too long to go to Crame and back—so I had to rely on information being relayed by the ABC crews in the field with walkie talkies, and pick up what information I could from the radio and television.

I wasn't happy having to report what other people were seeing, but there was no choice.

Veritas, the Catholic-owned radio station, had been broadcasting live play-by-play of the events. At least we all thought it was Veritas, but Veritas went off the air on Sunday afternoon. The Veritas transmitter had been blown up and the studios smashed by Marcos loyalist vigilantes early in the morning.

June Keithley, an entertainer whose broadcast experience was as an emcee for kiddie television shows, was the only broadcaster with the courage to carry on the fight. June was broadcasting from a secret location on a station she called "Radio Bandido." The Radio Bandido frequency skipped around the dial, but it was easy to find. Nobody else was broadcasting much of anything. June literally carried the propaganda machine of the revolution singlehandedly. Some of the information she was putting out over the radio was so unbelievable that it seemed she was deliberately misleading us or engaging in outright lies.

June sincerely promoted People Power. She directed groups of yellow-clad enthusiasts here and there to "People Power," away from the bad guys. It worked.

We found out much later that June was broadcasting from a tiny booth on top of a tower within sight of Malacanang. I know June was half-paralyzed with terror a good part of the time, but without the information coming from Radio Bandido, we would have been very much in the dark.

Marcos declared a six P.M. to six A.M. curfew in some half-hearted attempt to get the people off EDSA. He was getting desperate enough that I think he had finally decided to attack Enrile and Ramos. But it was too late. The curfew was cheerfully ignored and there were few signs that anyone even attempted to enforce it. Indeed, there was probably very little military power left on Marcos's side to enforce a curfew. By Sunday night there had not yet been massive defections to the side of Enrile and Ramos. It seemed that most of the military men were hiding out waiting to see which way the tide would turn. Marcos's power had dwindled so much that people simply laughed when they heard about the latest directive.

I felt like a human news machine. I kept doing radio spots and radio spots and more radio spots; but I was loving every minute of it. I had had no sleep, but the adrenalin was flowing and I had a strong sense of being a part of history unfolding. I couldn't have stopped if someone had tried to force me. Sleep was unthinkable. I was living in each moment, submerged in radio, the perfect medium for the story. I could tell a new story every minute, every time something changed. My colleagues who wrote for newspapers later told me they were extremely frustrated because they could only write once a day about the barrage of events. I felt very lucky to be where I was.

I had a phone line open all the time since it became impossible to dial in or out of the country. Frantic relatives in the States clogged the circuits trying to call to check on the safety of their families. ABC assigned me a "baby sitter" on the New York desk, Peter Salinger. Peter developed a great knack for making sure I ordered room service meals and had regular showers. He even made me tell him what I ordered from room service. I didn't tell him that, although the food was delivered regularly, I hardly ate a bite of it. Revolutions are highly recommended as a diet tool.

Peter Salinger informed me that Peter Cleaveland was being sent from San Francisco to back me up. I chuckled and went on with what I was doing. The airport was closed. I knew there was virtually no chance I would see Peter Cleaveland until the uprising was over. There was also word that Ted Koppel was camping in Hong Kong, trying to get in to do "Nightline" from Manila. He didn't have any better chance than Cleaveland.

I began to wonder how long this "revolution" could go on. The tension was too high. It had to be building to some sort of climax.

19

REVOLUTION—DAY THREE:
Monday, February 24, 1986

THE MORNING SUN STREAMED GOLDEN through the carved mahogany window screens of my room at the Manila Hotel. Even though I hadn't had any sleep since Friday night, I wasn't tired. The story was too exhilarating. I had placed myself in the rhythm of the biggest story I had ever covered, and it seemed like I could go on forever.

My room was neat and organized. I was relieved that the sticky fingers express that had plagued Terri and me throughout the election days was inoperative. I had the only key to the room, which was a convenient twenty-yard sprint to the bureau. I could make it in under five seconds.

My sense of purpose was shattered at dawn when the bellboy slipped a copy of the *Bulletin Today*, Marcos's pet newspaper, under the door. Large black head-lines proclaimed that Marcos planned to attack the crowds on EDSA and restore order. Of course that was an old story, but when I saw it in black and white the threat assumed a reality I hadn't felt before.

My stomach turned upside down and my eyes began to stream tears without warning. I thought of the hundreds of thousands of people out there, many of them my friends, and the possibility that this madman might really kill them. I was on an emotional roller coaster. I didn't really believe Marcos would shoot, but I was no longer certain of anything. My mood swing was astonishing. I was suddenly exhausted and frightened. I knew I was losing my grip. I don't believe in detachment in journalism. Maybe my emotional involvement is what has given my stories some life. But I realized that the overwhelming strength of these emotions that fourth morning of People Power was in danger of incapacitating me.

My baby sitter, Peter Salinger, talked me out of my funk. He suggested I might get out of the hotel and take a trip out to Crame to see what was going on. The change of scene was a good idea, but there was one big story that had to be unraveled first.

Radio Bandido was reporting that Marcos had left Malacanang at dawn and was heading up Roxas Boulveard toward the airport in a tank. A great effort was made to make the story sound good. They even interviewed a colonel identified as part of the palace guard who supposedly witnessed Marcos' hasty exit.

That didn't make any sense to me. First, Marcos had his own helicopters and pilots. We knew there had been discussions between Marcos and Cory and the American ambassador. There seemed to be no reason why Marcos should go anywhere in a tank, much less to the airport, that was by then held by a solidly anti-Marcos Air Force. It would make far more sense for him to leave Malacanang by helicopter and go to the American Clark Air Force Base, where his safety would be assured. It also didn't make sense that the bellicose madman who was threatening to attack the crowds at EDSA would suddenly turn tail and run. In view of the previous day's press conference that ended in a pledge for a resolution "without bloodshed," what did make sense was that Marcos was frightened. Much later, we learned that the story of Marcos's escape was a masterful bit of psychological warfare engineered by Ramos and assisted by Radio Bandido.

It achieved the desired effect. Disheartened military commanders, thinking the die had been cast and wanting to be on the winning side, began to announce their allegiance to the Enrile-Ramos cabal.

But in the street things were looking dismal. At Crame the crowds had dwindled to a few thousand people around Crame's main gate. People Power had faded dramatically, partly because people had gotten tired of the picnic and partly because there had been sporadic tear-gassing. What was lacking in people was made up in trash. EDSA looked like a garbage dump. The street was littered with banana peels, corn cobs, discarded newspapers, lost yellow ribbons, and the occasional rubber sandal.

A few people were dancing in the street in jubilation about the phony Marcos departure story.

I heard the familiar noise of chopper blades and looked up in time to count seven helicopters circling the camp. This time it seemed certain the attack was coming. The crowd seemed paralyzed, like deer frozen in the headlights of an oncoming car. I was sure the helicopters were about to open fire on the crowd. My sense of surrealism returned. I had no awareness of personal danger, no realization at the moment that I was part of that anonymous crowd. I forgot to feel afraid.

As the helicopters circled Crame a couple of times, I sprinted toward the main gate on EDSA. I arrived in time to see the first helicopter land on the Crame parade ground. The guards on the gate let me inside as the remaining six helicopters touched down. Everyone was puzzled. Soldiers and journalists flocked around the first helicopter as an officer stepped out waving a white handkerchief. (I later learned he was Colonel Antonio Sotello, who later became the Air Force commander.) The crowds inside and outside seemed to realize with simultaneous jubilation that these helicopters were not an attacking force, but defectors. What had been an illusion of strength had, in that brief moment, become reality. Ramos and Enrile now had their own air force. The tide was turning. There was a massive roar as the exuberant soldiers carried Sotelo and the other pilots to Enrile and Ramos.

The crowd's excitement over the defecting helicopters flagged quickly as more news spread: Marcos had hastily called a press conference to deny the story that he had left the palace.

I dashed back to the bureau in time to see it on the government's television station, Channel 4, the only television network with a live linkage to the palace. It was real. A handful of journalists had been able to get there with only a few minutes' notice. Marcos was definitely in Malacanang.

Marcos engaged in a masterful drama with Gen. Ver, who was pleading with him, begging to be allowed to attack the camps. But a patient and fatherly Marcos calmly told Ver he would never allow civilians to be harmed. A tearful Imelda and Marcos's terrified-looking daughters and grandchildren huddled behind him. Marcos said the palace had been attacked by a helicopter. With dignity he pleaded with the rebels to stop the attack. Marcos's 120-pound son, Bong Bong, attempted to look ferocious in his military fatigues. They were all pathetic. For the first time, I felt a little sorry for them, almost like I felt when I watched the despised and broken Richard Nixon leave the White House for the last time.

The fascinating Marcos drama broadcast from Malacanang was rudely interrupted when someone pulled the plug. My television screen went black. In sudden panic, I ran into another room, thinking something had gone wrong with my set. All of the screens were black. Radio Bandido began reporting that rebel troops were fighting for control of Channel 4. June Keithley asked for People Power at the TV station. Thousands responded.

If Marcos lost his television station, he would lose his most strategic asset: his ability to communicate with the people.

Our crews in the field confirmed the battle. For four hours, we monitored the black screen. Then we saw a flash of light: a flickering screen and a shaky picture showing the lovely freckled face of Ma-an Hontiveros, one of the Philippines' most respected television journalists.

She said, "I'm very proud to be part of the first free broadcast from this station. Rebel forces have now taken over. This is now People's Television."

It was heady stuff. I wiped away another tear. Marcos had lost a decisive battle, but he still hadn't lost the war. Not yet. For the first time, I had the barest of beliefs that this rebellion, coup or whatever it was, might actually succeed in dislodging Marcos.

The revolution seemed to have expanded exponentially. It was taking on its own life and character. I also began to wonder how much of it was part of the well-laid plans of Enrile and Ramos and the RAM boys, and how much events had gotten out of their control.

After the helicopter incident I was trapped in the hotel. The crowd had simply become too large and the travel time to EDSA was too long. I felt schizophrenically very much in the center of things and at the same time very isolated from the real events. I was watching the revolution on television and listening to it on the radio rather than seeing it with my own eyes. Yet I had access to far more information than anyone who was standing in the middle of EDSA, or possibly, even those inside the Crame war room.

I know that staying put in the bureau allowed me to get more data and stand further back to look at the whole picture, but the street reporter in me wanted desperately to be in the center of the action.

I was in Rumor Central. It was a Herculean task to sort out fact from fiction. I wasn't always successful. None of us were. The only way to be absolutely sure of a bit of information was if it could be verified by the crews in the field. Some of the rumors being spread by Radio Bandido were unconfirmable, yet too significant to ignore. I reported some of them, like the fictitious story about Marcos leaving Malacanang, couched in disclaimers about "unconfirmed reports."

I began to wish desperately for some help.

I kept thinking about Walter Cronkite and his fame as the-man-who-never-went-to-the-bathroom during his marathon coverages of uncounted crises. I am no Walter Cronkite. Fortunately, I had a bathroom easily at hand. I was grateful I wasn't on television. I looked a mess, wearing the same jeans and white T-shirt now for the third day, with unwashed hair and unmade-up face. It was small comfort to know that I didn't look any worse than anyone else.

It was funny to see the hastily assembled motley crew of broadcasters at the new People's Television Channel 4. They looked worse than I did, if that was possible.

During a momentary lull I called my apartment and was relieved to find Gerry safe inside. I had a tickling in the back of my brain that he might try to get involved in some CPP craziness and jeopardize his security. I asked Gerry to bring me a change of clothes, a toothbrush and to buy some batteries for my tape recorders. He didn't arrive at the Manila Hotel for several hours. I was too busy to worry about him. When he finally appeared, he said the suspicious security guards had made him wait downstairs for three hours since they were unable to call through on the house phone (which was my radio link to New York). Unassuming Gerry had waited patiently for a long time before he got exasperated and finally announced that he was a priest who had been asked to bring communion to the embattled ABC staff. Sheepish security guards whisked him up to my room immediately and announced shamefacedly that "Father Santos" had arrived.

Gerry uncomplainingly made himself useful translating Tagalog reports from the radio and TV.

The pace of the story was escalating. I was sure there would be a resolution soon. I started doing live double joins (reports for two of our internal networks back to back) at the top of each hour. They were tricky because I sometimes couldn't hear the anchorman, so I merely began talking blind at a specfied time. The desk in New York was ecstatic, but I felt like I was too stumbling, too uncertain. So much was happening and the story had become very complex. It was nearly impossible to explain it all in the forty seconds available.

Dramatic videotape was flooding into the bureau, including some of the battle for Channel 4: some loyalist soldiers sneaking away in civilian clothes, a couple of bodies, a man lying in a pool of blood from a head wound, the cheering crowds, the little girls dressed in their Sunday best, giving garlands of *sampaguitas* (jasmine) to the soldiers sent by Ver to fight for Channel 4, a loyalist soldier breaking down in tears and finally accepting a yellow headband. Demonstrators had started to gather at Mendiola bridge, just a quarter-mile from the palace gate.

I talked on the phone to my friend Dick Powell, who had begun to form the flying squads for active non-violence. Dick and his nephews—Steve Joseph and his brother Mike, who at six feet and 240 pounds looks anything but non-violent—were dispatched by radio to places where People Power tempers were getting a little frayed. Their task was to start praying the rosary very loudly. It is hard to tell whether it was the linebacker-like Mike Joseph or the rosary that cooled things off, but it worked.

Nervous soldiers at Mendiola Bridge fired off a few rounds to keep the crowd back. One of the bullets ricocheted off the pavement and hit my friend Melinda Liu, *Newsweek's* Hong Kong bureau chief, in the knee. After a quick patch job at the hospital, irrepressible Melinda was back in action.

I was being swept along with the tide of events impossible to analyze. My mind was constantly racing, trying to keep abreast of the rapid flow of information and the constant shift of events. The airport was still closed. Ted Koppel and the "Nightline" team were still stranded in Hong Kong. Peter Cleaveland was stranded in Honolulu. I told the New York desk to be sure that when the airport opened, Cleaveland had a first-class seat on Philippine Airlines with a sky bed so he would arrive well rested. I had no idea how much longer I could keep this up.

By the third night of the story, I was fading fast, but I still had no problem rallying myself when it was time to go on the air.

Rumors began to circulate that Villamor Air Base, the Air Force headquarters, was under attack. The People's Air Force had wiped out the remaining helicopters on the ground. There were some wild rumors that the pilots of the Malacanang helicopters had quietly slipped out of the palace, leaving Marcos trapped.

At dusk, Marcos appeared out of the cosmos on Channel 9, a patched-together low-budget station reportedly owned by his daugher, Imee. He was bellowing like a madman that he would not give up, and, finally threatened to attack Ramos and Enrile.

Marcos was obviously being backed into the corner. The noose was tightening around his neck. Now it seemed like only a matter of time.

Each time darkness fell I wondered if the morning would find the streets littered with bodies. Each morning I was alternately relieved it hadn't happened and fearful the worst could come at any moment.

20 REVOLUTION—DAY FOUR: Tuesday, February 25, 1986

THE STREETS WERE UNCANNILY QUIET as the fourth day of the revolution cautiously dawned. There were no bodies as I had imagined in my fearful fantasies. Manila was weary. It had been a short war, but the tension of waiting was wearing everyone down.

Tuesday was inauguration day. Both Marcos and Cory had announced they would be inaugurated that morning, Cory at nine A.M. and Marcos at noon.

Cory's people were at odds with Enrile's people, who wanted the inauguration to be inside Camp Crame. Enrile and Ramos thought the security risk of having the inauguration outside the rebel stronghold was too great. She was adamant. She wanted her inauguration on civilian soil at the historic Club Filipino to set the tone for a civilian government. An inauguration inside Camp Crame would connote military control. It would also imply greater power to Enrile and Ramos than she was willing to concede. The choice of Club Filipino, a posh private club for upper-crust Filipino families, set an aristocratic tone that made some of Cory's people feel uncomfortable.

I was already hearing reports from inside Crame that Enrile was enraged that Cory seemed to have co-opted his revolution without ever making an appearance. There has since been a great deal of discussion about whether Cory ever went to EDSA at all. She insists she was at the corner of Ortigas and EDSA on the Sunday afternoon when the tanks came, but I have never seen any photos or television footage to prove it. But she became the unquestioned president because she was the popular hero. Enrile and Ramos only served as instruments, although that was clearly not Enrile's intention.

Our crews were staking out the television stations that morning, particularly Channel 9, Marcos's sole remaining contact with his people. Channel 9 was only a stone's throw from the Aquinos' Times Street home. We could hear sporadic gunfire through the crew's walkie-talkies. It was hard to tell if the snipers were after Cory or Channel 9.

Even though her advisers were urging Aquino to back away from the Club Filipino inauguration because of the security risk, she insisted. The ten-minute inauguration went ahead at ten A.M., an hour late. Cory, dressed in a hand-embroidered yellow linen dress, was flanked by Doy Laurel and Ramos and

127

Enrile, all smiling nervously. People's Television Channel 4 proudly covered it live.

I remembered an interview I had done with Cory Aquino on February 25, 1985, exactly one year before she became president. I came away perplexed about the character of this woman who would become president of the Philippines. During that hour-long talk she had stubbornly refused to discuss politics. She talked about her children and her grandchildren. She talked about the best and worst schools. She talked about her daughter's ambitions to be a movie star. She talked about clothes. But she would not talk about politics. I wondered if she was guilty of assuming that, because I am a woman, I would be interested in clothes and children rather than substantive issues. If that were true, it would be one of the few times I had not been taken seriously as a journalist in the Philippines. It hurt if that rare assumption was made by a woman. Or, could it be, I wondered, that she was really uninterested in politics and her main concerns were really children and clothes? Or, I thought was Cory Aquino an extremely astute politician who masterfully avoided a delicate issue by appearing to be disingenuous?

Whatever the reason, the little woman with the yellow dress who served coffee to her husband's politician buddies had become the first woman president of the Philippines. I felt proud of her, on one hand, and fearful for the future on the other. Given the inherent sexism and mother-worship of Filipinos, I wondered how much real power she would be allowed to have. I had one of my uncanny prescient feelings that Cory would be a little doll who would be impervious to the poitical storms swirling around her.

Just as I was ready to go on the air with the report on Cory's inauguration, my telephone line went ominously dead. I wondered if Marcos had finally pulled the plug on all of us. It would be a strategically perfect time for his attack. It had crossed my mind before that Marcos could have ended this crisis easily if he cut the power and telephone lines. But the much-anticipated Marcos attack never came. The strongman was nearly impotent.

I screamed at the hotel operator in frustration. She meekly confessed she had accidentally pulled the plug on me. There was no way I could get a line out of the Philippines. After forty-five minutes of continuous and frantic dialing from the New York end, the line was reconnected and seized, so it couldn't be cut. I took a few deep breaths to calm my jitters.

The line was reestablished just in time for the Marcos extravaganza. Channel 9's cameras inside the palace showed us an array of nervous Blue Ladies (Imelda's minions) and Marcos cronies. The atmosphere was more funereal than celebratory. The diplomats had conveniently absented themselves with excuses of emergency trips abroad or illness. Many of Marcos's cabinet ministers were also conspicuously absent.

About 11:30 Marcos appeared on the balcony, looking ghastly. He seemed to be living in slow motion, like a man walking through water over his head. Imelda and the kids looked like their couturier was the Mad Hatter. Imelda, with a tear-streaked face, was wearing her usual queen outfit, this time in white with Swan Lake feathers, playing the scene for high drama. The daughters, Irene and Imee, looked fragile and fearful in virginal white. Bong Bong was twitching nervously, looking alternately like a speed freak or a child playing dress up in his too large fatigues and lugging an M-16 that seemed to dwarf him.

The desk in New York decided we should open the network line live at the top of the hour when I would talk about the Marcos inauguration. I tried to explain to them the concept of Filipino time and how nothing, but nothing, ever happens in a precise time frame in the Philippines. The inauguration could happen at 11:45 or 12:30 or anytime in between. The editors wanted to try it anyway.

At five seconds to the top of the hour, the Chief Justice of the Supreme Court took his place. The announcer introduced Marcos and I saw his face on the monitor for perhaps half a second. That was the last time the Filipinos ever saw Marcos. The screen went black. I knew in that split second the ABC network line had been opened. Millions of people were listening. I gulped for breath. My mind was screaming, "SHIT" in four-foot-high letters. It was my first moment of real panic since the crisis began. I had absolutely no idea what was happening.

I rattled on helplessly for nearly two minutes about the screen going black. I said that Marcos was supposed to be inaugurated at that moment. I didn't know if Malacanang had been attacked (we had a crew there) or, more likely, Channel 9 had been knocked off like Channel 4 the day before. Finally someone rescued me and let me off the air. I sprinted to the bureau. No one was in contact with the crew inside Malacanang because they had turned off their walkie-talkies during the inauguration ceremony. After about ten minutes an old John Wayne movie came on Channel 9 and our guys came back on their walkie-talkies. Malacanang was unscathed. The Channel 9 transmitter had been hit. Marcos had been inaugurated, but his last line of communication had been cut. It was just a matter of time. He was finished.

The desk in New York went through a laborious process trying to decide how we were going to handle the fact that the Philippines had two presidents. Were we going to say "President Marcos" and "President Aquino" in future spots? Were we going to proclaim the legitimacy of one over the other by calling one "President" and the other something else? I lost interest in the discussion, and frankly I can't remember how it was resolved because it became a moot point just nine hours later.

All day long there was news of military units defecting to the rebels. The Ramos psy-war machine was wearing down Marcos's remaining troops.

The people in the streets were getting angry and growing harder to control. Dick Powell's flying rosary squads were meeting some serious resistance from an astonishing variety of hotheads, goons, thugs, and other flotsam that had mysteriously surfaced. By early evening a huge crowd had broken through the barricades at Mendiola Bridge, threatening to break down the gates of the palace.

Inexplicably, the airport had reopened and Koppel and other reinforcements were on their way in.

Since the election, I had been placing daily phone calls to Major Tom Boyd, the public affairs officer at Clark Air Base. We had a standing joke about whether or not there was a C-5 supertransport warming up on the runway to take Marcos and his billions out of the country.

In a comparatively relaxed moment in mid-February, I had asked Tom if he would tell me the truth if Marcos was actually heading out of the country. He wasn't sure if he would be allowed to tell me. But I did get the next best thing from Tom, a trusted friend and professional contact: a promise he wouldn't lie to me.

As the crisis escalated, I called Tom Boyd every couple of hours. He always laughed and answered, "Not yet."

At nine P.M. the tension had literally reached a fever pitch. I called Tom again: "Well, is Marcos headed there yet?"

Ten full seconds of silence followed. That's a long time when you're on the phone and waiting for a crucial answer.

Finally his voice came back almost in a whisper: "No comment." That was the signal I was waiting for. Tom hadn't confirmed the story, he hadn't compromised himself as an officer of the U.S. Air Force, but he hadn't lied, either. I was absolutely sure Marcos was on his way to Clark.

The bureau had a circular staircase to the upper office where I had made the phone call to Boyd. I raced down that staircase to get to my telephone and file the story. I must have built up quite a bit of centrifugal force running down those stairs because I popped off them with the velocity of a cork out of a bottle of champagne. Ted Koppel, who had arrived at precisely that moment, got the full force of my explosion from the staircase. I didn't even stop to apologize, I just kept on sprinting to my room and breathlessly reported the news that Marcos had left Malacanang. I was told later that I was the first on the air with the news.

Then I just sat in silence for two full minutes. The hair on my arms was still standing on end. Goose bumps rose on my scalp. It was a moment of intense clarity. After so many years, after so many thousands of people marching so many thousands of miles against Marcos, I was jubilant that Marcos was finally gone. After so many lives lost, could it really be true that only a handful of people had died in this massive outpouring of communal effort that finally forced him out?

Channel 4 was on the air with a constant stream of "revolutionary heroes." A few minutes after I reported Marcos's departure, the announcement came. Someone handed a note to Radio Bandido's energetic June Keithley, who had closed Radio Bandido on Monday and moved over to People's TV. It was pure justice that June was on the air at that moment. I'll never forget the expression of disbelief, followed by joy, when she announced with tears streaming down her face, "Ladies and gentlemen, this is the moment we have all waited for. The dictator is gone."

That was the signal for the party to begin. The entire city of Manila seemed to pour into the streets to celebrate. Cars raced around the circular driveway of the sedate Manila Hotel, honking their horns. People couldn't seem to find enough outlets to express their joy. It was as though a heavy burden had suddenly been lifted and the Philippines became light again.

I was still doing radio spots, but there was a sense of finality. The Air Force confirmed that Marcos and a party of his followers, including General Ver, had arrived at Clark. They would be airlifted to Hawaii early in the morning.

The party quickly started to get ugly.

Moments after Marcos left Malacanang, the wildly celebrating folk broke down the gate. The notorious Presidential Security Guard, knowing that Marcos was leaving, had quietly disappeared. Some of them told me later they simply stripped off their uniforms and melted into the gigantic crowd. Left inside were the last, and unarmed, guard: the Kabataang Barangay, teenagers from poor neighborhoods whom Imelda had fashioned into a bizarre combination of Boy Scouts and street gang. Nobody had bothered to tell these poor kids that the show was over. They thought they were still stoutly defending the palace. Our videotape shows one KB kid taking a vicious beating from the crowd that broke down the main gate in those first few minutes. I never found out what happened to him, but I doubt he could possibly have survived. It was amazing how quickly this crowd of rosary-chanting peace freaks turned into hate-frenzied animals.

The mob surged into the palace with complete mindlessness. Papers were thrown out windows. Paintings of Marcos and Imelda were ripped to shreds. Hooligans bounced up and down in the red velvet throne chair where Marcos had sat a thousand times. Valuables were looted with complete abandon. It took a while for the rebel troops to arrive and restore some sort of order.

I was still an outside observer, trapped in the bureau, watching videotape and listening to reports on the walkie-talkie, the television and the radio. Peter Cleaveland was to arrive at midnight. I couldn't wait.

I did a few ROSRs—Radio on Scene Recordings—in the driveway of the hotel with the noise of the celebration behind me. It was the first time I had even been off the fifth floor since Monday morning. I felt a little like I was in a halfway house after serving a jail sentence. I wanted to be completely free.

I felt nostalgic. I talked about the Manila Hotel as the Marcos's private showplace, where the red carpet was literally rolled out every time they arrived. I prophesied that Ferdinand Marcos would never walk through those doors again, but I did not feel triumphant. Richard Nixon came to mind again. I felt pity for a greedy man who had squandered his place in history.

Jim Laurie, ABC's superb television correspondent, was feeding me ROSRs from the palace through his walkie-talkie. I wanted to keep on doing radio forever.

Peter Cleaveland arrived, somewhat the worse for wear. He announced he wanted to go to sleep. I suggested with all the sweetness I could muster from the depths of my exhaustion that the New York desk wanted to talk to him first. It was proclaimed that Cleaveland was to stay awake while I went to sleep.

How could I possibly sleep when history was being made? Sleep was impossible. I didn't even try. I had to see what was happening in the streets. I had to witness the birth of a new nation. I walked out the front door of the hotel about two A.M. A carload of people I knew from the Parliament of the Streets was circling the driveway, horn blaring. They picked me up and off we went to Malacanang. Near Mendiola Bridge we met a crowd of ten or fifteen people patiently dismantling the barbed wire barricades. I unabashedly joined in and came away with my only souvenir of the People Power Revolution—a three-inch piece of barbed wire.

By the time we reached the palace, it had been secured by jovial, but firm, soldiers. Several truckloads of soldiers lined J.P. Laurel Street in front of the palace, all of them with yellow ribbons wound around their heads or tied around the barrels of their guns. People kept running up and hugging them. The benign crowd was all around. The thugs and looters had already been dispatched. Several people announced triumphantly that they intended to sleep in the street in front of the palace, just because it was being allowed for the first time in years. Everyone was everyone's brother. It was Woodstock, Haight-Ashbury, Greenwich Village, hootenannies, and pot parties all rolled up in one. Like everyone else, I wished the heady moment could last forever.

I ran into Toshi Matsumoto, who was one of the first inside the palace after the Marcos departure. He told me about his photo of the table left with remnants of Marcos's last solitary dinner: fried eggs, soda crackers, and a huge bowl containing at least two pounds of caviar. One spoonful had been eaten, two pounds wasted. I have kept Toshi's description as a mental souvenir of the excesses of Marcos.

Finally the exhaustion overwhelmed me. I don't really remember how I got back to the hotel, but somehow I stumbled inside and fell into the bed in Cleaveland's room, which had been proclaimed the "sleeping room," as opposed to my room, which was designated the "working room."

My advanced state of weariness, combined with the adrenalin rush of the night, made it hard for me to sleep. I had drifted off for no more than an hour when the phone rang. It was the radio desk. Marcos's flight was ready to take off from Clark. Did I want the honor of reporting his actual departure from the country? Of course, I did. I was instantly awake again. Sleep wouldn't come for another fifteen hours, but nothing mattered but the story.

Marcos flew away in a cloud of ignominy, with many a backward glance. As evil as he was, I felt sorry for Marcos. I knew his heart was breaking.

As Marcos flew off into the dawn, I naively felt sure that a new day was dawning for the Philippines and that Cory Aquino had all the best intentions for her country.

21

REVOLUTION AFTERMATH:
February–April 1986

IN THOSE FIRST HOURS AFTER Marcos left, the face of the Philippines changed. Filipinos stood a little taller on the streets. They had a right to be proud after the changes they had made. There were reports that in the immigration sections of foreign airports, Filipinos, once treated with suspicion as prostitutes and cheats, were actually applauded by fellow travelers. The relatively bloodless People Power Revolution, as it was beginning to be known, had captured the imagination of a world jaded by bloodshed.

Maybe it was only my wishful thinking, but viewed through yellow-tinted glasses it seemed that there was already less garbage in the streets and Manila had taken on a magical shine. It was not my imagination that people were smiling everywhere. There was a new sense of shared achievement. Maybe this new beginning would initiate a new brotherhood among a people who had been so selfishly divided.

The new president announced her cabinet: Joker Arroyo would be the powerful executive secretary, better known as the "Little President;" Bobbit Sanchez was appointed minister of labor; and Rene Saguisag was named presidential spokesman. Many of the people with whom I had spent so many hours, marched so many miles, were now part of the established government. The street parliamentarians had overnight been catapulted from noisy oppositionists to the wielders of power in a country with enormous problems. I knew them well and I was willing to bet that if anyone had the will to solve the enormous problems of the Philippines, these new power wielders could. I believed they had the virtues most needed by their people.

In hindsight that was naive, unrealistic, and perhaps unfair thinking. But at the time I was as full of euphoria about the changes of the past four days as was the rest of the world. I had made an emotional investment in the downfall of Marcos. I fervently wanted to see Cory succeed. Perhaps my blind romanticism about the "Bloodless Revolution" was the greatest disservice that I could have done to the Philippines. With such unabashed optimism, my colleagues and I helped raise such absurdly high expectations of the Aquino government that it was impossible for those expectations to be fulfilled.

On Wednesday morning, only a few hours after Marcos's departure, I was feeling a little giddy, like a kid playing hookey. I had actually gone down to the restaurant in the hotel lobby and eaten a leisurely breakfast while I worked on political obituaries of Marcos and Imelda. I spoke of Marcos as "the man who lined his cronies' pockets while his people literally starved outside his palace gates" and Imelda as "the woman who fancied herself queen and dressed the part."

As I was returning to the office, one of the bureau's drivers popped out of one of the rooms facing Manila Bay, which we had turned it into a dorm for off-duty drivers. It was a sign that the story was winding down that four or five of them were in residence at that moment.

"Look at that," he shouted, pulling me inside and pointing at the pier that was just visible over the palm trees. Marcos's yacht, *Ang Pangulo* (The President), was slowly pulling away while a lone crewman stood on the pier after casting off the last line. The *Ang Pangulo* was not just a yacht; it was a seagoing luxury ship worth millions of dollars. We all banged helplessly on the windows, alternately yelling, "Stop! Shit! Somebody stop them." Somehow, perhaps through our shared emotional investment, the yacht had become common property. We felt very territorial about it. We couldn't let it get away.

I called the new president's office at the Cojuangco Building in Makati. After talking to a security guard and a secretary who were obviously totally bewildered by their new status, I got Ching Escaler, the president's new appointments secretary. I told her the *Ang Pangulo* was being hijacked. She asked if I was sure.

I told her, "I'm sure, unless Cory has decided to go waterskiing this morning."

Nobody had any idea what to do. The *Ang Pangulo* sailed unmolested over the horizon. When it returned, a week later, the captain told a lame tale that he had taken the yacht away for safekeeping from the mobs. Yet there were no mobs after that first night when Marcos left. A more plausible story came from a friend who told me he saw two vans come from the American embassy drive to the dock and discharge several passengers. I think those were the last of the Marcos entourage turned refugee. A week was just long enough for the *Ang Pangulo* to go to Hong Kong or Brunei. I suppose we'll never be able to prove so many of those delectable details.

The world was reeling with Marcos's arrival in Honolulu and the inventory of the goods brought with him in Pampers boxes: hundreds of thousands of dollars in cash in pesos and U.S. dollars, boxes of jewels, religious icons and documents belonging to the Philippine government. U.S. Customs had impounded most of the booty in Honolulu, claiming the U.S. government had no idea what was in the boxes of personal effects brought from Manila aboard the Air Force jet.

Information embarassing to the American government was beginning to surface. It cast some light on the overall American role in the events of that week and confirmed some of my earlier suspicions that the American government had been far less than candid with us and with the world.

I had been cultivating a particular source, whom I strongly suspected was a CIA agent, for some time. We had developed a symbiotic professional relationship commonly used by journalists and diplomats. It couldn't in any way be termed a friendship. Mark Jones (not his real name) had given me a number of excellent leads, all of which had proven absolutely reliable. I knew he was a bit of a renegade and I honestly never knew his motivation for feeding me information that was often detrimental to the stated interests of the American government. Jones had announced to me in December that he was going on a vacation for two months. I thought that was highly illogical since we were in the midst of the election campaign and things were extremely unstable in the Philippines. He said he'd see me at the end of February.

Indeed, on February 26, I phoned him at the embassy. Sure enough, he was back. We arranged to meet for lunch at a very intimate French restaurant near the embassy on Thursday. When I arrived, Jones warned me that embassy people were instructed to have no contact with the press, so he was courting danger by meeting me. He ordered a steak and insisted on ordering a double chocolate souffle for dessert.

He was bursting to tell me some details of the revolution that had not yet been made public. First, did I know that all of the defecting airplanes and helicopters had been sheltered at Clark Air Base? I didn't. And that Colonel Sotelo's group of seven helicopters had been refueled by the American government at Clark before they flew to Crame on Monday? That was also news. The only condition on the sanctuary was that the defecting helicopters would not attack Malacanang. In fact, one naughty helicopter pilot did fire off a few rocket rounds on Monday, destroying a blue Mercedes belonging to Greggy Araneta, Marcos's son-in-law, and succeeded in terrorizing the palace occupants.

It took one telephone call to confirm that story. The story was immediately denied by the embassy, but a shamefaced State Department spokesmen later had to admit it was true after the pilots began telling their stories of landing at Clark and interspersing their aircraft among the American planes on the ground to preempt any Marcos plan to attack.

Second, Jones wanted to tell me that the American embassy in Manila knew exactly what the Marcos entourage took out of the country.

How did he know that? I asked.

"Because I was one of the embassy officials ordered by [Ambassador Stephen] Bosworth to make an inventory when Marcos and friends arrived at the embassy compound Tuesday night," he replied calmly.

Without changing tone, Jones instructed me, "Hold my hand."

I was really startled. Had he lost his mind?

"Never mind, just do it," he said, reaching for my hand. "Al Croghan [the embassy's chief information officer who had notified us of the Ramos-Enrile press conference on February 22] just walked in the door. If he sees us, let him think we're having an affair."

I reached for Mark's hand, feeling foolish. I had my back to the door and didn't turn around.

Croghan didn't approach us. I never knew if he even saw us in the darkened restaurant.

Friday, February 28, was my thirty-eighth birthday. I had lost all track of time and didn't even remember the date. After I had the luxury of three hours of uninterrupted sleep, the ABC desk in New York woke me up with a loud whistle on the still-open telephone line. Everyone was singing "Happy Birthday." I told them they were all crazy. It wasn't my birthday. There was a knock on the door and a bellboy staggered in under the weight of a gigantic basket of orchids and a birthday card from ABC in New York.

"What day is it?" I asked groggily.

"February 28," they all shouted back.

"Damn, I guess it is my birthday. I feel like I am ninety-eight years old," I groaned as I rolled over in bed.

Minutes later my mother called on the bureau phone to wish me happy birthday and to tell me about her telephone conversation with an old kindergarten classmate. I admit I was half listening and half sleeping when I heard her say something about Marcos and 38,000 metric tons of gold bullion worth 240 billion dollars.

I snapped awake. "Did you say 240 *billion*?"

Mom assured me I had heard right. I got in touch with her old classmate, who was a gold broker. It sounded completely ludicrous, but in those strange times nothing was impossible. Through the ABC bureau in Los Angeles we got a copy of the offering made anonymously through some generals representing Marcos to sell 38,000 metric tons of gold bullion. It was only an offer to sell; no transaction ever actually occured.

Mom said her friend was not squirrelly and he had seen Marcos's personal chop on the document. Some checking showed that while it may have been an authentic document, there was no proof that Marcos actually had control of 38,000 metric tons of gold. Later, when tales of treasure hunts and discoveries of massive amounts of gold began to surface, I wondered if it was true. Even later, Marcos himself hinted to me he had found the fabled Yamashita treasure. I was sure that Marcos would never have dumped all of the gold on the market at once.

Our minds were being boggled daily by new tales of how much Marcos stole, but I couldn't get my mind around a number as big as $240 billion dollars. I don't think anybody could.

But it did call to mind some information provided by a rather naive Canadian friend a year before. She said she was dating an American helicopter pilot, who had been ferrying loads of gold bullion to Hong Kong for the First Lady all week. It seemed outrageous to me. I just couldn't imagine such a thing, although this friend was so apolitical she wouldn't have thought to make up such a tale. I asked if I could meet her boy friend and talk to him about it.

Two days later she phoned me, bewildered. Her boy friend had been transferred without notice. He hadn't even said goodbye.

Now I strongly suspect at least some of the gold story was true.

We'll probably never be able to prove the truth of so many of the wild tales that circulated in those first heady days. They may be puzzle pieces that will someday show us a more clear picture of the Marcos kleptocracy. They are certainly part of the gathering Marcos folklore.

Nick Thorne, a British diplomat and a dear friend, invited me to lunch at the Champagne Room of the Manila Hotel on my birthday. The elegant Champagne Room had been the Marcos's stomping ground. The opposition never went there. But the first person I saw when I walked into the restaurant was Chino Roces, the elder statesman of the Parliament of the Streets. Chino greeted me boisterously. He said he hadn't been in the Manila Hotel since martial law was declared nearly fourteen years before. He wasn't wearing his familiar slippers and peasant hat from the Parliament of the Streets that day.

As we sipped glasses of cold white wine, the pianist began to play "*Bayan Ko*" (My Nation), the theme song of the opposition that had been sung so many times in the past few months that it had become hackneyed.

For the forbidden "*Bayan Ko*" to be played in the elite Champagne Room would have been absolutely unthinkable just a week before. Imelda Marcos would have, at her most charitable, made sure that musician never played in the Philippines again.

Nick pointed out a man across the room whom he had last seen the previous Sunday while the two were leaning against a tank on EDSA. In the opulence of the Champagne Room, that seemed completely absurd.

Things were gradually getting back to normal. Peter Cleaveland followed Marcos to Honolulu and then went back to San Francisco. I plugged along, getting three, four, even five hours of sleep a night.

President Aquino decided to release the imprisoned leaders of the Communist Party of the Philippines. Among them were Jose Maria Sison, the founder of the CPP, whom I had interviewed a number of times. I found his deep intellect stimulating, so I was among those who accompanied "Joma" through the gates of Fort Bonifacio, where he had spent eleven years.

The release of the communist leaders seemed to set a tone for the Aquino administration. Left-wingers began to talk of "democratic space," something Marcos had never permitted. Many underground leaders began to surface. Some legal leftists were gushing in ecstasy as they talked about Aquino's promised land reform and sweeping social and economic reforms. I remembered her campaign rhetoric, but that was just the promises of a candidacy that was an impossible dream. Once she became president, I wondered if she would really follow through on those promises. I had my doubts. Over beers one night with my friends in Bagong Barrio, I theorized that Cory Aquino was a member of the oligarchy that had only temporarily been out of power during the Marcos years. It seemed unlikely that she would ever betray her elite social class. But in the euphoria of those first days, everybody wanted to believe the new social order had come to the Philippines at last.

I went back to my apartment to sleep. Gerry and my little cat, KK, made it cozy. It felt good to have Gerry there, but I wasn't exactly sure how far I wanted the relationship to go. It was such a relief to have a little quiet domestic life again that I was not willing to confront anything that required an emotional expenditure. I felt deliciously decadent the first time I wasted an entire evening watching mindless sitcoms on TV.

Gradually, I began to think about the future.

My relationship with Gerry was more needed than wanted. I knew that we had far too many differences for it to work on the long term. I was saddened by the realization, because I cared deeply for him. I even thought I loved him at one point. But I knew it was time for my career to go elsewhere.

The kudos and herograms were still coming in from New York. ABC was really high on my performance. My boss, Mark Richards, ABC's international assignments editor, called to ask me about my future plans.

I was ready for the question. I told him I would like to stay based in Manila and travel in Asia working on special projects and special events. Mark was dubious. There were lots of correspondents in Asia and there really wasn't room for that sort of thing.

Would I be interested in being based in Rome and covering the wave of terrorism which was at that time shaking up Europe, plus covering North Africa? It sounded great, although I was dubious, as a woman, about working in Islamic countries. I had heard nightmare stories from other women journalists and I remembered Jordanian men distastefully. But Rome sounded great. I asked for a few days to think about it.

I talked it over with Gerry, realizing painfully that the break with Manila and with him would be final. He knew it too, but he insisted I could not refuse an offer that would mean so much to my career. My life has always been blessed with gentle and supportive men.

A couple of days later, Richards and Peter Flannery, ABC's vice-president for radio, called back to offer me Rome and "everything from Cairo to Casablanca."

It sounded too good to be true. I was touched by ABC's faith in me. Decisions like these always seemed to come to me more by gut feeling than by logic. I accepted without further hesitation.

At an ungodly hour one morning in April, Gerry and Nick Thorne and I drank a goodbye pitcher of Bloody Marys in the airport coffee shop. I bade them a bittersweet goodbye and swallowed my tears as I stumbled toward the plane.

The lump in my throat would not go away as I watched the rugged beauty of the mountain ranges and the Philippine plains fade away beneath me as I flew north.

22 ROME: *May 1986*

R OME IS A STUNNINGLY BEAUTIFUL city. The Italians have protected it well from the ravages of the modern age, particularly from ugly glass and steel skyscrapers. The late afternoon light underscores the ochres and the slate greys and the alabasters of the ancient buildings that have survived almost beyond memory. I was excited about living in the midst of such antiquities.

I could see that my assignment in Rome would be different from Manila in a hundred ways.

There were perks I had never enjoyed before.

I was met at Fiumicino Airport by Carlo, the ABC bureau's handsome Italian driver, in a gleaming white Mercedes. Carlo whisked me off to an apartment I had arranged to take over until I found my own place. It was a sixth-floor attic walk-up in a crumbling building in a grubby part of town near the train station. The driver and I groaned as we dragged up my four heavy pieces of luggage. My cat, KK, was due to arrive by air-freight in a couple of days.

I had an office in the ABC bureau, even though it was in the Siberian part of the bureau on an upper floor with no other human beings around. I was surrounded by banks of bewildering machines, but the bureau chief, Chris Harper, attempted to alleviate my confusion with a quick orientation on my first day on the job.

Over a morning cup of cappuccino, Chris handed me a pocket beeper. I wondered if I would ever be free of those damned things. I was excited, but well aware that the new assignment entailed risks. Big ones.

As a free-lancer, I was accustomed to being free, to calling my own shots and working for a number of bosses, being controlled by none. The disadvantage to that is that sometimes there are too many bosses making demands at the same time. The advantage is that, if one boss turns into an asshole, I could stop working for him with very little pain.

In Rome, I would be almost exclusively affiliated with ABC. That frankly made me nervous, even though I liked the people in New York and they had treated me very well. The free-lance market in Rome had been tied up for years, so it would be difficult for me to find any other outlets for my work. If things went as promised, I fully expected to be traveling a great deal for ABC, so I wouldn't really have time to work for anyone else.

The only guaranteed income I had was $100 a week. That was a drop in the bucket in expensive Rome. At $50 per radio spot I would have to do a lot of radio to earn a living. I was certainly willing to work and work hard. I thrive on hard work. I prayed I could make enough to sustain a reasonably comfortable lifestyle.

The Chernobyl nuclear power plant accident and the bombing of Libya had happened while I was en route to Rome, so there were plenty of stories. For a first story I thought I would use the rudimentary Italian I had picked up through a tutor in Manila to interview people in the marketplace about the ban on the sale of leafy vegetables contaminated by the Chernobyl fallout. The Italians had no patience with my feeble attempts at their language. Many rudely walked away or, worse yet, maliciously corrected my grammar and laughed at me. No one seemed to speak English.

With tears of humiliation and self-pity stinging my eyes, I realized that Rome wasn't going to be as much fun as I thought it would be.

I was occupied with trying to make some contacts in the incredibly unfriendly and byzantine Italian bureaucracy. Again, virtually no one there spoke English, so I was very dependent on the Italian-speaking bureau staff to ask questions for me. If there was a bomb scare at Fiumicino Airport or the government resigned for the ninety-ninth time, I couldn't even find out the basic facts on my own.

I realized it was time for a crash course in Italian, so I signed up for a month of very expensive, daily, two-hour private lessons. I did OK, but I think the Italians had already intimidated me. I was afraid of opening my mouth for fear of being mocked. I also knew it would take several months, maybe a year before I would be able to competently interview anyone in Italian. That seriously squeezed my independent nature.

I found a fantastic apartment. The sixth floor walk up had become oppressive. Even KK, who had arrived humiliated because he had pissed on himself during the twenty-four-hour plane journey, hated the attic place because there were no windows. He leaped for the skylights in a vain effort to see outside. It didn't help that pigeons mocked him from the skylight ledges.

I think my life and KK's were echoing each other in terms of frustration and mockery.

The new place was glorious. It was a large one-bedroom apartment on the sixth floor of a renovated sixteenth-century building with black marble floors, high ceilings, and floor-to-ceiling windows with white gauze curtains that billowed in the breeze. There was even a pocket-sized balcony that KK promptly appropriated. It was at Piazza Risorgimento, adjacent to the Vatican. In fact, one of the things that I liked best about it was that my living room windows overlooked the Vatican walls on the side of the Vatican Museum. The loveliest fountain in Rome, the Fontana di Nave (Fountain of the Boat), was just below the balconied window. My new apartment had a feeling of open space, unlike many Roman apartments that look across narrow streets into other apartments. I could see the sky and trees and birds.

My rent was one million lire. It was hard to get my mind around paying a million of anything, even the overvalued lira, for anything. But it was about $666 at the current rate. That amount might seem modest by New York standards, and it was modest by Rome standards, but it was more than I had ever paid for rent. Given my financial situation, I would really have to hustle, yet I refused to consider having a roommate after the danger and scrutiny I had brought upon my roommates in Belfast.

The day I moved in I went to the corner grocery to buy some staples, including cat food and cat litter. Chris Harper had given me a little "cheat sheet" with the words in Italian. I carefully asked for "*il cibo per i gatti.*" The jolly grocer asked something that I assumed meant "what kind?" My cheat sheet didn't go that far. I replied, "*peche,*" meaning "fish." The grocer, who seemed to be a caricature of every Italian grocer, complete with grubby apron and drooping mustache, collapsed on the floor with laughter. I had asked for peach cat food. *Pesce* or fish would be more appropriate for poor KK. I was determined to stop taking offense at being mocked, so I laughed along with him. We became friends, but he refused to let my gaffe be forgotten. Every time I went into the store over those months, he offered me peach cat food.

I was homesick. I had never really missed the States, but I missed the Philippines. The Italians were a sour lot. They didn't smile like the Filipinos. I found their unfriendliness strange, since Italy is so dependent on tourism. I was lonely again.

Far worse than being homesick was the lack of work. The expected wave of terrorism had not materialized after the bombing of Libya. I felt like a vulture, sitting in Rome waiting for horrible things to happen.

I was bored doing stories about the new McDonald's that had opened on Piazza di Spagna. I went to see the PLO and they gave me a biography of Yasser Arafat—in Italian. I struggled through it and was rewarded for the effort with several intense headaches. I understood about 10 per cent of what I read. I felt like I was getting nowhere. I went to the office every day and sat in Siberia. I ate cheese and rolls for lunch at my desk.

I had attempted to make some headway with the Vatican, but that was definitely a closed city. Even getting a press credential was an amazing bureaucratic exercise, as was nearly everything in Italy. One journalist told me he had been covering the Vatican for fifteen years and he was only just beginning to be trusted.

I went to an ordination at St. Peter's, just to get a glimpse of the Pope and the feel of the place. But I only made myself angry looking at the banks of flowers around the altar, which cost enough to feed a village in the Philippines, or any other Third World country for that matter, for a year.

There was also the matter of friends. Italian society is very insular. Each Italian seems to have a small group of ten or twelve family and friends. He rarely has social interactions with anyone outside that group. A large part of the expat community seemed to have adopted that posture as well. After the first few days of friendly introduction, the ABC bureau people had left me on my own. There was some friction with Wolf Achtner, a free-lance producer I had met on a bus in London when I first arrived in Europe in February of 1984. Wolf had apparently wanted the radio assignment I got, so he was going to make life difficult for me. I learned to ignore him.

If it hadn't been for the warm and enthusiastic welcome I got from Jane Evans, Chris Turner, and Trey Haney, a great bunch of people who worked for Cable News Network (CNN) and Anna Clopet, a photographer for *US News and World Report*, I would have been terribly lonely. We formed our own little group, and when we were in town, we would have raucous dinners at quaint little trattorias two or three times a week. Others joined in as they arrived, including Julia Tawn, a British woman who was taking a year off to study Italian. There were even a couple of Italians, like the owner of the apartment Anna had rented and a woman I had hired as an interpreter. The only friends I had outside that group were Gordon and Maria Pirie, a British diplomatic couple who were friends of Nick Thorne. The Piries took me under their wing and invited me to several parties where I slowly began to make some contacts with government people.

Italy was a much more difficult assignment than the Philippines. I wondered if I had gotten lazy, but I was champing at the bit. I wanted to work, but there was little of any substance to do.

I gradually discovered I had been caught in the "Cap Cities Crunch." Capital Cities Communications had bought ABC a year before. The austerity measures imposed first on television had hit radio while I was en route to Rome. My champions were gone. Mark Richards had opted to take the early retirement program and Peter Flannery had abruptly resigned. Peter Salinger, my baby sitter during the revolution, was my new boss. I was left with new management people under severe budget pressures who knew nothing of the verbal promises made to me by Flannery and Richards. As far as they were concerned, I had been sent to cover Italy. There was no travel budget, yet I was frequently asked to do stories about Libya, since I had access to considerable amounts of information about what was happening there. It seemed ludicrous that I should be reporting about a country I had never visited.

I was suffocating. I had envisoned a dream job with Rome as a base, as a lovely place to return to. I had imagined traveling all over northern Africa and even in Europe covering exciting stories and making lots of money. It was all going sour very quickly. I was sitting in Rome, scraping for stories, struggling to put together four or five spots a week. Simple math told me that my savings were draining fast. Worse was the professional malaise. How many stories could I do about McDonald's or the tourists who had been scared away by the terrorism?

I made a solemn vow that I would make the best of it, work hard and succeed.

In June, ABC sent me north to Genoa to cover the trial of the hijackers of the *Achille Lauro* cruise ship. For the first time, I felt comfortable in Italy. The people of Genoa were warm and friendly. And they spoke Italian in a slow singsong way that I could understand. I actually had conversations with people in Genoa.

Things were looking better.

Then in July, my world came crashing down again. I found a rather large lump on my breast. I was terrified. I called an American doctor I had met a couple of times. He examined me and recommended immediate surgery. I spent an entire weekend looking at myself in the mirror and sobbing about my impending mutilation. Julia Tawn called and wanted to see me, but I didn't want to see anyone. I had never been so low in my life. I knew it was completely irrational. I tried to intellectualize the situation and convince myself that breasts had no physiological functions for someone like me who had decided not to have children. But my gut wasn't buying those arguments. If I had been told I needed some less mutilating medical procedure, like an appendectomy, I wouldn't have been happy, but I would have accepted it as fate. I was alternately hysterical and mournful.

Julia, sensing something was wrong, appeared at my door. She wouldn't go away until I let her in and told her the story. She offered great human comfort, for which I will always be deeply grateful. I finally was able to pull myself together and think rationally.

In Watertown I had done some medical writing and covered several malpractice lawsuits involving breast surgery. I knew that there were alternatives to surgery in cases like mine. I started to think rationally again. I called the American doctor and canceled the surgery; I told him I wanted a second opinion. In fact, I got two second opinions from Italian doctors. Both said the lump was almost certainly not malignant. One even showed me the cyst on his ultrasound machine and how it responded to touch like a balloon filled with water. Both recommended I wait a month and, if it did not disappear on its own, a needle aspiration would be done. A month later I had the needle aspiration, which was like inserting the needle into the water balloon and drawing out the fluid. It was done in the doctor's office and was almost painless. I was weak with relief.

But the melodrama of my life in Rome wasn't about to let up. In early August I was riding in a car on the Via Veneto late one night after a particularly long and boozy dinner with some fellow journalists. The driver, a free-lance cameraman for NBC, sideswiped a horse-drawn carriage. He insisted that it was not necessary to stop, despite his passengers' arguments to the contrary. We were in real trouble when the carabinieri stopped us a few blocks away and confiscated all of our passports. We had the bad luck to be stopped by the carabinieri, who are a sort of national police, rather than the regular police. The carabinieri were known for their absolute inflexibility. The two men in the car spoke no Italian. My Italian was about as fluent as that of a two-year-old. Marissa Perrier, a feisty Australian social worker, spoke about as much Italian as a five-year-old. Between the two of us, we attempted to apologize. That did no good.

At one in the morning, we were dragged back to the distraught carriage man, who was entertaining a crowd on the Via Veneto with his histrionics.

I was ensnared in another Kafkaesque nightmare. From there on we could understand virtually nothing of what was going on. We were asked no questions, but we were not permitted to leave. Hours went by. The cameraman who was driving the car thought we might be in deep shit. He confessed he had been arrested inside the NATO base at Sigonella in southern Italy two years before. He had been illegally taking television footage and was caught smuggling out tapes concealed in the door panels of his car. He was charged with espionage and put in jail. After three months he was finally released from jail at the personal request of the American ambassador. He had ignored court summonses on the case for over two years.

"Oh, shit, you mean they think we are spies?" Marissa and I slapped our palms to our foreheads.

Time passed. We stayed on the Via Veneto. Nothing happened. I tried to ask why we weren't being allowed to leave. No answer. I muttered something to Marissa about "Lieutenant Mussolini," the guy in charge of our "case." Marissa had some stronger words to say to him in Italian.

I was getting worried, so I dug my tape recorder and mike from the bottom of my bag. I stuck my mike in Lieutenant Mussolini's face and asked, very politely, why we could not go home. For an answer I was grabbed by the arms and shoved roughly into the squad car. Marissa was pushed in right after me. The police took off, leaving the errant spy and our other companion standing bewildered on the street.

I was being arrested. I couldn't believe it. I was outraged. No one explained why we were being taken in. Marissa and I were kept in a waiting room for an hour or so and then a burly matron (aren't they all burly?) arrived and conducted a very thorough strip search. We were photographed with numbers hanging around our necks like common criminals, and fingerprinted. Our bags, shoestrings and belts were taken away to prevent suicide attempts. An obsequious policeman then locked us up in separate cells.

For the first time in my life I was in jail.

I sat on the cell's dirty mattress, arms crossed and glaring at the peephole through which the police would watch. If I hadn't been so furious I probably would have freaked out over being locked up; I have terrible claustrophobia. In the recesses of my mind I told myself that someday I would laugh telling this story. At that moment it was a nightmare.

In the morning they actually loaded Marissa and me into a paddy wagon and took us to court. At least we weren't handcuffed. We were locked in a holding cell in the basement of the courthouse for about four hours. My anger was fading and my claustrophibia was beginning to get a foothold when we were finally brought to the courtroom, where there was an interpreter from the American embassy. She finally explained what was going on. We had been charged with using foul language to a police officer and for tape recording a police officer without his permission. She warned us that the charges carried a possible two-year jail sentence. Panic surged through me. God! Two years in an Italian jail! I would rather die. Couldn't I get someone to slip me a cyanide capsule?

I was immensely relieved when I saw Chris Harper standing at the rear of the courtroom. He had been alerted by our spy-driver who had not been arrested. Chris, our angel of mercy, bailed us out. I was never so glad to see anyone or so relieved to get out of a place. ABC hired a lawyer for me, and the foul language charge against me was dropped. Apparently the judge saw that my Italian-speaking ability was so poor that I couldn't possibly know the words I was accused of using. Due to intervening events and the slow pace of Italian justice, I never found out what happened to our case. I still wonder if I will be whisked off to an Italian jail if I ever have the misfortune to pass through Rome again. I am giving Italy a wide berth.

I began to spend a lot of time at the beach. I was totally disheartened. There was no work to do anyway.

In late August I had a big blowup with the New York desk over the revolutionary anniversary in Libya. It would be the first public appearance of Kaddafi since the bombing in April. I was most eager to go. But the powers-that-be said no, they planned to send someone from Cairo.

I swallowed that decision unhappily.

But when, during the weekend of the anniversary, I got a phone call from the desk asking me to do a story on what was happening in Tripoli, I blew up entirely. For the first time with ABC, I lost my temper.

"If you want to know what's happening in Tripoli, you can bloody well send me there. Remember where you called me? This is Rome, not Libya," I shouted.

I slammed down the phone, threw my beeper in a drawer and went to the beach. I didn't answer the phone for three days.

Finally I answered the phone. Mild-mannered Peter Salinger was on the line.

"I heard there was some problem over the weekend," he began tentatively. If he expected me to be contrite, he was surprised. I lit into him about the Libya call. Peter gently admitted that someone had made an error in judgment, and apologized.

There was a pause.

"I understand you're not very happy in Rome," he said. "What would you like to do?"

I hadn't really thought about it. But the answer came out of its own accord.

I answered, "Peter, I don't belong in the First World anymore. I am sick of the superficiality of people who only care about their Gucci loafers and the latest movies. Send me back to the Third World. Anywhere," I answered.

Two days later Peter was on the phone again. How would I feel about going back to Manila?

KK and I were on the next plane.

23 BACK IN MANILA: *October 1986*

Tears filled my eyes when I saw the blue-black mountains and the green rice fields and even filthy brown Manila Bay as my plane approached Manila.

My intuition was telling me there was still more for me to do in the Philippines.

I couldn't believe the animal inspector was actually waiting for me at the airport at six A.M. so he could clear KK through immigration. He was courteous, efficient and even lent me seventy-five centavos to make a phone call. Maybe some things had changed with Cory Aquino in the driver's seat.

As soon as I got outside the airport door, my love-hate relationship with the Philippines manifested itself once again. I knew my euphoria was too good to be true. I got in a ferocious fight with a greedy taxi driver who attempted the usual tourist ripoff.

I was home. I even moved back into my old apartment in Legaspi Towers. Over the next couple of weeks I saw Gerry Santos twice, but we had already said goodbye. It had to stay that way. Gerry was by that time working for a Japanese newspaper. He had recovered well from the pain of his separation from the party.

I began to look at the Philippines again. I was as guilty as the rest of the world, expecting miracles overnight. But I was disappointed to see the same squatters. The same beggers. The same garbage in the streets. The same ripoffs. The same crooked political games being played by new political faces. That glow of the first few days after EDSA was gone.

The hard-won pride and self-confidence had already disappeared. The people weren't smiling on the streets anymore. I was saddened to see the loss of that pride they had so briefly enjoyed.

I felt a strong personal loss. I had a major emotional investment in the success of the Philippine revolution, and I wanted to see the people finally fight their way out of poverty. There were few signs of change.

Again I felt like I had lost my virginity. Many Filipinos told me of their unbearable sense of loss, their grief, their feelings of betrayal. Over and over, people would ask, "What did we fight for on EDSA?"

Yet they still affectionately referred to their president as "Cory" or even as "*Tita* (Auntie) Cory." For Filipinos, Cory Aquino is a very personal property. I confess I even thought of her that way, too.

Aquino said she was a simple housewife. Maybe all of us were unfair in not taking her at her word. Maybe her people and the world should have let her remain a housewife rather than pushing her into an impossible job.

The country was being run by the people who had marched in the streets a few months before. At the outset I had every confidence that Cory had chosen the best the country had to offer. By November of 1986 I had doubts. Others had doubts, too.

Already there were tales of corruption surpassing the Marcos days. Over a cup of coffee in the lobby of the Peninsula Hotel, the newest political gathering place, one of my best sources in Cory's new government called the new corruption "frenzy feeding." He said that Cory's people, knowing their time might be limited, had decided to grab everything they could get. Peping Cojuangco, Cory's brother, was the man most often mentioned as the purveyor of the new corruption. People already believed Cory Aquino was unable or unwilling to stop her greedy relatives.

Already Cory had backtracked on some of her multitudinous campaign promises, most noticeably on her promise to place Hacienda Luisita, her family's 15,000-acre sugar plantation, under land reform.

Rene Saguisag was serving as a most miserable and reluctant government spokesman. He said he did it only because Cory insisted and because he couldn't refuse her. Joker Arroyo was obviously enjoying his power as the "Little President," executive secretary to the president. Bobbit Sanchez was still labor minister, but his tenure would be short. He was already being branded as a communist. Big business was clamoring for his head. Just days after the revolution, Joe Concepcion, chairman of the clean election group NAMFREL (National Movement for Free Elections), had violated his vow that none of the supposedly non-partisan NAMFREL volunteers should accept positions in any new government. Concepcion was the new Trade and Industry Minister. Butz Aquino was champing at the bit for a job, but Cory had promised she would not appoint any of her relatives to government positions. He had somehow wangled himself a position on the negotiating team that had, in September, committed some appalling gaffes in its dealings with the Muslim insurgents. Butz had negotiated an agreement that would allow the return of Nur Misuari, chairman of the Moro National Liberation Front, who had been waging a seperatist war against the government in Manila for fourteen years. Misuari, who had been in exile in the Middle East, returned to negotiate "peace" with the new president. In the guise of "consulting" the Muslim population, he traveled at government expense through Mindanao, rebuilding his guerrilla army. The strength of the Muslim rebel army doubled during that "consultative" period.

But some things looked good.

Foreign governments were pouring in aid money, largely as part of the post-EDSA euphoria.

There was the much-vaunted "democratic space." The legal left was operating much more openly and being given a credibility it had never known before. Cory had pardoned and released all of the imprisoned Communist Party leaders within a few days after she came to power. Some had even formed a radical political party, Partido ng Bayan (People's Party).

The Constitutional Commission had been formed. Some of those appointed to write a new constitution were among the country's best and brightest. Who would ever have imagined a year before that such an unlikely group as radical peasant leader Jaime Tadeo, conservative Jesuit intellectual Father Joaquin Bernas, radical nun Sister Christine, Tan and even Marcos's deep-thinking labor minister, Blas Ople, would be writing a constitution which would chart the future for the Philippines?

Cory had announced a firm policy of national reconciliation. In an attempt to bring about a cease-fire with the NPA, the government had been playing footsie with the Communist Party. The National Democratic Front, the communists' political wing, was receptive. It looked hopeful, although many party cadres did not trust the sincerity of the oligarchical Cojuangco and Aquino families.

The heroes of February were becoming the villains of November. There were incessant coup rumors, and one name was attached to them all: Juan Ponce Enrile.

"Johnny" Enrile was still defense minister, but he appeared to be ready to make good on a threat he had made the day after Cory took office: "We got rid of one president and we can get rid of another if we don't like the way you do the job." The defense minister had even appeared on the podium at a Marcos loyalist rally billed as an anti-communist rally. With a diabolical sneer on his face, the man who led the insurrection that overthrew Marcos led a thumbs-down chant, "Down with communism," which promptly evolved into "Down with Cory."

Like a cat cruelly teasing a mouse, Enrile was taunting Aquino.

The president left for Japan amid rumors that Enrile and his ever-loyal RAM boys would attempt a coup while she was out of the country. That was a typical Filipino non-confrontational tactic that would avoid the issue of what to do with a deposed president. She would be neatly forced into exile. It was even possible that it would work.

I knew from firsthand information provided by a young air force pilot that on several occasions Enrile had ordered air force planes taken out of Manila to strategic airports like Lipa in Batangas. While Aquino was in Japan weapons had been issued to RAM boys, and air force pilots were ordered to stand by for orders.

None came, apparently because Ramos talked the commanding generals out of supporting the intended coup.

A smiling Enrile was among those who saw Cory off at the airport. He was still smiling like the cat that ate the canary when she returned on November 13.

Less than an hour after Cory's plane touched down at the Manila International Airport, I got confirmation of the rumor I had been tracking all afternoon. Police had found the tortured and brutally murdered bodies of leftist labor leader Rolando Olalia and his driver. Olalia, who openly admitted he was a Marxist, led the Kilusang Mayo Uno (May First Movement), a large red-banner-carrying labor confederation. He was much beloved by the workers, and his murder was likely to cause some strong reaction. I wondered if that was the purpose behind his murder. The military would have to play a greater role to control rioting workers, wouldn't it? Who would gain the most from that? The answer was obvious.

I was sickened and angered when I saw Olalia's mutilated body. I had a prickly premonition that I would see many more mutilated bodies.

At a protest rally outside Camp Aguinaldo, Bernabe "Commander Dante" Buscayno, the recently released founder of the New People's Army, accused Enrile of ordering Olalia's murder. Near the gate I saw Joe Castro, one of the most visible and articulate leaders of the legal left. I had marched for many miles beside Joe over the years, and I always thought of him as tough and strong. As tears silently trickled down his cheeks, Joe Castro looked like a man who had lost his best friend. His voice broke as he told me that Lando Olalia was like a brother to him. I longed to reach out and give him a hug, but that is not done in this culture. I could only clutch his arm and helplessly offer sympathy. Standing next to Joe was Lean Alejandro, a radical student leader. I patted Lean's arm, too, and warned him to be careful. Somehow I felt Lean and Joe were both targets. My intuition was working again. Lean was killed nine months later in much the same way as Lando Olalia. Tragedy also touched Joe's life—but that is getting ahead of my story.

Olalia's funeral march was massive. More than half a million extremely well-disciplined people marched all day through Manila's streets, making a very powerful statement: the left had a firm following and the left would not be goaded into irrational reaction to the murder of its leaders.

At the head of the funeral march the Communist Party's underground leaders marched openly for the first time under a National Democratic Front banner, surrounded by masked security guards. They had surfaced to make their statement of outrage and, almost paradoxically, to voice their acquiescence to a cease-fire.

One of the leaders was Satur Ocampo. I had known Ocampo, a former journalist and one of the CPP's highest ranking members, since my first month in Manila. The quick-witted and affable Ocampo had been paroled briefly from prison to attend a symposium on press freedom at the National Press Club. It was apparently one of Marcos's interesting propaganda ploys. Ocampo and I had met and talked many more times when he was brought from prison to the military court for his intermittently conducted trial on charges of subversion and rebellion. I liked Satur. Most everybody did.

Less than a year later, Satur escaped from his military guard at another National Press Club function. At the time many journalists snickered at the military and secretly cheered Ocampo's escape. He was a wonderful propaganda tool for the party. At Olalia's funeral an exuberant Ocampo embraced me and asked what I thought of his face. It was certainly different. I laughed and told him that shaving off his mustache and combing his hair back had altered his distinctive cheekbones as I had never imagined possible. I was glad to see him.

Satur and his wife, Bobbie Malay, and NDF chairman Tony Zumel were to be the rebel negotiators if the cease-fire came about. The possibility of a cease-fire had dimmed, largely because of the anger generated in the left by Olalia's murder.

After the funeral events began to move very rapidly. On November 22, the president finally was fed up with Enrile's shenanigans. She summoned him to the palace one Sunday morning and summarily fired him. Aquino was displaying an uncanny ability to paint herself into a corner and then create an escape hatch that I had begun to think of as the "magic door" syndrome. She had taken up the gauntlet and fired the volatile and powerful Enrile, but would that spark a coup?

Unexpectedly, Enrile retreated, tail firmly tucked between his legs. But everybody who knew the ambitious Enrile knew he would return to fight another day.

Also unexpectedly, the cease-fire went through. In jubilant ceremonies at Club Filipino on November 27, Ninoy Aquino's birthday, a sixty-day ceasefire agreement was signed. Ocampo, Malay and Zumel appeared, wearing formal clothes. Malay, the guerrilla lady, was improbably clad in a pink suit and pearls. Government negotiators decided to play it lower key. Ramon "Monching" Mitra, the handsome bearded chief negotiator who is often mistaken for the Marlboro man, wore his famous green plaid shirt. Mitra looked far more like a rebel than the rebels.

The cease-fire limped along for a month. There were constant reports of violations by both sides. I heard that the NPA was using the hiatus to recruit new members, give old fighters a rest, and develop some new expertise with explosives. They were blowing up jungles all over the country for practice.

The military, typically, was taking a siesta. The government's propaganda machinery was nonexistent. That didn't really surprise me.

During the cease fire, I wanted to spend some time in a military camp with the veteran fighters, writing about how they saw the hiatus in the fighting. Even though I had official permissions on a dozen pieces of paper, I was never allowed to do the story. There were always a hundred excuses that resulted in a huge amount of wasted time. That has been my experience in virtually every dealing I have had with the Armed Forces of the Philippines in more than six years in the country. I have never figured out if they are simply bungling fools or if the sabotage is intentional. After three abortive trips to a military camp in Pampanga, I finally gave up on the military side of the cease-fire story.

The rebels had the upper hand in the cease fire. They were being interviewed constantly because they were available for the first time in years. Every talk show featured the Satur-Bobby-Tony trio. I thought the well-chosen team of Ocampo, Malay and Zumel had put a very human face on the rebel movement. They were clearly not the type of people who ate babies, despite the heavy-handed military propaganda. Yet I knew enough by then to be cautious in my dealings with the left. They were also not as trustworthy as they tried to lead us to believe.

By late January there was some unenthusiastic talk of extending the ceasefire another thirty days. A tragic land-reform protest rally at Mendiola Bridge brought an end to all hope for reconciliation. A group of rowdy peasants had gathered at the bridge to protest the lack of movement on land reform.

There were some strong words between those in the front ranks and the nervous police. The demonstrators began to throw rocks, clearly provoking the police. I felt like I was caught in déjà vu. I could only think of September 23, 1984, when the shooting began. Then the shooting began again. In unison, the first line of police sheltered behind the barbed wire barricade aimed their weapons, obviously in response to an order. Then they began to fire into the crowd. People fell, bloodied, to the pavement. Their comrades screamed, panicked, and began to scatter. One boy tried to pick up the lifeless body of a girl. The police fired again; he dropped her and ran. In minutes the street was clear and deadly quiet. There were abandoned leaflets and rubber flip-flops. And bodies scattered here and there. It was one of the most shattering sights I have seen in the Philippines. I knew this marked the end of "democratic space" and killed the last hope for reconciliation.

Within an hour, the NDF had announced the end of the cease-fire. The Philippines was back to business as it had been a year before. Almost unbelievably, repression had returned to the streets of Manila.

The days of legal protest in the Philippines died the day of the Mendiola Massacre, as surely as twenty-two demonstrators died. There has never been anyone charged with the murders of those eager young demonstrators. Neither has there been a viable street protest movement since, not because there is nothing to protest but because there is everything to fear.

24 HACIENDA LUISITA, THE PRESIDENT'S PLANTATION: *November 1986*

N o one ever denied that Corazon Cojuangco Aquino comes from a wealthy family. The Cojuangco family, as everyone knows, owns Hacienda Luisita in Tarlac, nearly 15,000 acres of prime farmland, that is one of the largest sugar plantations in the country. Cory Aquino was always telling us that she was only a simple housewife and a woman of her people. I was intrigued with that idea. I doubt very much she has ever washed many dishes or changed many babies' diapers.

Many of my colleagues had been wined and dined at Hacienda Luisita. Cory's brother, Jose "Peping" Cojuangco was fond of taking journalists on jaunts to see his flock of pampered fighting cocks, each tethered to the ground like a bouquet of feathers, each with his own little house to protect him from the sun and rain. Many families in the Philippines don't have it that good.

From what had been written, Hacienda Luisita is a storybook place. There is an elegant family compound containing several houses, a golf course, swimming pools, tennis courts, a private airstrip, all the toys of the rich.

I had seen enough of the trappings of wealth. I didn't need to see Peping Cojuangco's Hacienda Luisita. I wanted to get a glimpse of the lives of the 40,000 people who live and work on the plantation.

I couldn't think of a better tour guide than Bernabe "Commander Dante" Buscayno, the recently freed founder of the New People's Army and a longtime friend of the Aquino family.

I had met Dante on the leftist political circuit after he was released from ten years in Marcos's prisons. I was intrigued by his direct and simple politics. Dante is not given to the usual communist rhetoric, which bores me to tears. I think it is precisely because Dante comes from a peasant background and has little formal education that he assimilated his politics by living them rather than by reading books. He was refreshing.

The first time I saw Dante was in early March of 1986 on the day he was released from prison. We were in a room at the Cojuangco Building in Makati, from which the Aquino government running in those first weeks. Dante, Communist Party Chairman Jose Maria "Joma" Sison, and military turncoat Victor Corpuz had all been brought for a press conference. There was the usual animal show. Reporters and photographers were crawling all over each other. Everyone was shouting; fistfights broke out here and there.

I noticed a very thin man sitting behind a table in the corner, legs crossed, shoulders hunched forward as though he was trying to disappear inside himself. He was being mobbed by the reporters and blinded by the television lights. He looked absolutely terrified.

"Who's that?" I asked.

Someone answered, "That's Commander Dante."

I found it hard to believe that this gentle-faced, soft-spoken man could be the founder of the rebel army. After ten years of solitary confinement, Dante's voice was little more than a whisper. He was clearly overwhelmed by the sheer number of people in the room. It was impossible to imagine this timid man marching through the mountains at the head of an army, carrying an M-16.

I made it a point to get to know him.

After I returned from Rome, I ran into Dante at the Partido ng Bayan offices where he told me the story of Hacienda Luisita. We agreed we would go there together someday.

We saw each other several times during the week of Lando Olalia's funeral. In the months since his release, Dante had found his voice. He lambasted the military for Olalia's murder. He was magnificent. He captured his audience with his charisma, and I became a fan.

At a press conference the day before the funeral, Dante asked if I was still interested in a trip to Hacienda Luisita. I said I was, but I wasn't sure it was the right time to go. There was high tension in Manila. Everybody was sure there would be more killings. To me, Dante seemed like a prime target. Maybe we should wait a few weeks, I suggested.

The gentle, shy Dante still remained, but he had gained a self-assurance that was disarming.

"Why should I be afraid?" he asked. "If they want to get me, they'll get me."

If Dante wasn't going to chicken out, how could I?

The day after Olalia's funeral, Dante and his friend Nick Atienza, a professor at the University of the Philippines, picked me up at a shopping center on the northern edge of Manila. They were driving an eyeball shattering dayglo-orange Volkswagen Beetle. So much for being inconspicuous.

I climbed into the back seat and looked under the seat for a gun. There was none. I looked out the back window for a backup car. There was none. Dante said there was no security because sometimes the security attracted too much attention. That wasn't very comforting. I caught myself wishing for a gun. I wondered if I was becoming enmeshed in the Filipino gun mentality?

For two hours, we drove north through the plain of brilliant green rice fields edged with jagged purple mountains. I love the improbable chartreuse of the rice fields and the encircling arms of the mountains of Central Luzon.

I asked if we would have trouble getting onto the plantation. I had heard that the Cojuangcos had stepped up security because they wanted to keep outsiders off the hacienda. Dante and Nick looked at each other and laughed. Dante explained that, at the age of thirteen, he began working as a sugar cane cutter at Luisita. Later he had organized the Luisita sugar workers. Even later he lodged his rebel bands under the canopy of the mature sugar cane. He wasn't an outsider at Hacienda Luisita.

A uniformed guard stood by the gate as we entered the plantation. The guard looked into the car, saw Dante, and saluted. "Hello, sir," he said. Obviously Dante was well known.

Later, inside a small concrete house in one of Luisita's many small barrios, Dante introduced me to Pepe, a leathered man in his fifties. Pepe was carrying an M-16 and wearing a security guard's uniform. Pepe had been at Dante's side with the NPA in the hills for many years until age caught up with him. Then he became a security guard at Luisita.

"How many of the security guards at Luisita are like you?" I asked Pepe.

Everyone laughed.

"Most of them," he said, "You might call it an NPA retirement program."

We drove down miles of dirt roads, through ten-foot tall sugar cane plants ready for harvesting. Cars are unusual there, so the orange VW caused a sensation. Kids came running out of the houses screaming and waving. When they saw it was Dante riding in the car, they jumped on the hood, stuck their hands in the windows and nearly threw themselves under the wheels. The men came out of the houses, so we stopped the car and Dante quietly talked politics with them. The women and girls stood to one side, handkerchiefs covering their giggling mouths. They said Dante was handsome, which is stretching the truth a bit. But there is no doubt he has a strong appeal. I hadn't seen such adulation for anyone, not even Cory, in my stay in the Philippines. Dante was very self-effacing and almost shy about it. I joked that Dante should run for president. Heads nodded solemnly in unison while Dante blushed under his dark tan.

These people were obviously crushingly poor. Even through the smiling faces, I could see that the children were in very bad condition.

I was shocked to see the distended bellies and matchstick legs of advanced malnutrition right on the president's plantation. Cory Aquino constantly talked about social justice, and I thought she believed in it. I was disappointed that her family did not live it. The kids were dressed in rags, their legs covered with running sores and their eyes dull. My heart went out to them. They weren't quite like Joel Abong, but they looked as bad as any of the ambulatory kids I had seen in Negros.

In another barrio, we were welcomed to the modest home of a laborer. As the news spread that Dante and a foreigner were there, people began to gather quickly. About thirty people squeezed into the tiny house where Dante, Nick and I were served Cokes. I felt very uncomfortable drinking mine, because I knew the Cokes cost as much as a kilo of rice.

I asked some questions about conditions on the hacienda. There was a hospital and even doctors and nurses, but no medicine. One of Dante's many sisters worked as a nurse in the hospital.

A solemn-faced old lady handed me a glass of water. It smelled like sulfur. I politely commented it was the color of weak tea. They roared with laughter and said, less politely, it looked like piss.

Drinking water polluted by molasses discharge from the sugar mill was a serious problem.

They said the water was making people sick. I asked if any of them had children who had died. Two-thirds raised their hands.

We drove through a field being harvested by a couple of dozen heavily sweating workers. I remember the days when romantic American college students went to Cuba to harvest sugar cane and "help the revolution." It never seemed glamorous or romantic to me. Sugar cane cutting ranks with the dirtiest, hottest, and most miserable work in the world.

Dante explained that Hacienda Luisita had been mechanized for several years, which meant that the sugar cane was harvested by machines. But 1986 had been an unusually rainy year. The ground was too soft to support the heavy harvesting machines, so *sacadas* or sugar cane cutters had been brought in from Negros.

We stopped to talk to a grimy group of them resting beside the road at the end of their day's work. The homesick cane cutters were happy to meet someone who knew their towns in Negros. I chanted the names of some towns, "Kabankalan, Hinobaan, Sipalay, Murcia," and they cheered. We passed some time with stories about their homes and their families and how much they missed them.

As the sun was setting we grew quiet, just feeling the coming of the night. I asked a last question: "Have any of you lost children?"

Most of them raised hands, eyes cast to the ground.

A small wiry man sitting next to me said quietly, "Ma'am, I have watched four of my children die."

I was angry. I wanted to shake him. I wanted to make him tell me why he wasn't angry. I wanted to know why he wasn't in the hills carrying an M-16 instead of cutting sugar cane in Tarlac. My mind raged with a dozen questions. But I didn't ask them.

I touched his calloused hand in sympathy and said nothing.

How much could these people take? The answer was obvious: a lot.

Dante and Nick and I were all lost in reflection as we drove back to Manila through an achingly beautiful sunset. I reexamined my anger about the *sacada* and his dead children. I still hated the idea, but I realized that people like him had no choice but to fight. They had nothing left to lose.

25

UP THE MOUNTAINS WITH THE WEIRDOS:
January–March 1987

ANTI-COMMUNISM HAD BECOME the Philippines' latest fad. Suddenly there had been a spontaneous combustion of armed vigilante groups quietly sanctioned by the military. I thought it was very unusual given the divisive nature of Filipino culture that such groups had sprung up all over the country at once. The catalyst seemed to be in Davao City, which was a rebel stronghold at the time. I could see a strong possibility they would turn into death squads.

Between January and March of 1987 I went to Mindanao twice to look at the vigilante movement and the more-established and more-vicious phenomenon of anticommunist and anti-Muslim religious cultists who believed that they could not die.

In Davao City an organization called Alsa Masa (which meant, literally, Mass Uprising) was quickly pushing the NPA from its traditional stronghold in the city's huge Agdao shantytown. Part of the reason for the sudden upsurge of adherents to the Alsa Masa organization was the popular discontent with the NPA's revolutionary taxation program. But I was sure that some stronger force was behind the Alsa Masa.

Alsa Masa and similar groups in Cebu, Bacolod and Central Luzon seemed to be part of a very sophisticated plan that was totally contradictory to the Philippine culture, yet incorporated elements that appeal strongly to Filipinos. Filipinos like to join groups, but if there is strong leadership the group is likely to splinter. If the leadership is weak the group will be ineffectual. Alsa Masa had a godfather, Colonel Franco Calida, Davao's police chief. Nothing happened without his approval. It is important to point out here that nothing happens fast in this culture, so it was doubly suspicious that Alsa Masa seemed to spring full-blown from the mind of its unknown creator in a matter of months. Many Filipinos have love affairs with guns. There is a breed that is attracted to the feeling of power which comes from carrying a gun. The Alsa Masa members got free guns from Colonel Calida. Granted, some of the guns were pretty rough—old Garands, carbines, rusty .38s. But there was an unmistakable appeal. Carrying a gun for a living is definitely more fun than working as a fisherman, a tricycle driver, or a ditch digger. All of those elements composing the Alsa Masa added up to something suspicious.

I met Colonel Calida, a swaggering pot-bellied man dressed in fatigues and preening himself in front of a Rambo poster, on a January trip to Davao. Calida billed himself as the "godfather" of the Alsa Masa, but he was still trying to be a little discreet. (He pulled out all the stops a couple of months later.) Calida introduced me to a pack of small ratlike men whom he said were former members of Sparrow units who had killed hundreds of people in Davao. They were his bodyguards.

"Aren't you afraid they might turn on you?" I asked.

"Not a chance," the nice colonel replied with a wink. "They know we would go after their families."

Calida sent me off with a police sergeant to visit Agdao, once known as Nicar-Agdao because of its similarities to Marxist Nicaragua. I had to promise I wouldn't write that Calida's men had taken me there. "This is supposed to be a popular movement, you know," he said with another conspiratorial wink.

I had been to Agdao several times before. Only four months before, I had interviewed NPAs who lived and were sheltered inside Agdao. The people of Agdao were firmly in the camp of the rebels. In four months, things had changed dramatically.

Inside Agdao, there was a bunch of swaggerers waiting for me. They looked like clones of Calida. They all had M-16s festooned with stickers showing the hammer and sickle and a circle and slash mark through it. As if the international symbols wouldn't be understood, several others had stickers that said "No to Communism."

To a man, they told me they were former NPA members. Some of them probably were. They said that they were sickened by communist abuses. I was taken to a dirty beach where they said that two suspected military informers had been "salvaged" by the NPA. I knew the NPA was very capable of such activities, but the stories coming from the Alsa Masa seemed memorized. My bullshit-detector alarms were going off.

I was interviewing "the boys" in a small clearing, a sort of public square in the Gotamco neighborhood of Agdao. I had interviewed NPAs in exactly that same spot scant months before. The Alsa Masa was claiming that 100 percent of the residents of Agdao had converted from communist sympathizers to enthusiastic Alsa Masa supporters in the space of four months. I shouted a question to the gathered crowd, "Do you like Alsa Masa?"

"Yes!" they roared back.

I had noticed a man quietly standing to my right—he was one of the NPAs I had interviewed in September. I noticed he had not joined in the booming "yes."

"Do you remember me?" he asked out of the side of his mouth.

I didn't look at him. "Yes," I answered, looking in the other direction. He moved away. Point made. The other side was still there, but laying low.

A few hours later I went back to Agdao without my police escort, in hopes of finding someone who would talk freely. An old man was sweeping the flagstones in front of a small chapel. In the tiny yard, there was just enough space for four new graves.

He told me his son was buried in one of the graves.

"How did he die?" I asked.

"He was killed by the Alsa Masa because they thought he was a communist," he answered wearily.

I asked him, "What do the people of Agdao think of the Alsa Masa? Have they really joined?

He looked over his shoulder in both directions before he answered, "We have no choice. Many of those Alsa Masa are members of criminal gangs. They came in here with so many guns that there was nothing we could do. We are all afraid of them. They have already killed so many they say are communists. We are just quiet for now."

I returned to police headquarters in time to see six bodies sprawled on the grass in front of the main building. Calida proudly announced that his men had killed members of a criminal gang in a shootout with police a few hours before. I later learned the dead men were indeed members of a criminal gang, but Calida had not told me that they were also Alsa Masa. They had stopped giving the police a regularly allotted percentage of their booty, so they were no longer of use. I held my breath and shot videotape of the bodies. I noticed that there was no rigor mortis in the bodies arrayed before me, although Calida said they had been dead three hours. That should have been long enough. There was little bleeding from gaping wounds that looked like close-range injuries. One man's hand and another man's foot were nearly blown off. It didn't look like a shoot-out to me. I was sure they had been executed.

The recesses of my mind were screaming with the horror of the scene, but on the surface I kept myself detached. I just kept my camera running.

In February, Joe Conason of the *Village Voice* and I began to look into the activities of a retired American general, John K. Singlaub, in the Philippines. Gary Shepherd of ABC's Los Angeles bureau had encountered Singlaub in the Manila Airport in November. That aroused my suspicion.

Singlaub, a rabid anticommunist who had become notorious when he raised millions of dollars for the contras in Nicaragua, had moved to the Philippines several months before. Singlaub claimed he was engaging in a hunt for the mythical Yamashita treasure, but there was strong evidence connecting him to the rapid rise of the vigilantes. Joe and I broke the story in mid-February, but it was too late. Singlaub was in Hong Kong the weekend the story broke. He never returned, but it didn't matter. The vigilantes were already firmly entrenched. They still are, although their rigid organizational structure has broken apart somewhat because of internal bickering, as would be more typical of such groups.

On my next trip to Davao in March I met Colonel Calida again. He had read my January story and objected to being called the "cowboy colonel." He was less than friendly. That time he brandished a motley assortment of weapons and a captured communist flag in his office while posing for my camera. My companion on that trip was P.J. O'Rourke of *Rolling Stone*, an adventurer and gun freak. P.J. and Calida got along just fine, swapping gun stories. P.J. also got along well with Calida's personal gorilla, Nick the Goon. P.J. and I had a lot of different opinions about things.

On our first night in Davao, P.J. and Nick and some of Calida's other goons were settled in for a long night of drinking in the bar of the Apo View Hotel when I decided I couldn't stomach any more of the braggadoccio. I've never been very good at talking to people like that.

My phone was ringing when I got to my room.

"Have you heard what Calida is saying about you on the radio?" a voice asked.

It was an old friend in Davao who hadn't even known I was in town until he turned on his radio. It seemed that Calida and Jun Pala, his radio mouthpiece, were complaining about me over the airwaves. They were accusing me of being a victim of communist propaganda and making not-too-veiled suggestions that I was a serious nuisance to their cause. My friend was alarmed. He suggested I get out of town as soon as possible. He explained that he believed Calida was sending a message to his Alsa Masa boys that it would be all right if something happened to me.

It was eleven P.M. Even if I wanted to, I couldn't have left Davao until the next morning. But I told my friend I had no intention whatever of leaving. I would not allow Calida to intimidate me.

If I wouldn't do anything else, my friend strongly suggested I should change hotel rooms.

Around midnight, P.J. wandered upstairs and I told him what was going on. I was calm, determined and a little pissed off. I felt it was only fair to warn P.J. that there might be some trouble. He chivalrously suggested we exchange rooms, so I gathered up my junk and dumped it in his room. We sat in his room, dranking beer and talking for a while. After a half hour of Alsa Masa tales, P.J. was spooked enough to decide we should both sleep in his room.

I finished what I needed to do in Davao. We left two days later, but not before I called Calida on the phone and, in a very Filipino way, joked with him about how he had made me a celebrity by talking about me on the radio. I laughed and joked with him a lot, but I got my point across. I wouldn't allow Calida to intimidate me.

On another trip, when I made my obligatory appointment with Calida, he showed up with a dozen heavily armed and very strange-looking religious fanatics, his newest "boys." He obviously was trying again to intimidate me, but instead, I became very interested in them. Several of these cultists were dressed all in black. Their arms were covered with tattoos. They all wore vicious-looking twenty-inch butcher knives called *bolos*. Charming people. I interviewed them at length about their religious beliefs and their reputation for chopping people to bits. Some members of Calida's group had already been immortalized in photographs showing them brandishing the head of a young man they claimed was a rebel. Charming people! Calida was uncharacteristically silent during that visit. He had failed in another attempt to scare me off.

Nobody had been able to penetrate the religious fanatic cults and I had long wanted to do so. It was risky. I was far too stupid to realize just how risky it was.

But on the January 1987 trip to Mindanao, I decided to climb up the mountain in northern Mindanao to the headquarters of the Tadtads (which means, literally, chop-chop, for what they like to do with their knives). The Tadtads were the biggest group in a groundswell of these loonies who wore tattoos, amulets, and stinking magic oil that smelled worse than dime-store perfume. They practiced distorted Catholic rites, all of which were designed to protect them from harm.

Because of their belief that they could not be harmed by bullets, they were excellent cannon fodder for the military's campaigns against the rebels. If one of them was killed, cult leaders would explain that the magic had failed because the unfortunate victim had not said his prayers or applied his magic oil properly that morning.

It was probably crazy to go up to see the Tadtads alone, but it seemed to me that if they thought I was as crazy as they were, they might trust me. No journalists had been permitted inside their headquarters, so if I could make it inside I would have a good story. I took a bus to north Mindanao and landed in a dusty little market town called Initao. In the marketplace I hired a motorcycle driver to take me up the mountain to the Tadtad lair at a place called Barrio Casalingan.

I couldn't seem to get specific directions from anyone. I had no idea how far it was, but that's not unusual. Filipinos are not linear thinkers. Getting precise information like distances, times and dates is almost impossible. My motorcycle man and I set off up the mountain. For fifty cents, he was to take me to the Tadtad barrio.

After about a half hour's pleasant ride, we began to climb some serious slopes. In another five minutes, we came to a stop. We were in nowheresville. There was not a house, not a tree, not even a dog in sight.

I was sure I was about to be robbed. I looked at the video camera, still camera, and assorted electronic gear hanging from my shoulders and mentally said goodbye to them. What a stupid thing to go up there alone.

The motorcycle driver and I had no language in common, so I decided to go on the offensive by being abrasive. As a white woman, I had discovered an almost foolproof technique for getting out of sticky situations: when in doubt, be pushy. I demanded the motorcycle driver take me the rest of the way to Casalingan. By sign language he made me understand that the mountain was too steep. The motorcycle could go no further. Chastened, I conceded he was right.

"Where is it then?" I asked.

Even though he didn't understand the words, he knew what I was asking. He pointed. My spirits sank. Filipinos point by pursing their lips if something is close. They only point their fingers if it is really far.

I followed the driver's finger. I squinted in the noonday sun. It was really far. Two mountains away, I could barely make out the barrio perching on the mountain top. What else could I do but make the best of a bad situation? I picked up my cameras and began to trudge up the trail.

No arrangements had been made. I had no contacts. I began to realize nervously that no one in the world knew where I was and if I got hacked up by the Tadtads no one would know where to start looking for me.

When I got halfway up the second mountain, a bunch of kids came running down the trail to see what I was up to. As they escorted me to the barrio, they chattered like little parrots. It had never occured to me that the Tadtads might not speak English, but there was a sign at the barrio entrance, "Welcome to the Sagrado Corazon Senor" (Lord Sacred Heart Society, the Tadtads' formal name).

A gaunt-faced man came out immediately and cautiously greeted me in English. What did I want?

I explained that I was an American journalist and I was very interested in learning more about their group. Could I talk to the leader?

He glared at me. "Why did you come alone?"

My stomach lurched. I took the offensive. "Why not? Is there something I should be afraid of?"

He chuckled and offered me a seat and a drink of water while he went off to find someone. The barrio was so steep inside that it was almost necessary to crawl up the narrow pathways that served as streets. Nothing could grow there, there was no water that high up, but militarily it was perfect. No one could possibly attack them.

There were Philippine flags everywhere. People even wore paper ones around their necks. While I waited for the guide to return, someone explained to me that the Philippines was in danger of being taken over by the communists. But the Tadtads had vowed to fight for their flag. They told me with wide-eyed sincerity that each individual was willing to die for the cause, even for that little flag around his neck.

While I waited by the gate, a group of friendly people gathered around. All of them were wearing amulets, magic scarves, and tattoos. The sickly sweet smell of the *lana* or magic oil hung heavy in the unmoving air. It was beastly hot. I felt a little nauseated. They offered me some *tuba*, the potent native coconut liquor. I accepted, to calm my stomach and my nerves.

The first gatekeeper came back. He had only one question: Was I a communist? He warned me that the Tadtads hate communists. When I assured him I was not, he said I would be allowed to take a video of some of the rituals, but I could not interview any officials on camera. It wouldn't be possible to see the great leader with the weirdo glint in his eye. Master Sade was "indisposed."

There was a great deal of joking and nervous laughter as I was led to the first chapel, which contained several tombstones with names on them. At first some of my dozen escorts said these were "sacrifices," but then my guide corrected them and said the Filipino names on the tombstones were merely the "names of the Lord." I was dubious. The Tadtads were rumored to be adept in human sacrifice and cannibalism.

In an outdoor chapel two young men had already set up the implements of the notorious chop-chop ritual from which the Tadtads claim they took their name. Others say that chop-chop is what they had done to hundreds, maybe thousands of their unfortunate victims.

A young man with strange eyes lit a candle. The spectators were absolutely silent as he took the ferocious-looking twenty-inch native *bolo* knife, dipped the tip in a basin of "holy" water and muttered some fractured Latin incantations. Then he began to hack savagely, five, ten, fifteen times at the arm of the teenager next to him. The victim's arm was miraculously unmarked, "Because he has a lot of faith," they told me.

They handed me the knife and I ran my finger along the blade. It was sharp. Unexplainable things happen in the Philippines all the time.

They all fixed me with a double-whammy gaze and asked if I wanted to try it. My knees turned to jelly, but I had discovered that jokes often extricated me from tight situations. I joked that I was attached to my arm and I would like to keep it. They persisted. I laughed and said I didn't have enough faith yet. They continued to bait me. I kept laughing; they kept laughing. It was a Mexican standoff.

Finally I changed the subject. It was time for me to go. The sun was fading and I had a six-mile walk down the mountain. I didn't want to be in this place after dark. They said there was an escort waiting for me. I wondered if their plan was to do something to me outside the barrio, but I was much too far into the situation to change anything then. I rubbed my intact arm, grateful for its reprieve.

My escort came forward: three teenage boys, newly washed and newly slathered with oil, *bolos* hanging at their belts and magic scarves tied around their foreheads. It was convenient. They would escort me to Initao and see off one of their number who was going to join a fighting group in the eastern part of Mindanao. The fledgling fighter told me he was most eager to join his unit and "chop up some communists."

On the way down I followed at a distance while they carried my bags and incongruously sang at the top of their lungs, "We Are the World."

When we got back to Initao, I exhaled fully for the first time in hours as I boarded a bus going in the opposite direction I had intended. I didn't want them to follow me.

26 JOE CASTRO, A MAN FOR ALL SEASONS:
May 1987

I T'S STRANGE THAT I can't remember when I first met Joe Castro; it should have made an impression on me. We must have met at one of a thousand street demonstrations in 1984. His sharp intellect, his handsome face, and his impassioned political speeches, combined with a paradoxical gentleness, made him noticeable.

I once told a friend that Joe Castro was "the handsomest man in the Philippines, but he's not my type." That statement came back to haunt me.

Joe and I talked for hours as we marched together for dozens, maybe hundreds of miles through Manila's streets in the days of the Parliament of the Streets. On those marches we became friends. We would drink coffee together after press conferences or have an occasional long lunch. I was impressed with the depth of his commitment to free the Philippines of Marcos and of the sickness of greed that permeates the country. I thought of Joe as somewhat of a Don Quixote, tilting at windmills. He was achingly idealistic, but there was substance. He had ideas I thought were workable; his theories were sound. He was not a zealot, and not a communist, although some might, in the language of another era, call him a "fellow traveler."

Joe spoke often at rallies. He was always in the forefront of the leadership of the legal left. People quieted down to hear what Joe Castro had to say. He made sense.

Joe was an executive of a cooking oil company. At the age of forty-four, he had forged for himself a comfortable middle-class existence. He had worked in Singapore, Indonesia and Vietnam, so there was a cosmopolitan air about him.

Despite Joe's dark good looks and flashing eyes, I was not really attracted to him until our paths crossed a few times during the congressional campaign in the spring of 1987.

I was doing a television story about the emergence of idealistic young politicians. Since Joe was one of sixteen candidates for Congress in one of Manila's poorest districts, I thought he would be a good subject.

Canadian Television Network had agreed to buy my first "one-man band" piece, for which I would be the cameraman, producer, editor and correspondent. It was fun.

The focus of the Castro for Congress campaign was in the squatter areas along

168

the railroad tracks in Santa Mesa, where Joe grew up. He is one of the few Filipinos I know who raised himself above his lower-class origins. Joe's success was directly attributable to his hard work and native intelligence. He had devoted most of his time to politics since 1983, when Ninoy Aquino was killed. Fortunately he had a sympathetic boss.

In 1987 Joe honestly believed that the end of Marcos signaled the end of the corrupt political system. The congressional election of May 1987 was the beginning of a new era, Joe said, where the people would elect politicians who would truly represent them and work for their welfare. The days of corrupt politicians who would hand out a few basketballs and a few pesos on election day were over. People Power had proven that, he firmly believed.

In total contradiction to a political system entrenched through the generations, Joe refused to buy votes, bribe election inspectors, or even to pay his youthful campaign staff.

He wanted to help the poor empower themselves. He insisted the barrio folk could learn how to pressure city hall to build community water pumps or to clean up the filthy drainage canals. Joe's campaign was more of a teaching exercise. He taught them how to resist the depredations of greedy landlords. The greatest shortcoming of the masses, he said, is their belief that they are helpless in the face of the bureaucracy.

I was excited by his optimism. I wanted him to be right, but I have always been more cynical than that. Old politics and old habits die hard.

One sunny Sunday morning eight days before the election, I joined Joe's campaign for a walk up the railroad tracks that split his district in Old Manila. We walked through miles and miles of shantytowns where people cling with such tenacity to the tiniest scrap of land, the flimsiest piece of plywood they call home. Hundreds of ragged urchins followed us every step of the way.

Some of Joe's enthusiastic campaign workers had rigged an ingenious battery-powered sound system, a cart that could be pulled along the railroad tracks. Every few minutes we stopped and Joe delivered another of his impassioned speeches. He had some of the charisma of Dante Buscayno. The crowds loved him because he was one of them. He didn't talk down to them; he projected just the right blend of camaraderie to the men and sex appeal to the women. Joe Castro seemed like a sure winner.

Just after noon we stopped at a small store. While the campaign workers sat around chugging Cokes to ward off dehydration caused by the sweltering sun, Joe led me inside a ramshackle house.

"This is where I grew up," he announced as he introduced me to assorted brothers, sisters, in-laws, cousins, nieces and nephews who still live in parts of the ancient house that Topsy built.

It was hard to imagine this urbane and witty man as one of those snotty-nosed bare-bottomed kids living in a shack and running up and down the railroad tracks. I knew he was something very special.

We walked ten miles that day. The more I watched Joe Castro in action, shaking the grizzled hand of a worker, patting an old lady on the arm, or tousling a child's hair, the more I realized that we could be more than friends.

It had been a long and lonely time for me. There had been almost no romance since I left for Rome more than a year before. I thought I was ready for a new relationship. But I was afraid of the pain.

Over the next few days, Joe and I met several times so I could complete the Canadian Television story. One day he gave me several fragrant *sampaguita* necklaces. It was a sign that something was beginning to blossom between us.

On election night, Joe invited me to his headquarters to watch the returns. By that time I was confused about whether my motives were professional or personal. I arrived just in time to accompany Joe to the old elementary school to watch him cast his ballot.

When the polls closed at three P.M., he checked on his poll watchers and delivered boxes of juice and rolls to sustain them through the long count.

The evening dragged. The returns trickled in. A slow count usually means fraud. It was not encouraging. At about nine P.M., six hours after the polls closed, the bad news started to come in. There had been massive vote buying. Huge numbers of votes were being thrown out. What hurt most was that some of Joe's own poll watchers had defected to other candidates who bribed them. Joe was losing.

I held Joe's hand and watched him wilt when it became clear that the election had been lost to those with more money and fewer scruples. The defeat in his face touched my heart. I didn't want to see him lose that rare idealism. I firmly believe that those who change the world are the ones who dare to dream improbable dreams, the ones who don't have enough sense to recognize what cannot be.

Joe came in seventh of sixteen candidates. It was a respectable defeat, but not an honest one.

Over the months Joe and I found ourselves wanting to be together more and more. There were romantic candlelight dinners while we got to know each other. We talked half the night, each excited by the other's ideas, sharing insights of past failed marriages. We both wanted to avoid the mistakes of the past in this budding new love, and we admitted we were afraid to reach out for fear of failure.

Joe and I took a couple of human potential seminars together during that exquisite summer when we were learning how to love each other. After my mistakes with Bert, I realized that I had a lot to learn about relationships. My infallible intuition told me that Joe and I were together for a reason, that we had something to learn from one another. Our already good communication improved. The seminars helped us to build a firm foundation for our relationship.

Over a period of months, we fell in love.

One night in September we were staffing one of those seminars when we learned that Lean Alejandro, the fiery young student leader, had been ambushed and killed a couple of miles away. Joe thought of Lean as a brother. Counting Lando Olalia's murder, that was two men very close to Joe who were murdered in nine months. I remember thinking superstitiously that bad luck comes in threes. We drove at breakneck speed to the hospital. Joe's tormented voice broke as he said he was sure Lean's death was also the work of police or soldiers.

We arrived at St. Luke's Hospital where Lean's broken body had been taken. Hundreds of friends and journalists were already wandering around the lobby and the parking lot in shock. It was an agonizingly familiar scene. Lean's widow, Lidy, was sobbing as she tried to give an interview to a local TV crew.

Joe asked someone to take us to see Lean's body. We walked down endless brightly lit hospital corridors to a room with a locked door.

"Inside, there," the attendant told us.

Joe put his hand on the doorknob.

I put my hand on his arm. "Do you really want to remember Lean this way?" I asked. Without a word, we turned and walked away together.

Lean's murder was another in a series of bitter losses for Joe. Later in the night of Lean's death, Joe appeared on television and accused the Aquino government of complicity in Lean's murder. It was a chillingly cold and calculated accusation, devoid of the passion and idealism I associated with Joe Castro.

I was afraid for him. I knew that whoever was killing these leaders of the left would find Joe an easy target. He went to the same office every day at the same time. He parked his car in the spot marked with his name. Since he had never been a part of the underground left, let alone the Communist Party, he had no security guards. He had no ability to move through the aboveground and underground movements as his fellow leftist leaders had done.

Telephoned death threats began to come to his office. A sinister man's voice would warn, "We got Lean Alejandro and we'll get you next, Castro."

Big men, carrying leather clutch bags of the type that usually contain pistols, began to hang around his office building. Suspicious cars began to cruise the street in front of his apartment at night.

A few days after Lean's death, my friend Margo and I dropped by to see Joe. He was amazingly cool when he told us that three suspicious cars had been cruising the street all evening. I insisted that we would all three sleep there in his bed that night.

While Margo was showering, Joe and I sat on the bed watching the news on television.

"I want to teach you something," he said, opening a drawer and pulling out a .38 caliber revolver. I jumped off the bed in horror.

"Where did you get that? What are you doing with it?" I demanded.

He jingled a handful of bullets and calmly told me to sit down.

The gun was legal. It was registered. And it was unloaded. Joe wanted me to learn to load it.

It was like a scorpion lying there on the bed. I couldn't touch it. He forced me. Tears ran down my cheeks.

"I don't want anything to do with guns," I begged, but he insisted.

He guided my hand while I loaded and unloaded the gun several times. That cold metal seemed to burn my hands. I hated it. But I realized he was right. I should know how a gun works.

As we were drifting off to sleep, Joe put his arms around Margo and me.

"Life isn't bad," he laughed. "I have two beautiful women in my bed!"

We have laughed many times about how we were a threesome on the first night Joe and I ever spent in the same bed, but my strongest memory of that night is the feel of the .38 in my hand. It was the first time I ever held a gun. I knew then that I would use that gun if someone attacked Joe. I was changing. I asked myself if it was merely a case of adapting to my violent environment or if the violence in which I lived had somehow insidiously penetrated my basic belief system.

Joe led Lean's funeral march. The organizers of the day-long march were fearful of agents provocateurs in the crowd. Joe thought they might start a riot as a means of applying pressure on Aquino to give more power to the military. Several friends laid elaborate plans to escape if we were trapped in the funnel-like maze of streets leading to the cemetery. The exercise seemed melodramatic, but I had seen enough to know the danger was real.

Joe and I began to go everywhere together as a security measure. I wanted to be with him anyway. I thought my white skin and my status as a journalist might be a deterrent to assassins. Joe slept in a different place each night.

One night the underground made its meager contribution to Joe's security. Two Sparrows gave us a short course in personal security. We were taught some valuable lessons: how to tell if someone is following you in the car; how to use a back-up car; how to always keep the gas tank full because the military and police notoriously have very little gas, so they'll run out before you do; how to vary your routes and your schedules.

I had never imagined I would need to know those things.

We often traveled around town in two separate cars. I would pretend to comb my hair for hours, using a small compact for a rear view mirror. Sometimes we were followed, so we took circuitous routes and kept moving. Eventually we always lost our pursuers.

Security precautions made a great deal of sense, but it was difficult to live with that constant shifting, and Joe felt very constricted by it. He thought I was being silly and paranoid. He complained he felt like a prisoner. Gradually the threats diminished and we relaxed our security precautions. But we never really forgot the black cloud hanging over our heads.

In October we found an old Spanish-style house to share. There were spacious and airy rooms, a big screened porch, and, best of all, a yard with a wealth of green growing things. KK and his new companion, Oinky, loved it. Life was good. I felt whole for the first time in years.

My Mom and stepfather came to visit for Christmas and gave Joe their stamp of approval. It was a rowdy family occasion with all of Joe's four children and three grandchildren, a nine-foot stick Christmas tree and tons of gifts.

On December 29, 1987, in the midst of his losing campaign for a seat on the city council, Joe Castro asked me to be his wife. I didn't hesitate for a moment. I knew I wanted to spend my life with him.

I was excited about the idea of being his wife and a second mother to his two youngest children. I had especially grown to love Talya, his beautiful seven-year-old daughter. Finally, I would have a family again.

Our wedding was set for August 26, 1988, but other events got in the way.

27 DANTE: *May–June 1987*

DANTE BUSCAYNO, THE FOUNDER of the New People's Army, was running for the Senate on the ticket of Partido ng Bayan (PNB), the far left's party.

Dante and I had formed an easy friendship. I still found his company refreshing; his creative ideas made him different. Someone had called Dante the "destroyer turned reformer." I thought he was a builder, too. I still could not imagine this sensitive man carrying an M-16 in his slender artist's hands.

In early May I joined the seven PNB senatorial candidates on a bare-bones campaign swing through the Bicol region. The PNB's campaign was a dramatic contrast to Cory's candidates, with whom I had traveled a couple of weeks earlier on an elegant air-conditioned bus. On the Cory campaign we ate twelve times in one day. It was gross overconsumption. The PNB was markedly different. We rode through the shimmering summer heat in open jeepneys which seemed to have no springs. After a while, I couldn't tell one dusty road from another. We frequently made whistlestops in public markets. While the candidates shook hands, campaign aides had learned to jump out and buy bunches of bananas. The next meal was always far away and beds were nearly unheard of.

Newsweek wanted me to write a profile of Dante, to explain his transformation from warrior to candidate. The campaign trip provided an opportunity for me to get to know him better.

Very late one night we arrived in Legaspi City after sixteen hours of continuous campaigning. We were to fly back to Manila early in the morning, so the thrifty campaign organizers decided not to pay for hotel rooms. The thirty or so of us, candidates, aides and local hangers on, would camp at the office of a local human rights group for the five hours of the night remaining until it was time to get on the plane for Manila.

Some of the exhausted workers promptly fell asleep on the floor, but Dante and I found ourselves sitting outside in the cool of the night, unable to sleep after the bedlam of the day. We shared a couple of beers and enjoyed the quiet of the night.

There in the dark, as we gazed at the shadowy silhouette of Mayon volcano's perfect cone, Dante started to tell me of his life. I clicked on my tape recorder.

He told me of the earliest years, his childhood in Tarlac and how the military decapitated the father of a friend. Of how the overseers would beat the children who sucked on sugar cane to ease their hunger pangs. Of how the rebels, precursors of the NPA, would use young Dante as a runner. Of how he grew into membership in the Hukbalahap rebels and how he quit the guerrilla forces in anger when he discovered the corruption that had permeated the rebel army. Of how he met Joma Sison, an ideologue, in 1969. The ideologue and the warrior forged an alliance which eighteen years later had grown into a powerful rebel force. Of Dante's special relationship with Ninoy Aquino and the Cojuangco family. Of years spent in the mountains and housing his band in the cane fields of Central Luzon. Of how he became careless and was captured in 1976. Of ten unspeakably lonely years in prison with no human companionship. Of the spark of hope in 1986 when he heard of the events at EDSA and the simultaneous fear he would be killed before he could be freed.

Dante's story was a moving one. I still think of writing it in great detail. The *Newsweek* piece was far too short to do justice to such a complex man.

As we parted at the airport, I felt saddened by the parting. I admit, I had toyed with the idea of an affair with Dante. The relationship with Joe was embryonic at that time, but that had nothing to do with it. Something else held me back. Neither Dante nor I were suited for flings. I sensed that a relationship with Dante would be intense and frustrating. I knew the clashes of two strong wills would be more than I was prepared to handle. I decided I was much more capable of dealing with a friendship with him.

I didn't see Dante again until the night of June 8. Since the end of his losing campaign for the Senate, I had tried without success to reach him. I wanted to spend more time talking. And I planned to propose an idea to him: I wanted to write his biography.

I finally heard that Dante was to be a guest on a live talk-show the night of June 8. One of his friends told me I could track him down there. I joked to Joe that I would "ambush" Dante at the television studio at the end of the show.

When I walked onto the set just before midnight the show was almost over. I saw Dante squinting into the lights. His face lit up when he recognized me. As soon as the show ended he rushed over with a grin and gave my arm a squeeze. He said he was going to the Trellis, a popular leftist eating and drinking place. Did I want to join him?

There was a bit of shuffling about who would ride in what car. I had my car and a driver, so I declined Dante's offer of a ride. Jun Sibal, Dante's campaign aide who had also become my friend, got in my car. Jun's brother, Danny, and Danny's pregnant wife, Fatima, climbed in the back seat of Dante's car. Nick Atienza, my old friend, the professor of the orange VW fame, was driving Dante's shabby Toyota. While I was waiting for my car, they drove past and

Dante once again offered me a ride, which I again declined. Pauline Sicam, a reporter for the *Manila Chronicle*, was standing a few feet away from me on the sidewalk. Dante offered her a ride, too, but she already had one.

After Dante's car pulled away from the curb, time began to pass in slow motion. My car came. Jun and I became engrossed in conversation while we waited in a long line of traffic queuing to get out of the television station complex. The gates were being guarded by soldiers, as were all television compounds since EDSA. When we finally came to the head of the line, a soldier insisted we had to open our trunk for inspection. I had never been subject to an inspection on the way out of a television station. I snapped at the guy, "Do you think we are stealing a television camera?" He didn't find it amusing. In hindsight, it is clear that the inspection was an intentional delaying tactic.

When we arrived at the Trellis ten minutes later, we were surprised to find that Dante and his carload weren't there. We knew that Dante's car was at least five minutes ahead of us. Jun and I sat in the deserted restaurant, puzzled, for two minutes when a taxi came speeding up and two young women jumped out.

They shouted, "Dante's been shot, come with us!"

I felt like someone had kicked me in the stomach. We jumped in my car and raced back toward the television station by a different route, the route Dante must have taken. It took us a lifetime to get there.

A couple of hundred yards from the gate we found the car. A crowd had gathered, staring and pointing at the car, which was riddled with bullet holes. The glass was smashed. The front end was accordioned in where it had crashed into a wall. Jun and I ran toward the car. I was irrationally yelling, "Dante!" and Jun was yelling for his brother. There was no one inside. The car was full of broken glass and blood. There were huge blood spots where Danny and Fatima sat in the back seat and a smaller blood stain on the front seat where we remembered Dante was sitting.

My heart was hammering. Jun kept yelling. "No. No. NO!"

I was horrified. The onlookers were buzzing. Somebody said Dante had been kidnapped by the armed men who had ambushed his car. I ached with fear. If that was true, there was no hope. They would finish him off, I knew.

"Where are they?" I shouted to the crowd. Nobody said anything. Jun was yelling impotently for an ambulance. I calmed down a bit. We wouldn't learn anything if we both were hysterical. A sensible-looking old man on the fringes of the crowd told me they had been taken to East Avenue Medical Center.

We raced to the hospital. The emergency room was bathed in a sinister flickering light. The power had failed, so the emergency teams were forced to work by candlelight.

Frantically, I searched the tables. I saw Danny Sibal lying on the first table, blood oozing slowly from a wound in his right buttock.

Fatima was on the next table, in terrible condition. Her life was flooding from a dozen bullet holes. The blood was literally dripping into pools on the floor.

On the last table was Nick, lying stoically on the cold metal table, his eyes fixed on the ceiling, his ankle shattered. Blood seeped from a hole behind his ear.

I shook Nick's shoulder. "Where's Dante?" I screamed. No answer. I felt like I was moving through a pool of molasses.

In an abandoned corner of the room, I saw a cart with a covered body. Slowly, shaking, I approached. I held my breath as I pulled back the blanket to expose a face I had never seen before.

"Where's Dante?" I screamed again, feeling guilty because I was relieved the dead man wasn't Dante.

None of the gathering crowd knew where Dante was.

The panic increased. Dozens of friends were joining in the clamor. The rumors traveled swiftly through the flickering candlelight of the emergency room. Dante was safe and had gone into hiding. Dante was dead. Dante had taken refuge inside the television station. Dante had been kidnapped by his attackers.

There were no answers. In a daze, we sat down to wait. It was agonizing. I comforted a screaming woman. Someone told me she was Mila, Dante's ex-wife.

As I held Nick's hand, he continued to fix his gaze on the ceiling. He gave my hand the tiniest of squeezes, which was an indicator of the massive control he was using to battle his pain and fear.

Jun was holding his brother's hand. Danny was complaining about pain, but he wasn't getting much attention. He didn't seem seriously injured. All of the medical attention was focused on Fatima. It seemed impossible that either she or her baby would survive.

Suddenly Danny's eyes rolled back in his head. His body went rigid. We shouted for a doctor. One came quickly and examined Danny, discovering an overlooked bullet hole behind Danny's ear. The doctor explained to Jun that the medical center couldn't handle so many serious emergencies. He recommended that Danny be transferred to the Heart Center next door. It was a better hospital, anyway. We agreed. Danny's body relaxed after a few minutes and he lapsed into a coma. Danny died two days later without regaining consciousness. Miraculously, Fatima and her baby survived. The little girl, named Dana after her father and her godfather, Dante, was born, healthy and beautiful, six months later.

While we were waiting for the ambulance to take Danny the few hundred yards to the Heart Center, someone came in with happy news. Dante was in the emergency room at the Heart Center. He was wounded, but it wasn't serious.

I didn't wait for my car. I just ran to the Heart Center. In a bed in the emergency room, Dante was lying on a stretcher, the blood drying on his face from a dozen small cuts. He was bare chested. There were bloodstains on his jeans. His face looked terribly tense. He relaxed a bit when he saw me, and held out his hand to me.

"I thought you were hit," he gasped. "I thought you were in the car right behind me."

I couldn't speak for a minute. I just stood there holding his hand, afraid I would cry.

Dante's eyes widened. He looked down at my skirt. "Were you hit? Whose blood is that?" he demanded.

I looked down. The entire front of my blouse and skirt were soaked with blood. I have no idea whose it was. I was numb.

I stood there for hours, exchanging a few words here and there with Dante and his friends and family who had gathered. Dante laughed off his own injuries. He had been wounded far more seriously during his guerrilla days. He showed me a perfect square of four bullet holes on his right shoulder. They were not deep.

Dante's luck and his alertness born of years as a guerrilla fighter had warned him that something was wrong when they turned into the street outside the television station. When he saw the first man with an M-16, he hit the floor. The assassins were inexperienced or afraid or both. They failed to fire until the car had passed, so the bullets traveled through the car's trunk, through the bodies of Danny, Fatima, and Manny Santos, whom Dante had picked up in the parking lot. It was Manny's body I had so fearfully uncovered. By the time the bullets got to Dante, they had slowed down to nonlethal speed.

Who would do this? The answer was obvious, although unspoken. The police or the military would have a strong reason to want to eliminate Dante. He was a recognizable figure of the left. His NPA days had made him a romantic hero. It was possible that Dante's former comrades were his attackers, but I thought it was unlikely, for one major reason: they failed in their mission to kill Dante. To put it simply, the NPA wouldn't have botched the job. The leftists might have had reason to go after Dante for some of his less-than-sympathetic statements made during the campaign, but it seemed unlikely to me. Dante was a potent propaganda tool for the legal left. They wanted to keep him alive.

The fact that no one was ever arrested for the Dante ambush made it all the more clear who the attackers were. The military almost never arrest their own.

I couldn't relax. I knew Dante was OK. I knew Nick and Danny and Fatima and Fatima's baby were all in serious danger and Manny was dead.

I had crossed a line. It had never occurred to me, as a journalist, that Dante's ambush was a news story. Only hours later, sometime after dawn, the journalist in me clicked back into place. I realized that I should file something.

I clutched Dante's hand. He clutched back. I don't know if I was comforting him or he was comforting me.

I looked down at our clasped hands and saw Dante's, brown and bloody, and mine, clean and white. The rage swelled in my chest. I wanted to scream out my anger. How dare they do something like this to my friend?

How many more times would I hold a friend's bloodied hand? How many more would they kill until all of the best were gone?

28 COUP: *August 28, 1987*

I T'S FUNNY HOW NO ONE CALLS the events of August 28, 1987 an "attempted coup" anymore. It became simply "the coup" until another coup eclipsed it. Although it didn't succeed, it came damn close.

I spent the evening of August 27 with a departing friend from the American Embassy. Over the years I have become close to many diplomats, but I don't think I'll ever become accustomed to the pain of their inevitable departures. I vowed I wouldn't pursue any more friendships with diplomats, but they always happened anyway.

My American friend and I drank too many glasses of wine and talked about the changes in the three years we had each spent in the Philippines. The recent shootings and killings had depressed both of us. We were becoming cynical about the much-touted "restoration of democracy." We drank more wine and speculated about the future. She said that she thought there would be a lot more violence before things calmed down. We both thought Cory's chances for political, and perhaps even personal, survival were slim.

I fell into bed about one A.M., grateful I didn't have any early appointments because I had indulged in far more wine than usual.

For some reason I cannot explain, I left my ABC hand-held radio in the "on" position when I put it in the charger for the night. I had never done that before because it takes much longer to charge that way.

Exactly forty-five minutes after I fell into bed, I snapped awake. The ABC crew was talking on the radio. That was unusual at that hour. I heard excited chatter in Tagalog, then, "shooting at the Palace." I was wide awake, instantly sober.

I ran for the phone and first called New York radio and then called my backup, Brian Allan, a dedicated Canadian journalist/Anglican priest.

I faced the age-old journalist's dilemma. Should I stay in one place and try to gather information from as many sources as possible by telephone or should I go out to the story? I decided to let Brian go to the scene while I worked the phones. At the time neither of us gave a thought to the foolhardiness of rushing into the midst of a coup, although many of our colleagues have died in coups around the world.

180

It is always amazing to me in these fast-evolving situations how much I can file when there is so little hard information available. Every tidbit is another radio spot. In that first hour, I had only one hard fact: There was shooting at the palace. I didn't know who, how many, or why. I began calling sources.

Brian arrived at the palace. "Shit, you wouldn't believe this. There's a war going on here," he yelled through his radio. I could hear gunfire in the background. I told him to keep his head down. I recorded some of the crackly gunfire from his radio and sent it to New York.

Brian said there were soldiers everywhere, skulking through the bushes and approaching Arlegui Street, where Cory Aquino lives. Could they really be trying to kill the president? There didn't seem to be any organized defense of the palace, just a couple of dozen soldiers running around after a couple of dozen more soldiers. Obviously, the palace guard had been caught with its pants down.

Our cameraman, Sarni Ocampo, was on the scene with his camera rolling in the dark. The result was black video, but good audio. Sarni didn't dare turn on his lights for fear of drawing fire. I could hear Sarni talking on the radio, describing a scene with "Bodies everywhere." God, this was serious.

After a few minutes the Presidential Security Guard closed off the area and threw out all the journalists. No one was talking about what happened to Aquino, although we knew there had been shooting very close to her house.

I began to get more information. The man behind the coup was Colonel Gregorio "Gringo" Honasan, Enrile's security man made famous at EDSA for his bravado and his macho good looks. Gringo is the Philippines' version of Rambo. Enrile was nowhere to be found.

I talked to one source who had just talked to Joker Arroyo, the president's executive secretary. He said Joker was laughing. Knowing how Filipinos laugh when the situation is truly desperate, I asked, "Is it that bad?"

"It is THAT bad," my source said as he hung up.

Where was the president? Was she hit? Killed? Kidnapped?

Around four A.M., I made a mad dash to the office so I could be in touch with all available information. I arrived in time to hear Aquino's voice on the radio. She told people to stay calm. She assured them that General Ramos had everything under control. It sounded suspiciously like a tape recording I had heard eight months before when some lunatic Marcos loyalists had taken over a television station. I didn't believe Cory was there and feeling fine.

I called Captain Rex Robles, the thinker and strategist of the RAM boys. Either Rex and his wife, Marilyn, deserve Academy Awards or they really didn't know anything about Gringo Honasan's most recent adventure. Rex had become so close to so many foreign correspondents over the years that I thought it was possible he had been left in the dark deliberately for fear of an unintentional leak. This coup was an extremely well-kept secret. There hadn't even been any rumors. I should have recognized that the absence of *tsismis* (the Tagalog word for gossip, pronounced "cheezmees",) was a danger signal in itself.

Between telephone calls and cranking out radio spots, I kept dialing Joe's apartment. The phone was on the first floor but he slept on the second floor, so the phone rang and rang and rang. He never answered. Joe's apartment wasn't far from the palace and I thought he might even be able to hear the gunfire. I was worried he would wake up, hear about the coup and go out. I didn't know how dangerous things were, but I was very worried there might be a roundup of lefties. If there was, Joe would be a sure target.

The palace was sealed off. We had no idea what was going on inside there, although there didn't seem to be any more gunfire.

By dawn there was shooting at Camp Aguinaldo and the television stations. We tuned in to Channel 4 and watched in fascination. We knew that for an hour or so there had been a battle for control of the station. There was a live evangelical healing service on the air. The terrified teenaged choir kept singing and singing and singing. Other than the obvious fear on the faces of those kids, there was no indication that anything was going on. After an hour or so of the singing siege, a couple of soldiers wearing bloody bandages around their heads stumbled onto the set and asked to be healed. The kids kept singing. The preacher prayed over the wounded soldiers. It was dawn of a bizarre day. I had a jarring realization that by nightfall the Philippines could have a new and very unknown government.

The military was full of discontent. Soldiers felt that Cory had not lived up to her promises. They were looking for true leadership and didn't find it in her. Enrile and the RAM boys had been carping at Cory's perceived leftist tendencies and accusing her of giving over the government to the communists. Corruption in the military was still rampant. Pay was still low. I guessed it wouldn't be that difficult for Gringo to gain support.

As the day progressed, the success of Gringo's adventure would be measured by how many soldiers had the guts to jump onto his side of the fence. The soldiers would hedge their bets and jump to the side that looked like it was winning. Since there had been no warning or even any rumors about the coup, Gringo was fighting for time while his fellow soldiers made up their minds. If he could hold out long enough, I thought he would win.

There was no ABC-TV correspondent in town, so my duties to ABC expanded to include television. At six in the morning our time, I was live on the telephone on "World News Tonight." Joker Arroyo had been on live just before me. He said everything was OK and we should be calm. I said everything was not all right and the government was not being totally honest with its people. That made Joker mad as hell. He told me so very specifically a couple of days later.

By mid-morning, we were preparing to do a live shot with Ted Koppel on "Nightline."

Brian was outside Channel 7, pinned down under fire. I could still hear gunfire through his walkie-talkie.

Brian thought he was going to Channel 7 with government troops who were going to take it back from Gringo's boys. Instead, he found himself in the middle of Gringo's renewed assault. At dawn an Australian photographer had been killed in that same spot when he stupidly stood up and took a flash picture. I was again pleading with Brian to keep his head down.

Too many things were happening at once. I needed more help, so I picked up Trisha Thomas, a young American woman just out of college. Trisha, who had only been in Manila a few weeks, was very young and very naive. But she was hanging around the bureau pleading for a chance. I needed her, so I gave her a radio and sent her off to Camp Aguinaldo.

I begged for time to wash my hair before I went live on camera for "Nightline," but the producer in New York said there was no time. When I went into the bathroom to take a tremulous look in the mirror, I discovered my hair was standing on end. I had never even combed it when I vaulted out of bed eight hours before.

As I sat in the chair waiting for the satellite to go up for the Koppel show, Brian's wife, Frankie, who is a production assistant for ABC, came in to tell me that Brian was again pinned down under fire at Channel 7. Trisha was hiding in a bathroom in the headquarters building at Aguinaldo, which was also under fire.

The "bird" went up. I looked a little wild-eyed, and I felt awful. I had never asked staff people to do anything I wouldn't do, and I was sitting here nice and safe inside the Manila Hotel. I knew that Brian's and Trisha's lives were in danger. I knew I could not forgive myself if anything happened to either one.

I know someone has to sit in the studio during these things. Peter Salinger made it clear that the studio work was my job as radio "bureau chief." I chuckled about the promotion. It meant I was the boss of myself.

We did the first "Nightline" shot with no hitches. Koppel also interviewed Marcos live by phone on the same show. Marcos seemed smug. There was no evidence Marcos was directly involved in the coup attempt, but there was no way of being certain.

Sometime after noon came the first opportunity for us to take a breath. We were between shots for Koppel for the East coast and West coast feeds. Radio's voracious appetite was satiated for the moment. By my side was a McDonald's hamburger with one bite taken out of it. In ten hours there had been time for exactly one bite of food.

Every television station was under seige. Military headquarters at Camp

Aguinaldo was under the control of Gringo's troops. More troops were moving toward the city. We didn't know if Brian and Trisha were going to be able to get out.

There was a brief silence in the bureau. Out of the unaccustomed stillness someone said, "You know, these bastards could win."

It looked like it. My stomach twisted. What would the Philippines be like under a military government? After the Lando Olalia murder and the Dante ambush, I had no delusions. A government under Gringo's boys, and presumably Johnny Enrile, would be very hard indeed. Anticommunism had become very fashionable. Anyone who had ever had an idea originating from left of center would be branded by a military government. That meant Joe, too. I was sick with worry because I was still unable to reach him.

I thought about reports that the marauding soldiers had opened fire and killed several people they came across near the palace who had the audacity in the pre-dawn hours to chant, "Cory, Cory." These guys were really brutal.

Brian had gotten out of Channel 7 in an armored car inexplicably being driven by an American marine who was obviously some sort of intelligence officer. The marine told Brian that Aquino was safe, but her twenty-six-year-old son, Noynoy, had been wounded.

We still hadn't seen the president, but we kept getting statements out of Joker Arroyo that everything was OK. That was a credibility destruction pattern that would be repeated in the future.

By early afternoon, when it was time for the "Nightline" West Coast feed, Gringo's boys seemed to be gaining momentum. The television stations were changing hands by the hour. It was very hard to tell who was holding what.

A group of baby-faced young lieutenants and captains appeared on Channel 13 saying they were a group of "idealistic young soldiers" acting for their families and for democracy in the Philippines.

I remembered a conversation I'd had two weeks earlier with one of my American military sources. He told me that a group of young and very intelligent military officers had approached him, told him about their plans for a coup and asked for support from the American government.

"Why are you asking me?" he asked them.

"Because you are a CIA agent," their leader answered.

He told them he was not a CIA agent, and they went away disappointed.

I got my American friend on the phone.

"Did you see those guys on the air?" I asked.

"Yes," he replied.

"Are they the same ones you talked to two weeks ago?"

"No," he answered.

"Do you mean there are more?" I asked, incredulous.

"It appears there is another even smarter bunch," he said.

Joe finally got through on our jammed bureau phone lines. Talking to him relieved the part of my mind that had been preoccupied with him all day. He was holed up with a bunch of leftie strategists making contingency plans about what they would do if Gringo succeeded.

Trisha Thomas came stumbling back into the bureau, safe from the siege of Aguinaldo but looking a little shell-shocked. I was much relieved that Trisha and Brian were no longer in the field. By that time artillery shells were being lobbed across EDSA between Gringo's boys in Aguinaldo and Ramos's troops in Camp Crame. Little kids were running in between, picking up the spent brass shells, which were valuable as scrap.

Dozens of civilians had been killed. The death toll among the soldiers was low, leading to speculation that the brotherhood of soldiers was holding. They didn't want to kill each other. Finally General Alfredo Lim, the police chief of Manila, with no notions of that "military brotherhood" nonesense, led his men in an assault of Channel 7, killed a few RAM boys, and regained control. Then he routed out Gringo's boys holed up in the Camelot Hotel across the street. The tide was finally beginning to turn against Gringo.

To our collective sigh of relief the president finally appeared on television, looking pale but alive. She was in her tough-guy guise. She ordered that the rebellion and the rebels would be crushed without mercy. On the air, she ordered Ramos to attack Camp Aguinaldo and take it back at all costs. She also confirmed what we already knew, that her son, Noynoy, had been shot while riding in his car near the palace at the beginning of the action. He was not seriously wounded but his mother was obviously outraged. The president also said her house had been attacked but her guards had repulsed the rebel soldiers. It was a Cory Aquino we hadn't seen before.

As soon as the president was off the air, ancient World War II Tora Tora planes in the hands of loyal pilots dropped bombs on rebel-held military headquarters at Camp Aguinaldo. I was immensely grateful that Trisha was no longer in there. In fact, I think there was probably some sort of warning before the attack came, because Gringo and friends scurried like rats out of the doomed building moments before it was razed.

Gringo escaped over a wall, although there were wishful and false rumors that an unmarked white helicopter had swooped down and swept away the glamorous rebel leader.

The rebellion died as quickly as it began. Gringo and his boys were unable to hang on that time, but emotions still run high in the military. I had no doubt they would try again. Each adventure seemed to bring them closer to success.

29 PIDDIG REDUX: *February 1988*

I WAS ON A PULSE-TAKING TRIP around the Philippines. The object was to visit as many parts of the country as possible in as little time as possible to find out what people were thinking about, talking about, worrying about.

I had done a couple of these trips before. They were exhausting, but fun. They made for a great newspaper story that could be sold to several of the newspapers that had been publishing my stories. These trips offered a chance to re-establish contact with old friends and make new ones. That, to a journalist, is what a wallow in the good old mud hole is to a *carabao*, the Philippine water buffalo. I felt a bit like a *carabao*, buried in mud up to my nostrils.

I went south to Davao and Zamboanga, and to see the Muslim rebels in horrible Jolo, a place so depressing that many journalists called it "Hole-O." I went east to Leyte, Imelda's home province; and Bacolod; and Iloilo, a city of churches in the western Visayas region. At last, I went north, to Ilocos Norte, the Marcos stronghold, where the former president is still much loved and much missed.

I took an unusually decrepit jeepney to Sarrat, Marcos's birthplace. I remembered Sarrat from a previous visit. It is a sleepy, rather charming little place with a row of elegant homes built by cronies, a large and beautiful cathedral from Spanish times, and a crooked tower that houses the town hall.

Marcos's daughter, Irene, was married in that cathedral in an outrageously ostentatious ceremony in 1984. A few months afterward, an earthquake nearly destroyed the cathedral and the tower. Those who opposed Marcos said that God was angry with the greedy Ferdinand and Imelda. The people of Sarrat, Marcos-lovers to a man, remained silent.

I got off the bus in the center of town and looked for a little restaurant where I could buy a Coke.

I have discovered that, as a foreign woman traveling alone, I am very rarely alone for long if I am interested in company. Friendly Filipinos try to pick me up and take me home to Mom. I have a pretty good built-in bullshit detector, so it is not difficult to weed out the ones with spurious intentions. It's a great way to see a country, learn about people, and see how they live.

It took only me thirty seconds to find my tour guides in Sarrat. Inside the *carenderia,* or small restaurant, three gentlemen were sharing a bottle of local rum. From their merriment I surmised this was their second, or maybe even their third, bottle of the day.

"Hello!" they shouted at me as I walked through the door. "What are you doing here?"

I told them I was a journalist who wanted to learn more about Marcos's home town. That was all it took. It was hard to get them to stop yarning and filling me with tales of Marcos, their hero.

Bertie, the most vocal of the bunch, fell in love. He grabbed at my hand continuously, which made it difficult to take notes. To break the sexual impasse with Bertie, I asked them if they would give me a walking tour of the town. I was fairly certain Bertie couldn't walk very far.

I was right. Bertie fell into the gutter just in front of the restaurant. Unable to rise, he lay there pleading, like an overturned turtle, while we walked away.

"I love you!" he shouted to my back.

My two remaining guides, brothers Peding and Doming, were in only slightly better shape than Bertie. We lurched and stumbled through the streets of Sarrat, peeking in the windows of the house where Marcos was born. We tiptoed through the broken glass in an elegant guesthouse Imelda had built of bricks cannibalized from some of Sarrat's ancient buildings that had miraculously survived the second world war. The basement of the guesthouse was being used as a pigsty. Peding and Doming posed for me in front of the Marcos homestead, arms around one another, less out of brotherly love than out of need for physical support.

We made our way past the heavily guarded, but by then unoccupied, mansions belonging to General Ver and Marcos's relatives, eventually winding our way back to the carenderia. Bertie had miraculously righted himself and was perched precariously on a tipsy stool.

"I love you!" Bertie shouted as soon as he caught sight of me.

I slipped the waitress twenty pesos (about a dollar), enough to keep them in rum for the rest of the day.

"Thanks guys and have fun!" I waved as I boarded the jeepney to Laoag.

"I love you!" Bertie shouted one last time.

In Laoag, I was greeted warmly by my old friend Bishop Abaya. The bishop delighted in telling the story of our detention over and over. In the time elapsed since the event, the story had been embellished a bit at my expense and was far more hilarious than when it happened.

I told him I wanted to go back to Piddig, the scene of my detention more than two years before, and write about the changes under the new government. The bishop shook his head, clicked his tongue, and jabbed a finger at me. He warned that, if anything, the NPA infiltration of Piddig was greater than in the Marcos days. I accused him of acting like my father. The bishop chuckled and pleaded guilty.

I was adamant, so the bishop set about finding me some effective bodyguards. He made me swear on everything I held holy that I wouldn't try any shenanigans, that I would abide by his every instruction to the letter. I swore, with no fingers crossed behind my back this time.

I was to be escorted by the mayor of Laoag and the new mayor of Piddig. That seemed safe enough. Both mayors remembered our detention in 1985 which had apparently caused quite a sensation in Laoag and Piddig.

Despite my intellectual certainty that no harm would come to me in that company, my stomach was roller-coasting as we drove a few miles from town down the familiar rutted dirt road to Barrio Estancia.

Everything still looked the same. The rice fields were still that supernatural shade of green. Even in the morning sunlight, the spot where Sergeant Augustin and the Scout Rangers held us, near the little dyke, still seemed sinister.

In fact, everything was very different.

Piddig's Mayor Daisy Raquiza, who had a strong part in getting us released in 1985, had been kidnapped by the NPA during the election campaign just before Christmas of 1986. Mayor Raquiza was defeated in absentia in the January elections. There were rumors she had been killed, but Bishop Abaya said NPA emmissaries had assured him that she was alive and unharmed. (Mayor Raquiza would be released unharmed, but substantially thinner, after nine months in captivity.)

Young Tina Remegio was dead. Bishop Abaya assured me that her death was not a violent one, "She just got some strange disease and wasted away." Although unexplained deaths are fairly common in the Philippines, I had my doubts. It could mean Tina had gone to the mountains to join the NPA.

Father Ted Remegio had been released from prison before the election of 1986 and was back in his parish.

Sergeant Augustin, our drunken captor, had been sent on his way, the only positive result of the military's investigation of our detention. I have no doubt he is happily terrorizing people in some other part of the country.

At Estancia's only jeepney stop, we met four teenaged boys lounging in the waiting shed. Two of them had what appeared to be toy pistols. They told us, somewhat mysteriously, that they were "training." Then they told us how excited they were about the course in "democratic principles" they had been given by the military the previous week.

"We especially liked the movie *Killing Fields* 'cuz it showed what communism is really about," one of the boys confided.

There was an ominous hush in Estancia. The only townspeople we saw were the boys and a couple of old ladies carrying their market bundles on their heads. There was none of the usual hustle and bustle of the barrio. There were no women gossiping as they washed their laundry at the community tap, no naked children running here and there, no men working in the rice fields, no dogs lazing in the sun. Not even the roosters crowed.

We saw why when we rounded the bend to the main part of the barrio. At the intersection of the road and a foot path, two tanks and two jeeps squatted like giant locusts. A dozen soldiers in full battle dress busied themselves around the tanks. The "friendly" handful of Scout Rangers commanded by a corporal who offered coffee and guns in August 1985 had been evicted from the perch on the hill.

In their place was a well-equipped full company of soldiers. In command was a very officious colonel who nervously hurried over to our car as soon as he saw it.

The colonel announced that we were in a "heavily infested" area.

I immediately reacted negatively to the colonel. We weren't tourists. We knew exactly where we were.

"Where are all the people?" I asked. I had heard of hamletting, mass evacuations and food blockades in NPA strongholds as part of the military's plan to "isolate the fish by draining the water from the pond."

The colonel changed the subject. The mayors introduced themselves. They chit-chatted for a few seconds.

I went back to the point. "Where are all the people?" I asked, looking directly into the colonel's eyes.

He looked away. "They are out working in their fields," he said, vaguely waving his arm.

I could see several fields from where we stood. There was not a soul in any of them.

"Are the people of Estancia still NPA sympathizers?" I asked.

"I wouldn't know that, ma'am," he replied shortly.

"Are there many NPA's in this area?" I persisted.

"Some," the colonel answered unhelpfully.

The colonel said his men were preparing to go on an "operation," so would we please excuse him? He suggested, not subtly at all, that it was time for us to leave, since "this is a very dangerous area, you know."

Translated, that meant there was likely to be an encounter with the NPA any minute.

It looked like my return to Estancia was going to be even less productive than my first visit, when people were too frightened to talk. This time there was no one to talk to at all.

The two mayors were anxious to leave. The quiet in the place was eerie.

As we drove back down the washboard road, I thought how much Estancia typifies the drift of the Philippines. Despite government claims that the insurgency would go away after Marcos was gone, the military's own figures showed that the insurgency had gotten worse. Marcos was a convenient scapegoat, but he was obviously not the cause of the insurgency. Maybe the communists are clever propagandists. But maybe there is truth in the tale told by so many: the people listen to the communists because they offer some hope of escape from the misery of their poverty.

For the people of Estancia, wherever they were, it was clear that they are trapped with no prospects to continue their lives in peace. Whether they are supporters of the military or of the rebels, their lives are destined to be filled with fear and violence.

The Philippines seemed to be deteriorating. I remembered an article I read years before. It compared the people's tolerance for the escalating violence in Lebanon to frogs placed in a pot of water over a fire. The frogs allow themselves to be cooked because they are unaware of the increasing temperature until it is too late to jump out. Certainly that analogy applies to the Philippines.

30 KIKO—DEATH COMES CLOSE:
March 28, 1988

O N THE MORNING OF SATURDAY, March 26, Joe woke up with a terrible pain in his right hip. There was no explanation for it, but the pain got worse as the day went on. Joe is not a hypochondriac, so I was really concerned. To make matters worse, I was scheduled to fly to Zamboanga on Sunday to work on a documentary on the Muslim rebellion for Spanish television.

By Sunday morning Joe was in excruciating pain, but he insisted I should go on with my trip. I phoned him during a stopover in Cebu and he said a doctor friend had come over and given him a shot, so he was feeling better, but there was still no explanation for the pain. He was to have x-rays the following day.

Monday the 28th was a completely messed up day for me. The Spanish TV camerawoman, who was on her way back from the States, had been bumped off her plane in San Francisco. Word came from Manila that the crew couldn't arrive for at least two more days. Contacts made weeks in advance were not to be found. The scheduled shoot couldn't possibly happen. It was more than the usual screwup. I was frustrated, tired, and still worried about Joe. My psychic alarms said I should go home. Now.

About 3:30 in the afternoon, I went to the airport and begged a seat on the evening flight to Manila, pleading a family emergency. I didn't know at the time what I was saying.

I burst through our front gate about ten PM, expecting to be greeted with a surprised smile and a big hug from Joe. No one expected to see me for at least two more days. Joe was nowhere to be seen, but several people, including Joe's son, Carlo, and Joe's brother, Efren, were hanging out in our living room. That was strange. They greeted me with grim faces. I panicked. Something was wrong. Something had happened to Joe.

"Where's Joe?" I asked.

They pointed to our bedroom.

I started toward the door. Joe opened it, sobbing, and threw himself into my arms. I couldn't make any sense of what he was mumbling for a while, then I understood the words.

"They shot him. They shot Kiko. They killed my brother," he wept like a wounded child.

Oh, God! Kiko, Joe's thirty-one-year-old imp of a brother, dead? How could he be dead?

I stared at the wall over Joe's shoulder and repeated incomprehendingly, "No. No. No. No."

The next few minutes were very confused. We were both talking and crying. But finally the story came out. Joe had asked Kiko to do some errands for him that day because the leg was still too painful for driving. Kiko was on his way to the repair shop with Joe's car about 3:30 in the afternoon when several men in a white Toyota pulled up next to him at a stoplight on busy Aurora Boulevard. They coolly opened fire with M-16s, then sped away. Kiko was apparently injured, but not killed, in that initial volley. Somehow, unbelievably, he got the car into reverse. A security guard at the school across the street told Joe he saw Joe's car rapidly moving backwards. The gunmen apparently saw it, too, so they turned their car around and went back and fired several more rounds to finish Kiko off.

"They blew his brains out," Joe told me in a dull voice.

Those words blew apart our lives.

My mind could not comprehend the horror of the thing. Worse yet, it was clear that Kiko was followed from Joe's office and was plainly the victim of mistaken identity. Joe, because of his anti-establishment political beliefs, was very obviously the target. The apolitical, happy-go-lucky Kiko only had the misfortune to be driving Joe's car that day. He never understood Joe's politics or cared about them.

I could only sit and let the tears pour down my cheeks. Selfishly, I was relieved that it wasn't Joe. As I clung to his warm body I felt guilty about that selfish gratitude.

I was haunted by memory of a mustachioed Kiko grinning and patting his round tummy on Christmas Day and announcing he didn't want any more to eat because he had "a full tank."

Kiko and his two kids had been to the airport early that Christmas morning to say goodbye to his wife, Baby, who had signed a contract to be a singer in Japan. Both Kiko and Baby thought that the money she would earn would raise them above the rundown house on the railroad tracks. Kiko had been so blue when she left that Christmas afternoon. Afterward, I thought many times of the two of them sitting at our breakfast table, sadly holding hands in their last moments together.

There were lots of witnesses to the murder. It happened just across the street from a school that had just recessed for the day. There were hundreds of children on the streets who could have been hit by the bullets. The school crossing-guards, a bank guard, and dozens of passersby saw everything. Yet no one wanted to talk. They were all too afraid. That meant only one thing: the killers were military men or police. It happens time and again in the Philippines. I asked myself bitterly why I should be surprised anymore.

We groped for a reason for this third brutal murder to tear apart our lives in fifteen months. I kept thinking back to the death threats that came six months before, after Lean Alejandro was killed. Joe thought Kiko's murder was a revenge killing. The mayor of suburban Navotas had been ambushed early the morning of March 28. Six of the mayor's bodyguards riding backup in an ambulance died in the attack.

The military immediately blamed the Navotas ambush on the NPA. Incredibly, one tabloid newspaper even pointed out that a brown Mitsubishi Lancer, like Joe's and like 5,000 others in Manila, had been seen at the ambush site.

Only months later was there evidence that the Navotas ambush was not an NPA operation, but the work of a criminal gang.

Joe was a convenient and easy-to-locate figure of the legal left, an easy target for revenge. If he had been affiliated with the underground, the ambush wouldn't have been so easy because he would have had security guards. Whoever planned the ambush knew Joe's regular schedule to and from his office each day. They knew that he always drove his own car. They knew he had no bodyguards. The attackers could be assured no one would shoot back.

My rage re-surfaced. I remembered the blood on Dante's hand. I saw Lean Alejandro's handsome face, mutilated by assassin's bullets, unrecognizable in his coffin, not very well repaired with the embalmer's wax. I saw the wire that bound Lando Olalia's hands and the expression of agony frozen forever on his face. I raged helplessly. My throat was in knots. I felt as if I couldn't breathe. I could do nothing to change these outrageous injustices. I was powerless. The only power came from those with guns in their hands. My reverence for the sanctity of life was fading. I was beginning to wish for a gun in my own hands to extract revenge from those monsters.

Part of my consciousness seemed split. It was watching with detachment as I raged, and wondering what happened to the peace freak, what happened to my innocence? Why had I chosen to live this way? I wondered if I was becoming emotionally unbalanced. I was so far away from that safe and comfortable American lifestyle.

The murderers had missed Joe this time, but what would happen next week, next month, next year? Would they continue to stalk him?

Joe was consumed by grief, anger, guilt, and a whole catalog of emotions. In addition to my grief and anger, I was afraid. When would they strike again?

Joe's nephew, Danny, a Quezon City policeman, assigned himself to be Joe's bodyguard. His brother-in-law, Doming, a Manila policeman, similarly assigned himself. Various other friends and relatives took it upon themselves to move in and protect us. Their support was touching but painful. We were surrounded by guns in our own home. Danny very matter-of-factly showed me how to operate his M-16, but I couldn't bear the biting touch of the cold metal.

It terrified me to sleep surrounded by men with guns. It wasn't the same as being in the hills with the NPA. That was more of a romantic game. This was real life. Yet, there was a strange sense of security in knowing the guns were there.

The second day after Kiko's death, real life hit home with even more graphic horror. Danny came back to the house with Joe's car. The car was full of bullet holes; the seats were soaked with blood. Some of Kiko's brains were still inside and beginning to rot. The horrifying stench was worsened by the knowledge that it came from part of a man we had loved.

Someone had given Joe a bookmark that had been hanging from the rear view mirror of his car. It said "Yesterday is over. Tomorrow is a vision. But today, well lived, makes every yesterday a dream of happiness and every tomorrow a vision of hope." The book mark had four bullet holes in it. I gently took it from the car and put it in my desk drawer. Sometimes, I still take it out and look at it. There are days when it is impossible to hang on to a hope for a better future for the Philippines.

Hysteria kept rising in my chest at unexpected moments. The car was like a specter in the driveway. I ordered Danny to cover it with sheets, but nothing covered the horror of that machine. I complained that the house was full of flies.

"It's because of the stuff in the car, ma'am," my maid told me in a quivering voice.

I came totally unglued. I couldn't comprehend that I could be living this nightmare. Kiko was murdered. There was a car full of bullet holes, blood, and brains in my driveway. There were armed men all around me. I screamed my grief and Joe comforted me. Joe screamed his grief and I comforted him. I wondered if we were both losing our minds.

I burst into tears every time I saw that ghost of a car. Finally I begged them to take the car somewhere else. I awoke one morning to find it gone, much to my relief.

Somewhere in the middle of all the blackness, KK disappeared. I have never found out what happened to the little cat who had been my helpmate for so long, through the bad times in Rome and the lonely months in Manila. I think maybe the terrible vibrations of violence were too much for him. I don't want to think that KK may have been a smaller victim of the kind of violence that killed Kiko and that permeates this society. People here do kill cats for fun. Sometimes they kill people for fun.

KK's loss compounded my sorrow. I didn't think I could bear all the grief and fear.

Fortunately there were details to occupy us. Joe wrote a statement condemning all violence, not only Kiko's murder, but condemning the killers of the Navotas mayor's bodyguards.

Kiko's widow, Baby, was having difficulty getting out of Japan. Her employer was insisting on holding her to her contract. What else could be expected from an employer who insisted she had to leave her family on Christmas Day? Several phone calls finally sorted that out, but they opened more wounds on our hearts.

There was a wake every night for nearly a week: the first night at a funeral home, and on subsequent nights at the family home by the railroad tracks. There were many visitors, but precious few from Joe's former comrades on the left. I learned for the first time the meaning of true friendship. In fact I was surprised to see those who had the courage to come, including a couple from the American embassy whom we strongly suspected had CIA ties, and a Singaporean diplomat who had only arrived a month before but who had reached out in friendship several times. Those little things meant a great deal.

We had nowhere to go, but we knew we had to get out of the Philippines. A friend in Hawaii kindly offered to pay for our plane tickets. We would leave just after the funeral.

Since Baby couldn't get home until Good Friday, we scheduled the burial for Easter Sunday.

There were thirteen kids in Joe's family, all of them and all of their children and their children's children good Catholics. Yet not one Catholic priest could spare a moment to come to the house and say a traditional blessing over the casket, much less say a mass. Our only religious solace in those black days came from our old friend Brian Allan, the journalist/Anglican priest. Another Protestant minister who was a friend of the family also conducted a service one night.

I am not a Catholic and I strongly disapprove of many policies of the Catholic Church, none so much as the policy against birth control. The Church's neglect of the family's needs after Kiko's death was to me an example of the callousness of the Church towards its smallest members. It embittered me.

The official Church policy is that funerals are no longer permitted inside the church, we were told.

Why?

Because there are too many people.

Why are there too many?

Because the bloody Church doesn't believe in birth control.

What a sick and vicious cycle designed to keep the believers in misery.

Joe was told that we could bring Kiko's coffin past the church and, for a fee, a priest would come out and bless it. That made me absolutely furious. Who did the Catholics think they were? What of all of this talk about the blessed are the poor for they shall inherit the kingdom of God?

I got on the phone and began to call every priest I knew. All of them had "other plans" for Easter Sunday that obviously did not include a funeral. Perhaps we should have asked Kiko to die at a more convenient time.

I couldn't believe it. I asked one priest what we should do. Should we just throw the coffin into the ground and say, "So long, Kiko, it's been nice to know you"?

I was bitter and hurt.

Finally I called Brian Allan. I had hesitated because we were not members of his church, but Brian said he was honored that we had asked him to conduct the service. Yes, he had plans for a family dinner on Easter afternoon, but that could wait. His ministry was to those who needed it. His vows would never permit him to turn away anyone in need.

Brian gave a moving eulogy and told us that it was time to bury our guilt along with Kiko and look for what God intended for us all for the rest of our lives. I squeezed Joe's hand, but he shook his head.

Joe blamed himself for Kiko's death, which wasn't surprising, but how could I help him move away from the guilt?

Strangely, the pain in Joe's leg had disappeared the moment Kiko was shot. My sixth sense told me it was a strange affliction sent simply to save Joe's life. What else could it be? I asked Joe to examine why it was Kiko who died and not he. Wasn't it possible that Joe had some mission left in life?

The pain and the guilt were too much. The healing took a very long time.

The president ordered a special task force to investigate Kiko's murder. Joe and I laughed bitterly when we heard that. What had ever come of investigations of Lando and Lean's murders, Dante's shooting? Nothing. And nothing would come of this investigation, we were sure.

We were right. Despite the creation of yet another in the never-ending series of task forces, no one has ever been arrested for Kiko's murder. In fact the only tidbit of information the police were able to uncover was that the killers had used a stolen car. I am certain that Kiko's killers were policemen or soldiers and that is precisely why no one has ever been arrested.

Joe and I left the Philippines two days after Kiko's funeral. We spent a week in Hong Kong waiting for Joe's U.S. visa, and then went to the States to heal.

The healing was slow. My Don Quixote who was always tilting at windmills had become cynical. Gradually he began to recover his idealism and his desire to change his country, but it is still tainted with a distrust that will never disappear. It hurts me to watch him struggle with himself and his dreams.

I recovered, cynicism intact, but I am still afraid.

I am afraid that every time I kiss him goodbye it may be the last time.

31 MARCOS IN HAWAII: *April 19, 1988*

H AWAII SEEMED LIKE a perfect haven, a respite from the violence of Manila. The horror started to fade a bit as Joe and I lazed on Honolulu's sunny beaches and drank pina coladas on palm-tree-shaded terraces.

One night we went to see *Good Morning, Vietnam*. We were happily walking back to the condominium we had rented in Waikiki, chattering about the movie and playing back the funniest lines for each other. A block away from our building we were stopped by a policeman who had set up a barricade. The cop told us there was a drunk with a gun holding two women hostage on the top floor of the building. We couldn't go any closer.

I was shaking. I couldn't tell whether I was trembling from anger or fear. I wasn't really afraid that I would be a victim of some loony-toon on the top floor of a condo in Waikiki. I know I won't die that way. It just seemed like the specter of mindless violence was pursuing me everywhere I went. The palm trees and the white sand beaches lost their luster. I felt suddenly very depressed. We sat on the grass of a nearby park until three A.M. when the guy with the gun was finally persuaded to give himself up and we were allowed back into the building.

Our somewhat batty benefactor, a Honolulu gynecologist, was extravagantly celebrating his forty-fourth birthday that week with a huge bash. One of the guests was Ma-an Hontiveros, a well-known Manila journalist, the television voice of the People Power Revolution and a good friend. The doctor was definitely out to impress the foxy Ma-an. He couldn't meet her plane since he had to see patients, so he sent Joe and me to meet her at the airport in a shiny black Lincoln stretch limo that looked like it was ninety feet long. We had the liveried chauffeur, a huge lei of orchids, and a bottle of champagne in the silver ice bucket. Best of all, we had the limo for the entire day.

Ma-an was suitably impressed with the reception. We sipped the champagne as we drove through the morning traffic into Honolulu.

After a rest and a change, we drove off in the limo to Ala Moana Mall and treated ourselves to a Baskin-Robbins ice cream. I guess not too many folks in limos go to Baskin-Robbins. Especially not too many folks who looked like us. Ma-an and I were dressed with a certain elan, but Joe was wearing jeans, a baggy T-shirt and loafers with no socks. He looked like a beach bum. The chauffeur was taking great delight in opening doors and laying out the limo's little red carpet and addressing Joe as "Sir." We created quite a sensation.

We planned to eat our ice cream, sip champagne, and have a leisurely tour through Waikiki and Diamond Head.

Tourist spots. An idea flashed into my mind. What is Honolulu's biggest tourist attraction? Ferdinand Marcos. Why not pay him a visit?

The idea, and the champagne, sparked our excitement.

We drove high up the mountain to the high-priced real estate on Makiki Heights and asked directions to Marcos's house. Everybody knew where it was.

We stopped in front of the heavily guarded gate. While we continued to sip champagne and giggle, we sent the chauffeur to present our business cards.

Our business cards generated a parade of gawkers from inside the Marcos compound. The first one peered inside the car and wordlessly checked out the three of us coolly sipping champagne. A second, holding my card and Ma-an's, scrutinized our faces, glanced again at the cards and also departed without a word. We had apparently passed some esoteric test. The third gawker was Gemmo Trinidad, Marcos's spokesman.

Trinidad ducked his head inside the limo and said in a not-unfriendly manner, "Oh, it really is Ma-an Hontiveros. And you must be Kathleen Barnes? What is it you want?"

In her most syrupy tone, the Voice of the People Power Revolution told him we had "come to pay our respects to President Marcos."

Trinidad disappeared. We called our doctor friend on the car's phone to tell him about our adventures, and while we were talking the gates opened. We were told to drive inside.

"Gotta go. We're driving through the gates. Talk to you later," I yelled to him as I hung up the phone.

We had actually gotten inside! But what were we going to do with Joe, one of Marcos's most fervent critics for so many years? Would he be in danger here? No, this is America. They wouldn't dare try anything, would they? Maybe they wouldn't recognize him. Maybe they would think it was funny. I shoved my camera at him. "You're the photographer," I proclaimed. We didn't have a tape recorder, a video camera, or any of the equipment we needed to seriously interview Marcos. I ripped a few pages out of my notebook and handed them to Ma-an. She rummaged in her bag for a couple of pens.

There was no time for any more discussion. We were ushered inside a large home with a spectacular view, furnished in the nouveau kitsch so favored by Imelda Marcos.

Trinidad left us on the patio, seated at a table still decorated with plastic Easter bunnies and jelly beans left over from the holiday two weeks before.

Ma-an whispered, "I forgot to tell you, when I left Manila there was a rumor that Marcos is dead."

Trinidad said the President was resting, but Mrs. Marcos would see us. Our champagne-induced smiles faded. Imelda is famous for her excruciating eight-hour non-stop interviews in which the interviewers become virtual hostages. God! How could we get out of this one? We were trapped.

We sat on the patio, sipping coffee with Trinidad and Marcos's congenial security man, Colonel Art Aruiza. It seemed like nothing was going to happen.

We quite deliberately neglected to introduce Joe. That is sort of like ignoring a big pink elephant sitting at your elbow. But in the Philippine culture that is not as rude as it might seem. Everyone in the Philippines seems to have lackeys, flunkies, and factotums who are unimportant and therefore never introduced. We hoped they would think Joe was unimportant and would also ignore him. Certainly Joe doesn't look like a flunkie despite his casual clothes, but they were too polite to ask who he was.

After an hour, and three cups of coffee, I went in search of a bathroom. As fate would have it, I bumped into Marcos when I lost my way. He was just emerging from a room in the wing, dressed nattily in a white sport jacket, tie, and brilliant red wool vest. I seized the moment and walked right up and shook his hand. So much for the rumors of his death.

"Hello, Mr. President. I don't know if you remember me, I'm Kathleen Barnes from ABC."

At sixty-eight he already looked like a very old man. "Of course, you're the one who wrote about Hacienda Luisita. I'll be right out to talk to you."

I was baffled. Why should Marcos know about or remember that little piece I had written about my trip to Hacienda Luisita with Dante in November of 1986? Why wouldn't he remember the dozens of less than laudatory things I had written about him?

We were escorted into the dining room. Aruiza took Joe off into the living room to shoot off a photo, just to be sure the camera was not a bomb. There were more tacky Easter decorations on the big dining room table. Trinidad said they "help cheer up the President."

Marcos shuffled into the room on the arms of a couple of aides. With a sigh he seated himself at the head of the table in a chair with a needlepointed cushion proclaiming "Ang Pangulo ng Pilipinas" (The President of the Philippines). He clutched a newspaper clipping in his hand—my Hacienda Luisita story published in the *Toronto Star*. They must have a file on me! I wondered what else was in it.

Marcos was lucid. He was more than lucid. He may have been physically feeble, but mentally he was very sharp indeed. He greeted both of us with a cordial handshake. We did not introduce Joe. He winked and quoted the obvious Mark Twain rejoinder to the rumors of his death.

We spent a fascinating two hours talking to the man who had been the devil of the Philippines. As we drank Cokes and choked down Spam sandwiches at his table, I couldn't help but think of the hundreds of people who had disappeared, murdered in the name of Marcos. I couldn't help but think of the misery he had visited on millions of his people who had become beggers because of his greed. I couldn't help but think that even Kiko's murder just three weeks before was somehow the result of the military machine Marcos had set in motion.

And I couldn't help but admire the intellect and the persuasive abilities of this diabolical man. Everything he said made perfect sense.

He talked in veiled terms about negotiations with Aquino relatives for his return to the Philippines, about corruption in the Aquino government, his predictions of an economic collapse and the imminent communist takeover of the Philippines within two months. With a twinkle in his eye, Marcos humbly offered "Madam Aquino" his help in sorting out the problems of the Philippines.

When Ma-an touched delicately on the subject of February 1986, Marcos patted her on the shoulder and said, "Oh, it's all right, Ma-an, I always knew you were really on my side."

I nearly choked on my Spam sandwich. Ma-an? On the side of Marcos? This was the lady who, aside from Radio Bandido's June Keithley, is most identified with the broadcast coverage of Marcos's demise.

Ma-an tactfully changed the subject. Somehow, inexplicably, she got him on the subject of plastic surgery and liposuction.

I wasn't following very well. Joe had been sitting to my right snapping photographs. I had gradually become aware that I hadn't heard the camera's shutter click for several minutes. There was plenty of film. What could be wrong? I didn't dare look at him. Then I realized. He had finished a roll and didn't know how to load the camera.

God! How could any journalist have a photographer who doesn't know how to load a camera? Shit!

I surreptitiously reached my right hand out to him. He deposited in it the camera and a fresh roll of film. Without removing my gaze from Marcos, I loaded the camera and slid it back to him. The exchange wasn't lost on Aruiza and the security men. They sidled closer but Marcos didn't seem to notice. He was too wrapped up in telling Ma-an about the newest fad in fat removal.

The conversation rambled and became more bizarre.

Marcos began to talk about the rural banks and the Aquino government land-reform policies. I wasn't very interested until I caught the end of a sentence about farmers, "They are taught the question of, you know, worms."

"Earthworms?" Ma-an asked.

"Worms?" I echoed.

Marcos plunged on, "Earthworms are sort of held in contempt. Earthworms are part of the, what do you call that, McDonald's . . ." His voice trailed off as he searched for the word.

"I don't believe it!" I gasped. "They put earthworms in McDonald's hamburgers? Yech!"

"Ya! Extenders," Marcos blurted, having found the word.

I don't think I'll ever again walk into a McDonald's without thinking of Marcos and his old-man's mental wanderings.

He began to talk about his wealth and the legend that he had found the Yamashita treasure after World War II.

Marcos claimed that General Tomoyuki Yamashita had surrendered to him at the war's end in 1946, "and so he is supposed to have left a map with me. That's how I got this Yamashita treasure."

He admitted having a share of the gold taken from captured Japanese in Northern Luzon at the end of the war. He hinted it might be something in the neighborhood of 200,000 bars of gold. It was an easy explanation for the "unexplained wealth" of a man who never earned more than 650 dollars a month in his twenty years as president. I didn't buy it. But he insisted he didn't take the fabulous 2,000 pound jewel-encrusted Golden Buddha. Legend also said that Marcos had melted down that priceless treasure.

As far as I could tell, all of the treasure stories were fairy tales.

It was nearly seven P.M. We had to go, but this rather pitiful old man didn't want to let us go. I think Marcos was lonely. I found myself again feeling that vicious pity for him, much the same way I felt when Nixon had to play golf alone after he lost his presidency. He deserved to be where he was.

Marcos hung on to us for a while longer.

Thankfully there had been no sign of Imelda. Trinidad asked if Marcos didn't want to hear "Mona Lisa." I feared Imelda's entrance signaled our coming entrapment. Imelda is famous for inflicting her screechy songs and crocodile tears on every visitor. I exhaled in relief when an unseen pianist and soloist plunked out the tune. Later our chauffeur told us that Imelda had escaped out the back door ten minutes after our arrival. Apparently the disgraced former First Lady did not want to encounter television's Voice of People Power.

Marcos turned his sharp gaze on Joe. Here it comes, I thought.

"And what did you say your name was?" Marcos asked pointedly.

"Joe," the flunkie answered monosyllabically.

"Joe what?" Marcos persisted.

"Joe Castro."

No recognition. So far so good.

"Are you from the Castro family of Pampanga?" Marcos asked innocently.

Castro in the Philippines is as common as Smith in the U.S.

"No," Joe answered, not giving an inch.

"Where are you from, then?" the former dictator pressed.

"Manila," answered my momentarily inarticulate lover.

"And what do you do?" Marcos asked with icy formality.

"I am a businessman," Joe answered with equal politeness.

Marcos dropped it. But I am sure it took no more than ten minutes after we departed for Trinidad and friends to discover Joe's identity. Trinidad told us later they had a good laugh over the idea of a leader of the Parliament of the Streets sitting at Marcos's table.

Marcos beckoned to an aide, who brought over two copies of a Marcos 1971 paperback entitled *Today's Revolution: Democracy.*

He inscribed mine: "To Kathleen S. Barnes. This is an introduction to the New Society which you have come to be acquainted with in our country. Let me congratulate you on your excellent articles that picture the Philippine society today, especially the ones on Hacienda Luisita. Sincerely, Ferdinand Marcos."

That dedication was a prize! I wondered if Marcos meant to congratulate me on *all* of my stories. How about the one about being detained? How about Joel Abong? How about Smoky Mountain and a dozen more? I was angry with him for being so self-centered and a bit angry with myself for liking him.

We took our leave quickly, firmly declining Marcos's invitation for dinner. As we walked out the door, Joe snatched a copy of *Today's Revolution* from a pile on a table. His wasn't autographed.

We tumbled into the car, popped the cork on another bottle of champagne, hooted and hugged each other in delight at the success of our caper as the limo glided into the Honolulu night.

32

AFTERMATH: *June 1988-September 1989*

W E SPENT NEARLY TWO MONTHS in the States attempting to cope with the complete uncertainty of Joe's future. Finally, with nearly everything unresolved, I returned to my real world in Manila and left Joe in Honolulu. We knew it was not possible for him to return to Manila in the short term, possibly not even in the long term.

I was miserable without him, but I knew I would be even more miserable if he had been with me and I spent every moment wondering if the killers had finally gotten him. I cried in supermarkets and generally felt sorry for myself.

In addition to the pain of separation, Joe was suffering from a burden of guilt over Kiko's death. That, in addition to being alone and nearly friendless in Honolulu, made it a difficult and painful phase of Joe's life. I was too far away to be of much help, which caused some rough times in our relationship. It wasn't long before I became his emotional punching bag. I was walking the razor's edge between being supportive of the man I loved and being a target for all of his pain. I didn't like myself or him very much in those dark days.

I was alone, too. Sleeping with the gun next to the bed and hating my life. It seemed that the more internal resistance I raised to my life the more tumultuous it become.

On top of all of the turmoil our relationship was undergoing, I was struggling financially. After an unplanned two-month hiatus in my income, Joe's forced unemployment and the monster phone bills we racked up, the financial situation was becoming desperate.

And my inner turmoil seemed to be paralleling the Philippine political situation.

In July, several human rights lawyers were killed in what seemed like a nationwide pogrom against the left. Joe's friend Dr. Nemesio Prudente, the well-respected left-wing president of Philippine Polytechnic University, was ambushed for the second time in July. The first ambush in November of 1987 had injured Prudente and killed two of his companions. The second killed two of his bodyguards. Miraculously Prudente was only slightly injured. It was clear that our August plans for Joe to sneak in to Manila for a few days for a visit with me and his kids was out of the question.

The danger signals were extremely intense in those days. Everyone was on edge wondering who would be hit next. Several Manila policemen were arrested for the Prudente ambush, but no one really thought that the death squads would stop their work. The legal left-wing organizations began to disappear as legal workers became frightened and quit or became hardened and went underground.

The political situation was deteriorating dramatically in those days. Cory Aquino, the simple housewife, had been found wanting.

People Power and spirit of EDSA were dead. Stone dead. There were periodic feeble attempts to revive it, but I could see that Aquino had missed her chance. She had not acted quickly when she had that adulation. And she had allowed unscrupulous people to squeeze themselves into positions of power.

I was greatly disappointed. I remembered the electricity of those shining moments on EDSA when I had seen the hope in the faces of the people. I knew that the catalyst was there for change. But people had become disheartened again. I could see it on their faces as they waited glumly in the rain for hours to catch a jeepney ride home from work. I could see it in the increased numbers of ragged children begging on the streets and the piles of garbage everywhere, including on my own street. I could see it in the potholes that made driving and riding hazardous on Manila's streets.

Cory Aquino's presidency was plagued with inadequacies. Her presidency remained a teflon one, but there was so much dirt around her that it was clear to me that soon she would get dirty herself. She had trusted the wrong people.

In August of 1988 Vice-President Salvador "Doy" Laurel split with Aquino, calling her leadership "weak and indecisive" because she had failed to control the people around her. Laurel, himself no paragon of public admiration, formed an opposition party with Enrile and some Marcos loyalists. The political wheel had rotated full circle. By September of 1989 Laurel was openly calling for Marcos's return and castigating the Aquino government for even refusing to allow his body to return after his September 28, 1989 death in Honolulu. After the Enrile-Laurel alliance, there was talk about a coup engineered by the still lively military rebels of RAM with Enrile and Laurel as civilian participants.

There was still a strong belief that the Aquino government was massively corrupt. Taxi drivers in Zamboanga, waiters in Laoag, students on Mendiola campuses, and mestizo *ilustrados* at swanky Manila dinner parties all sang the same tune.

The lion's share of allegations of corruption was carried by Cory's brother, Jose "Peping" Cojuangco. The popular belief in the massive corruption of Peping Cojuangco reminded me of the Marcos days. Despite the fact that none of the allegations against him could ever be proven, the people believed them. This is a country where perception becomes fact.

In fact there was so much smoke about corruption there had to be fire. In

October of 1988 my friend Louise Williams of the Sydney (Australia) *Morning Herald* published an investigative story that said that Cojuangco and his wife, TingTing (the same TingTing Cojuangco who saved the young man who had been shot at the rally in September 1984), had extorted one million dollars from an Australian businessman who wanted their help in obtaining a gambling concession. The Cojuangcos promptly sued Louise in Manila and in Sydney. For the next few months Louise received constant harassing telephone calls. It got so she couldn't sleep at night because the phone threats would continue all night long. She was followed. Sinister-looking men with clutch bags hung around her apartment. A year later she left the Philippines, partly because she was so distraught over the constant harassment. Eventually the Sydney *Morning Herald* paid a settlement to the Cojuangcos on the Australian portion of the libel case. Louise could not return to the Philippines, where her husband's family lived, for more than a year, until the case was revolved in Manila.

One high-ranking American official told me the Philippine government had "democratized corruption." He explained: Under Marcos, corruption was rampant, but it was strictly controlled. Only those carrying Marcos's imprimatur could collect bribes. Under Aquino it was "equal opportunity corruption," with everyone with a finger in the pot.

One government official told me that under Marcos the routine bribe for a contract was 20 percent. The official receiving the 20 percent would take care of everyone under him with that amount. But, he said, under Cory the volume had quadrupled or worse: "Now you have to take care of each layer of bureaucracy individually. It is completely out of control."

Allegations of corruption were everywhere. The director of the National Food Authority was fired after he faked the sinking of a barge carrying several thousand tons of rice. But he was never charged criminally and he was later quietly given another government job.

Port officials were caught allowing in hundreds of luxury cars duty free.

The agrarian reform secretary was fired for a scandal in which the payments to landowners were grossly inflated.

The newspapers were full of allegations of corruption every day. It seemed like some of Aquino's bureaucrats had studied the bribery system at Marcos's knee and learned their lessons well. Yet still there were no criminal charges brought.

Aquino promised action. She promised to catch some "big fish." But the big fish were too wily or the fisherwoman's will was too weak.

The graft cases against Marcos and his cronies went equally slowly. The government had filed several dozen civil suits against Marcos and the cronies, but no criminal charges. They perferred to allow the American government to prosecute Marcos and Imelda, since that would remove the necessity of allowing them to return to the Philippines to stand trial.

And there had still been no proseuctions of military men for human rights violations. I knew that the human rights commission had taken direct testimony from several torture victims against military stalwarts of the new government, but no charges were filed.

In October of 1988 I traveled around the country working on a piece I called "The Fragmentation of the Philippines." I was surprised to see that the frustration people were feeling seemed to be transforming itself into anger. But Filipinos are more placid that the Latinos; they don't engage in instant mass uprisings. I continued to wonder how much abuse they would take.

In March of 1989, when rice prices began to skyrocket, I couldn't imagine how the poor could survive. I began to ask people what it would take to infuriate the Filipinos to the point that they would rise up. Food shortages? Massive sickness? The deaths of their children? Increased military repression? None of those dire possibilities seemed to be the trigger.

One day I thought I found the answer. Truck drivers were on strike at the Coca Cola bottling plant. A week passed. No Coke was delivered. This was becoming a serious problem for a country that is fueled by Coke. People were going through withdrawal. There was no Coke on the shelves. Then one day, as I was driving home, I spotted a Coke truck outside the little grocery down the street. "Aha!" I thought. The strike has been settled.

Then I saw two squad cars, each with four men inside, each man with an assault rifle, guarding the scab driver who was making sure that the Coke got through. What dedication! That was how important Coke is. Maybe that was a clue to future revolutionaries about how to get people stirred up.

I wasn't sure where all of this aimless frustration would go, or if it would go anywhere at all. More than a year after the 1987 coup attempt, military sources told me they were still unhappy but the time for action had not yet arrived.

I was tired. Tired of living alone in Manila. Tired of the day-to-day frustrations of daily life, the nonoperational telephones, the garbage in the streets, the pollution, the nonworking government offices. Tired of the cultural separation. Tired of the war with Joe. Tired of spinning my wheels. By late August, when Joe decided to risk a quick visit, I was ready for a showdown. I knew we would resolve the problems between us or I would end the relationship and leave the Philippines.

I knew that if it had not been for my love affair with Joe, I would have left the Philippines sometime in 1987. I thought of all of the loneliness before Joe. I wanted someone in my life and I wanted a home. But I realized that the misery I was feeling with Joe wasn't a price I was willing to pay for companionship. It was like having gangrene. If I couldn't cure it I might have to cut off my own foot to save my life. It would hurt like hell but I would go on.

I was prepared for the amputation and in a combative mood when Joe came home from Hong Kong, where he had been trying to set up a business. We fought ferociously for several days, and one night, I reached the end of my rope. After yet another day of doing battle, I opened the door and threw him out of the car on EDSA. I told him not to come back. Doggedly, he did come back, shattered to realize that our relationship and even our friendship were nearly destroyed. We stayed up all that night, talking, crying, and finally holding hands and pledging to rebuild our friendship. I couldn't venture any further than that. We slept in separate bedrooms as his visit stretched to three weeks. We needed the time to see if we could survive the crisis. One step at a time, it was a long, hard process. There were setbacks, but by Christmas we knew we were back on the right track.

Joe began to divide his time between Manila and Hong Kong. The business in Hong Kong was an excruciatingly slow and expensive process. We hated being separated, but we agreed the threat to his life still remained in Manila. We avoided setting any patterns in his visits.

I continued to work and write. I settled a bit, although I was still frustrated with the political state of affairs. Every time Joe came home he would agonize over the failures of the government. I wondered, and I still wonder, how long he can stay away from the driving desire to change his country.

I continued to sleep with the gun next to the bed, although I still hated it.

My health was not good. Joe and I had dreamed of trying to have a baby, although we both knew it was just a pipe dream. Our ages (forty-one and forty-six) made it difficult. Our life-style made it impractical. And finally, my physical problems made it impossible. It was hard for me to accept the fact that I would never hold my own baby in my arms, even though years before I had decided that motherhood was not for me. How could I climb mountains with rebels or sleep in barrios or do half the crazy things I had done if I had a baby?

And I had Joe's family. His beautiful eight-year-old daughter, Talya, had become like a daughter to me. His seventeen-year-old son, Carlo, was handsome and bright, everything I could want in a son, I argued to myself.

After months of seeing doctors and trying to find a way, I finally gave in to the inevitable and had a hysterectomy in March of 1989. Joe stayed by my side, not only through the traumatic operation, but through the more difficult emotional recovery.

Our love had blossomed again. Finally, we were ready. Joe and I were married in Indianapolis, Indiana on June 2, 1989, surrounded by my loving and wacky family, where he was easily accepted as one of the gang.

In September Joe began a new job in Manila, as president of a real estate marketing and managing company. I agreed to put in some more time in Manila to give him time to recover financially and emotionally. Mutual support had become the keystone of our relationship.

33 A GOD FORSAKEN PLACE:
Eastern Samar, October 1989

THROUGHOUT THAT SULTRY Eastern Samar day on the River Delores, whose name means River of Sorrow, the words of an old American spiritual kept running through my head:

> The River Jordan is chilly and cold.
> It chills the body, but not the soul.
> All my trials, Lord, soon be over.
> Too late, my brother.
> Too late, but never mind.
> All my trials, Lord, soon be over.

I'm not very religious in the traditional sense, but throughout those bleak days at the end of the earth in Eastern Samar, biblical allusions kept coming to my mind.

Eastern Samar was the saddest place I had seen in a country of sad places. It is alone on the Pacific coast, open to the fury of typhoons and tidal waves, exploited for its minerals and wood and its people abandoned, forgotten by the government, uncared for, desolate. It seemed that even God had forgotten Samar.

Emiliana (Manna) Villacarillo, the mayor of the Town of Delores at the end of the road in Eastern Samar, had welcomed me like a long-lost sister. It was immediately apparent why many of her constituents call the round woman with a ready smile "Mother."

Manna seemed to be alone in her struggle to help her people help themselves. Even her husband, Tony, who is enamored of the United States, continuously entices her to leave behind "this God-forsaken place."

Manna had made a nuisance of herself by knocking on political doors hoping for help for her people. In Borongon, the capital of Eastern Samar, and in Manila the answer was always the same, "Everybody needs money." Manna didn't make much headway. Often she couldn't even find anybody to hear her pleas. Neither did I when I tried to find responsible public officials. In Borongon I looked for the governor, only to find he was in Manila. The vice-governor was attending to his law practice in Tacloban, a three-hour drive away. The same story held true for the provincial military commander, members of the provincial board, and even the bishop. No wonder people in Eastern Samar felt abandoned.

"Why?" I asked the lone person with authority I was able to find in the capital.

"They are rarely here. Why should anybody want to live here?" he asked, with a sweeping gesture that indicated the barren hillsides, the precariously leaning shanties and the rickety jeepney with thirty people crammed inside and ten more hanging from the outside.

Eastern Samar has an annual budget of $800,000. That comes to about $2.50 per person. I thought of the ornately refurbished provincial capital building in Tarlac, Cory Aquino's home province. That project alone cost $1.2 million. I wondered how many rice seedlings that would have bought for this "God-forsaken place."

Manna Villacarillo invited me to go on a boat trip up the river through her town. Delores was lucky in only one respect: because the river serves as the town's highway, its people have far more access to markets than residents of less fortunate places. The homemade plywood pumpboats that cruise up and down the forty mile stretch of river are Delores's buses.

"What will we see when we go upstream?" I asked in the flickering candlelight over the remains of dinner in Manna's comfortable middle-class home. Electricity is only a "sometimes thing" in the populated areas of Eastern Samar.

"You'll see poverty like you have never seen," she answered, dropping her good humor abruptly. In less than a year, it seemed that all of the plagues invented by God had been dropped on the heads of the people of Delores. And then some.

Manna chanted the sad litany of the plagues:

In November of 1988 a raging typhoon took even the smallest morsels of food from the mouths of the subsistence farmers. It destroyed 80 percent of the rice crop, uprooted tubers and knocked the ripening fruits from the trees.

The farmers planted again.

In January, just two months later, a flash flood wiped out dimly returning hope when it drowned 100 percent of the tender new rice crop and hundreds of carabaos (water buffalo). Without their carabaos, the farmers could not plow their land.

Disheartened, but determined, they planted again, in ground tilled by their own stamping feet, using the last of their hoarded pesos to buy new rice seedlings.

In June, just when harvest was in sight, a plague of stinkbugs sucked the life from 70 per cent of the maturing grains of rice virtually overnight.

There was nothing left to eat. A lucky family might be able to scrape together one meal of roots and leaves a day. Families foraged in the forest for tubers, snails, anything edible. A little girl died after a snake bit her during a foraging expedition. A boy died from eating a poisonous tuber. Government relief was minimal and lackadaisical. The farmers' skinny children became scarecrows. Their bellies began to balloon.

Then the fourth plague hit. The children began to die. A measles epidemic in July killed 137 children in fourteen of Delores's forty six villages. A further count was impossible because of the ruggedness of the terrain in the remotest areas, but it is fair to guess that the death toll was two or even three times what Manna Villacarillo was able to document.

Manna proposed to take me to Jicontol, one of the hardest-hit villages, three hours up the river and a two-mile overland hike to the village.

I have seen so much in the Philippines, I couldn't imagine that it could be worse than the starving children of Negros or Smokey Mountain. But each time I think I have seen the worst, I have to invent another superlative. So it was with Jicontol.

After a three-hour river journey the pumpboat dropped us at the river's edge and we set off, barefooted because of the sucking mud. We forded a small tributary that despite its mud and the danger of leeches, was refreshingly cool. But the coolness soon turned to stickiness as we tramped barefoot over parched rice fields. Manna explained that the government was building an irrigation project, which would allow the farmers to grow two crops a year. That would double their income and release them from their dependence on the unpredictable rainfall. It seemed promising.

"How long have they been building this irrigation project?" I asked Manna as I barely missed stepping barefoot into a *carabao* pie as big as a bushel basket.

"Since 1981," she answered cheerfully.

I scowled at her in disbelief.

She winked and crossed her heart and hoped to die without breaking her purposeful stride over the partially complete irrigation dike.

"Are there any NPAs around here?" I asked, shading my eyes with a gritty hand as I scanned the mountains that ringed us.

"Oh, of course. They are everywhere," Manna answered. "Maybe we'll even see some. They often walk along with me and we share ideas when I visit the barrios."

Manna explained that the NPA and the military in Delores seemed to have come to an uneasy peaceful coexistence: "The NPA stays upstream and the military stays downstream. Nobody gets killed that way."

She pointed to an abandoned building a mile away across the valley. "That used to be part of a military camp, but they scared the people up here so much that this whole area was abandoned in the late seventies. I made the military get out so the people could go back to their farms."

The "peaceful co-existence" ended a month after my visit to Jicontol. The military began a massive counterinsurgency campaign there that frightened the people from their homes and on the journey three hours down the river to the population center. To add to the miseries of the people of Jicontol, the military is considering re-establishing its camp there.

We walked in silence for a while until we came to a small schoolhouse. The teacher said there had been no books since the flood washed them all away. Well, no, she admitted, there weren't any desks, either. Or chairs, for that matter.

The government mandates that all instruction must be in English or Pilipino, the national language. The people of Eastern Samar speak Waray, which has no similarity to either English or Pilipino.

I turned to a group of children crowding in the door and chucked a little boy under the chin.

"What's your name?" I asked him in English.

Doubt crept into his bright eyes. He looked to his companions for help.

I repeated my question slowly.

They all shrugged.

I turned to the teacher and asked how many years the boy had spent in school.

"Three," she replied wearily.

The teacher translated my question into Waray. All the children jumped up and down, eager to tell me their names. I wondered what the hell they were learning in school.

We walked on to Jicontol, where the people greeted Manna like a queen. We were offered coconut water under the shade of the village shed as we passed pleasantries in typical Filipino style.

Then Manna called out one of the men.

Remegio Incio sat on a bench in front of us like an errant school boy. He was only twenty-six years old, but his face betrayed a lifetime of grief.

Remegio struggled to fight back the tears as he told us of the deaths of three of his four children two months before. "They just got sick. I didn't know what to do. There was no medicine, There was no food," he said with the voice of a man who has lost all hope.

It wrenched my guts.

I tried to draw the story from him as gently as possible, but I had lost all heart for the interview. I could barely hold back my own tears.

Later, Remegio squatted to one side of the gathering, staring apathetically into space while his neighbors finished his story for him. When the first child died, Remegio and his friends built a crude wooden coffin. While they were in the chapel praying over the tiny emaciated body, a second child died. While they were building the second little coffin, the third died.

Another family buried two children under the house because the parents were unable to leave the remaining sick children to give the dead ones a proper burial.

The afternoon shadows grew long. The horror stories went on and on.

The people of Jicontol were already falling victim to the fifth and most terrible plague: apathy. The despair and blank hopelessness were reflected on every face.

I had to escape, so I left Manna in the shelter talking with the village elders. During that softly quiet moment just before sunset, I wandered through the small collection of carefully built bamboo huts.

Along a short concrete drying strip, an old lady with nimble fingers meticulously collected every individual grain of her precious supply of rice that had been drying in the sun. Yes, it was all she had, she told me. The whole lot couldn't have weighed more than ten pounds.

A little girl shyly took my hand in silent offer of companionship on my tour of the village. She was wearing nothing but a faded pink T-shirt air conditioned by a dozen holes.

At the end of a walk, silhouetted by the last of the sun gleaming softly on the coconut fronds, a woman smiled the smile of a madonna and greeted me in perfect English. My diminutive guide chirped a greeting. The woman hugged the little girl with unabashed love.

"I am Eusebia Trinidad, and I am Rosita's mother." She smiled as she held out one work-calloused hand and stroked the child's hair with the other.

She clapped a ragged conical straw hat on her head and we continued our stroll together. Eusebia was gossiping about this family and that family as though I were a part of the village. I couldn't help but think of my countless sunset strolls in small-town America past white clapboard houses with lilacs in the yard. What American resident of such a clapboard house would ever suffer the loss of even one child to such a horrible death, let alone three?

Suddenly Eusebia clutched my arm and began to sob.

"Help us," she begged. "Please help my people. God has abandoned us. We don't know where to turn anymore."

I hugged her hard, allowing the afternoon's unshed tears to finally fall.

Indeed it seemed that even God had abandoned Jicontol. Eusebia's husband, who never told me his name, joined us as we began our hike back to the river.

"We haven't seen a priest here for more than a year," he confided, confirming God's abandonment.

That was shocking in a Catholic country.

"Why?" I asked.

"We can't afford it," he admitted shyly.

I was shocked again. "You can't afford a mass? Isn't mass free?" I asked, puzzled.

"Well, you see, ma'am, the priest charges 800 pesos [about forty dollars—a small fortune, far more than a month's income for two or three families] to come out here," he mumbled, embarassed by his poverty.

I thought about Jesus and the money changers in the temple. I wanted to march to the church in the town, bang my fist on the altar and confront the priest. But of course I didn't.

We made a stop at the weed-choked cemetery on our way back to town. Although it was a jumble of brambles and wildflowers somehow appropriately run riot, it was easy to see that the vast majority of the graves with crudely lettered wooden markers were tiny ones. The children are the first victims of violence wherever it strikes, I thought, as I brushed some dead leaves away from a little wooden cross that I thought read "Incio."

34 TANKS IN THE STREETS: *December 1, 1989*

THROUGHOUT NOVEMBER, the wheels of the Manila rumor mill had been grinding overtime. Someone at the American Embassy told me that they were receiving an average of a rumor and a half per day. I was getting at least that many myself. It seemed to me like the boy who cried "wolf," or perhaps it was the perfect camouflage. If you talk about coups often enough, people will either get bored, or be relieved when the inevitable finally happens.

The quality of life in Manila had deteriorated. For two months there had been daily blackouts. A public transportation shortage forced office workers to spend four to six hours a day just getting to and from work. Garbage in the streets, mammoth potholes, and skyrocketing prices were making life unbearable. Cory Aquino was being blamed.

Rumblings were coming from within the military camps. Soldiers and officers were expressing the same complaints as the ordinary citizens.

I had a sneaky feeling something was up. Again, it wasn't anything I could exactly put my finger on. It was just my intuition working. I tried to convince myself that I was simply overtired. It was time for a vacation. Joe and I planned a post-Christmas trip to a remote island paradise.

On the night of November 30, I joked to Joe that I hoped there was no coup that night since I was too tired to cover it. I was getting ready for bed at 11 P.M. when the phone rang. It was the ABC radio desk in New York. There was a wire report that General Renato de Villa, the armed forces chief of staff, had reported the arrest of several men attempting to sabotage a military communications transmitter outside of Manila. I got on the phone. De Villa's spokesman said it was another crushed coup plot. Somehow that didn't ring true. I did a radio report on the arrests, but I knew it wasn't time to sleep yet.

We started monitoring the local radio. Strangely, most of the radio stations had already signed off. The only station on the air was DZEC, a Marcos loyalist station, which was reporting troop movements near Villamor, the Air Force headquarters a few miles south of our house. I wouldn't have put it past DZEC to promote a scam, so I was cautious.

I called my old friend Colonel Vic Belo who lives inside Villamor. His sleepy voice came on the line.

"Vic," I said, "I think something is happening there at Villamor."

"What?"" he asked groggily.

"I think another coup is starting."

That woke him up.

"I'll call you back," he said hurriedly.

Just after midnight DZEC was saying that marines who had moved into the air base were wearing white diamond-shaped countersigns on their left arms. They had several tanks with them. I made a few more calls. Something was definitely up.

Vic called back.

"Don't worry about it," he said. "They are a marine blocking force because of this coup rumor. They've secured the ramp and the gates."

"Look again, Vic," I said. "Are they wearing diamond-shaped arm patches?"

"Yeah," he answered uncertainly.

"Vic, I think you have been taken over," I said quietly.

"Oh, my God," he replied.

A few minutes later he was on the phone again.

"You're right," was all he said.

Later Vic told me that the air force command team had been called to an emergency meeting shortly after eleven P.M. that night. During the meeting, General de Villa telephoned for General Jose de Leon, the air force commander. The marines had left their barracks and they might be on their way to Villamor, General de Villa warned. At that precise moment, there was a rumbling noise outside. The air force officers ran to the window. Outside were two tanks with their guns trained on the air force headquarters building. They had been taken over with no resistance at all.

I started doing radio spots, still mildly concerned that the more reputable Manila radio stations were still not on the air. I phoned a dozen contacts. All of them were aware something was up, but there was very little information. One of my contacts had driven through the army headquarters camp at Fort Bonifacio late in the evening. He had been surprised to see the marine barracks in complete blackness. "But I guess it makes sense, in hindsight," he said.

I called Frankie Joaquin, one of our ABC bureau production assistants. She was skeptical and suggested extreme caution. I was equally sure something was happening, so I proceeded.

I sat on a stool next to the bed, talking on one phone while I kept the other one open to the radio desk in New York. I knew from experience that soon it would become impossible to get an international line. Joe propped himself up in bed and monitored the radio for me. For some odd reason, it never occured to either of us to move into the office, which was only fifteen feet away and where things would have been far more organized. Perhaps it was because in those early hours, I was having a hard time coping with the reality of it. Later I thought about the stealth of the rebels in the night; while most Filipinos were sleeping soundly, they nearly lost their country.

Other local radio stations came on the air and began reporting the same story as DZEC. I felt far more comfortable.

I could feel the adrenalin beginning to pump. And I could tell that this was different from the previous military adventures.

If the marines were involved, it had to be very serious. As in the United States, the marines are the elite, highly trained, believed to be incorruptible, of unquestioned loyalty. Because of all of that trust, they had managed to walk into the air force base unchallenged. They had obtained substantial air power without firing a shot. They moved easily into the domestic and international airports, which share the same runway complex with the air force. They had surrounded the Department of National Defense at Camp Aguinaldo where General Ramos was holding a command conference. They had control of part of Fort Bonifacio, the army headquarters, and an air force base, Sangley Point, across Manila Bay. They had taken two television stations, including Channel 4, the government's network, again without resistance. There were reports that rebel troops had taken control of military camps in several parts of the country.

I knew that there must be thousands of rebels to enable them to take that much territory. They were meeting almost no resistance. It was clearly a wide conspiracy born of enormous military discontent with the way Aquino was failing to run things. Already it looked like Cory Aquino was in very hot water.

Yet the rebels remained ominously silent. I was pretty sure the rebels were still being led by the RAM (Reform the Armed Forces) group, although there were several other dissident groups including Marcos loyalists. RAM had gradually been transformed from heroes of the EDSA Revolution to villains trying to unseat the virgin queen. In fact, I knew there had always been a certain amount of villainy and power hunger in RAM. The common roots of the original RAM colonels were in their roles as torturers during the black years of martial law. I was fairly certain my friend Rex Robles had a role in the murder of Rolando Olalia in November of 1986. The handsome RAM star, Colonel Gregorio "Gringo" Honasan, and the magnetic northern commander, Colonel, then Governor, Rudy Aguinaldo were reputed to be master torturers.

But whoever the rebels were, they weren't telling us anything.

Sometime after two A.M., a call came through from the foreign desk of ABC-TV. They wanted me to do a story for "World News Tonight." That was a big break for me. The adrenalin began pumping harder. The story was nearly impossible to write because it kept changing every few minutes. I would shout a spot to radio and go back to the television script. Teresa Albor, my radio backup, carried a lot of the weight by going to the scene and filing on-the-scene reports.

Already I had the sinking feeling I was going to be stuck covering yet another dramatic story from inside the bureau.

Somehow, I made a mad dash to the Manila Hotel in time to get script approval from the show's New York producers, throw on some makeup to cover the already forming circles under my eyes and do an on-camera standup.

Just before four A.M. the president came on the air with the shocking assurance that everything was under control. That was clearly untrue. She asked the people to stand by in case she needed to call on them for People Power. I couldn't believe she was saying such things. Radio bulletins urged everyone to go to work and school as usual. That seemed to me the height of irresponsibility. There were so many areas where there had been sporadic shooting, it was impossible to tell where it would break out next. I took the head-in-the-sand posture as a signal the government was in very deep trouble and was willing to compromise the lives of its people, even its school children, to project some semblance of normalcy.

People Power was an impossible idea. Aquino had lost that magic. If she pushed the idea of People Power hard enough, the popular frustration might turn against her.

About 6:30 in the morning, the ABC story was done, the "bird" (satellite) was gone and the spot had been received in New York in ample time for World News. We all paused for a breath for the first time in more than six hours.

At the moment of that first calming breath, our cameraman, Gamay Palacios, shouted, "Oh, my God, Tora Toras!"

He grabbed the camera and ran for the window. We saw two small specks in the sky: antique T-28 trainer planes known as Tora Toras that the Philippine air force uses as bombers. We huddled on the floor, Gamay with camera rolling, and watched, stunned, while the T-28s began to circle Malacanang Palace.

We all breathed "shit!" when we heard the "pak-pak-pak" of distant gunfire. There were booms from the anti-aircraft weapons inside the palace. "Christ, I didn't know they had anti-aircraft inside Malacanang," somebody whispered, as if the Tora Tora pilots could hear us. We huddled on the floor, Gamay with the camera out the window. I held the telephone out the window so radio could to try to record some of the shooting. It was too far away. They heard nothing in New York, but we in Manila certainly did. It wasn't loud, more like the sound of shoot-em-up on a western on television in the next room. Would they really kill a president, a woman president at that? They seemed to be far more determined and far better organized than in August of 1987. The Tora Toras began to turn toward the Manila Hotel. As they flew directly toward us, I felt, in a moment, panic and complete vulnerability. Were they madmen, planning to hit the hotel too? But they circled back to the palace for another shot. It had stopped being just an exciting story and become a deadly struggle for the survival of Aquino's government, perhaps for the freedom of the Philippines, conceivably even for my own survival. For the first time I realized that despite all of Cory's shortcomings, she was a damn sight better than the RAM boys. I had a creeping fear that Cory couldn't make it.

That day we frantically revised our television spot. It set a precedent. Each day the story would change dramatically at dawn and each day, in mere minutes, we were forced to throw out a story that reflected a night's labor and patch together something new.

The airport was closed. There was no possibility of getting any other correspondent into the country. It was my ball game. Even though I was already weary, it was exciting.

The ABC-TV news shows were voracious: "Prime Time Live." "Nightline," "Morning News," "World News Tonight," It seemed like a never-ending cycle. In between there were demands from others: *Business Week, Maclean's*, Canadian Television. *The Australian. The Observer. The Melbourne Sunday Herald.* Radio Television Hong Kong, *Deutsche Welle*, German short wave radio. I had known that during the quiet period I had overextended myself in my commitments to various newspapers, magazines, radio and television. I had feared for months that I would be unable to handle the load if a major story broke, but I needed the income from a wide range of clients during the lean times. During the December coup, I took care of all of them as best I could, feeling guilty that I couldn't give my best job to each.

Early that first afternoon, we heard the sonic booms of fighter jets circling overhead. The sound didn't immediately penetrate my consciousness because I grew up hearing such booms, but the sounds of jet fighters were definitely not part of the Filipino psyche. The bureau staff was instantly alert.

"Those aren't F-5s," someone yelled. "They look like Phantoms."

We stared at each other. The Philippine air force has no F-4 fighters (Phantoms). The jets had to be American.

It couldn't be.

It was.

The Americans had rescued Cory at her darkest moment. I wondered what price she had paid. She had made herself beholden to the American intervention for her political survival, and for her physical survival. Everyone immediately surmised the tradeoff for survival was a new lease on the U.S. military bases.

The F-4s circled ominously over Manila for the remainder of the afternoon on what the Americans called "persuasion flights." They didn't really do anything. Their mere presence speeding through the skies was spooky.

A couple of hours later someone from the L.A. Times bureau next door ran into our office, shouting that there was a huge black cloud of smoke on the horizon to the south. We crowded into their south-facing window. The Philippines' F-5s had hit Sangley Point and destroyed most of the rebel air force that had been frightened to the ground by the F-4s. The Americans insisted that the F-4s had not fired a shot. As far as I could determine that was probably true, but the local press had a heyday with unsubstantiated and hysterical reports that the Americans were killing Filipinos.

It seemed that the American intervention would end the battle, if not the war. But the rebels hung on and on. They obviously had a well-planned multiphased strategy.

Aquino crowed victory on Friday afternoon, but she was far from victorious. As quiet fell with dusk, there was a wary standoff and no sleep as little events tickled the fancy of radio and television almost throughout the night.

Just before dawn Saturday, the rebels marched out of Villamor and Fort Bonifacio and began moving to consolidate their forces at Camp Aguinaldo, the military headquarters. We had some eerie pictures of snipers in buildings along EDSA and tracer bullets going back and forth.

There was sympathy for the rebels at Camp Aguinaldo. They reinforced their numbers inside with little resistance. There had been some skirmishes inside Aguinaldo, but there was a great deal of confusion about who was on what side.

There had been some activity at the port, just behind the Manila Hotel. I thought it was logical that the rebels would want port facilities because they would probably try to bring in reinforcements from other parts of the country. That meant that the hotel and the bureaus of all of the American television networks might be vulnerable to a rebel occupation. I wondered if they were sophisticated enough to know where we were and how easy it would be to take journalists hostage. There was a squad of soldiers hanging around the hotel, but they appeared to be loyal.

At noon Saturday Aquino claimed victory again and told the last holdouts to "surrender or die." I couldn't see any reason behind her statement: she was still in serious trouble; it was far from over.

Senator Juan Ponce Enrile, Cory's nemesis, called his own press conference at mid-afternoon at the Hotel Intercontinental in the affluent Makati commercial district, about six miles from the Manila Hotel. As Enrile denied any involvement in the coup, rebel soldiers took up what appeared to be protective positions around the hotel. Tanks began to rumble incongruously up Ayala Avenue, the main street, which was already decorated for Christmas with millions of twinkling lights. Rebels moved determinedly toward obviously preassigned positions in high-rise apartment and office buildings.

My imagination was stretched even further. Makati, the home of the rich, was in the hands of rebels. If I put aside my rising certainty that Cory was about to lose her government, I could see it was a brilliant strategy. They had control of the high ground, literally. There were thousands of affluent residents and tourists and, more significantly in the international eye, thousands of Americans, British, Canadians, Australians, and other nationals living in the condominiums and staying in the four luxury hotels in the new rebel zone. All of the civilians had become de facto hostages, since there was shooting in the streets and no one dared go outside. And there were five large supermarkets and countless restaurants in the rebel controlled area. They could hole up for weeks.

I called people I knew who lived in the area. Teresa called some hotels and asked to talk to American guests. Over the next few hours we established an invaluable network of contacts who drew us into the drama and emotion of being trapped in the midst of a war most of them didn't understand.

One friend, John James (not his real name), a retired American colonel who has lived in the Philippines for ten years, was trapped in his apartment inside the rebel zone. John, who made his career in Vietnam, could see nothing, but by sound he could identify exactly what was being fired and where it was coming from. I talked to him on the phone every couple of hours. John, as someone quite used to living under fire, was calm and analytical for the first couple of days until he ran out of whiskey and cigarettes. Then the pressure even got to him. Over the next few days, there were times when John and I couldn't even hear each other, the shooting was so close to his apartment.

Those who had never heard a shot fired in anger didn't handle it as well.

There was a marvelously funny woman from Brooklyn who was inside the Peninsula Hotel. A friend from the Australian Embassy was there as well. And there was a businessman from New Jersey inside the Intercontinental who had formed a close relationship with one of the rebel soldiers. They all kept me very much in touch with what was happening inside the no-man's land, sharing their feelings and fears. There was a strong bond of dependency among us. I was their link with the outside world because they had virtually no information. Unlike during the peaceful revolution of 1986, all of the radio broadcasts were in Tagalog. Those who didn't understand the native language were quite literally in the dark. In retrospect, I think that was one of the major failures of the Western governments, who never requested the radio stations to broadcast situation reports in English from time to time until it was far too late.

Threats against Americans were being broadcast by local radio stations. The threats allegedly came from rebels angered by the American military intervention, which had been invisible since the Friday afternoon F-4 flights.

At dawn Sunday the government launched the battle for Camp Aguinaldo. Since the rebels had been knocked out of the air, the government could, with impunity, use air power to blast away at troops on the ground. And they did. Also, from the air, it was impossible to tell rebels from loyal troops. They killed ten of their own soldiers who were on patrol in a suburb adjacent to the camp.

Unfortunately, their aim wasn't too good, so they demolished many of their own buildings. Equally unfortunately, civilians in their plush homes didn't know what to do. Some of them ran and were mowed down.

There are a number of images from those few days that have imprinted themselves on my mind.

Perhaps the strongest is one of a ferocious tank battle taking place at almost the precise spot where the nuns knelt in front of the tanks in 1986. Less than thirty feet away, scores of spectators watched the battle like they were watching a tennis match.

Most of the casualties were civilians. Maybe they had seen too many war movies and had no sense of the reality of the situation. At least 70 percent of approximately 100 people who died during the nine-day coup attempt were civilians. At least ten soldiers were killed by friendly fire. That leaves only twenty "real" casualties among the soldiers in nine days of fighting.

The low casualty count says something about the seriousness of the soldiers who were supposed to be fighting each other. Although the war was noisy, it was not very bloody considering the heavy firepower that was being used. There were antitank weapons, bazookas, 90 mm, 50 cal. machine guns, and I don't know what all. I am not an ordnance expert, but I learned to identify the different types of gunfire by listening over John James's phone. After it was all over I expected to see buildings half falling down, looking like bites had been taken out of them. In fact I was surprised there was so little damage. There were a few broken windows, some bullet holes in walls. Nothing too dramatic. I called John on the phone.

"John," I asked, "have you surveyed the damage?"

"Yeah," he said vaguely.

"As someone who has spent a lot of time in Vietnam and under fire, do you think the damage matches the type of shooting that you heard in Makati?" I pressed.

"No way. They had to have been firing in the air," he insisted.

On Sunday afternoon Cory and Ramos claimed victory again and said all that was left was "mopping up." I was once again amazed. There was still a tank battle going on in a suburb less than a mile from Camp Aguinaldo, but the rebels had been cleaned out of the headquarters camp. The rebels were in complete control of the heart of Makati. How could the president say it was all over? I said in several stories that Aquino was losing credibility every minute she claimed to be in control when that clearly was not true. Those reports made the palace unhappy.

By Sunday night I was completely exhausted. I had slept for a total of four hours since Wednesday night. I didn't know how much longer I could hold on. There were rumors the airport would open Monday afternoon. I prayed those rumors were true. There were hundreds of correspondents in Hong Kong clamoring to be on the first flight and they would take some of the weight off my back.

Monday was undoubtedly the worst day. Early Monday morning a death threat was phoned in to the bureau. A woman said that the American networks had been "tasked with convincing Aquino to resign before the end of the day or we will begin killing Americans."

I felt a moment's fear. I had guessed this might be coming, but there was nothing we could do about it. After asking the desk in New York to pass on the information to the network powers that be, I almost forgot about the death threat.

An hour or so later I sat on the stairway outside the bureau with Maggy Sterner of NBC, sipping coffee and exchanging feelings. Maggy confessed that she was a little scared, too, after the death threats came.

As if on cue, Gabby Tabunar of CBS passed by.

"Gabby, did you get your death threat yet?" I called down the hall.

Without missing a beat, Maggy pointed out how far downhill we were all sliding. She asked, "Whatever happened to 'Good Morning'?" as the exhausted Gabby stared at us blankly and we collapsed in nearly hysterical laughter.

Monday's shooting began again at dawn and intensified throughout the day and into the night. The civilians inside the zone were becoming increasingly panicky, especially in view of the escalating number of reports that the rebels were preparing to take American hostages. Several foreigners had bolted for safety. Some had made it; a few had been caught in the crossfire.

My newfound friends inside the zone insisted that the rebels were being extremely polite and non-threatening. But my contact in the Intercon had bolted to freedom on Sunday night. He had been warned by his rebel buddy that there were discussions about taking American hostages.

Reinforcements finally arrived on Monday afternoon in the midst of a great uproar about foreigners being shot. Bill Redeker, the ABC correspondent from Tokyo, was aboard the first plane in from Tokyo. Mark Litke was on a plane from Hong Kong a few hours later. Finally the pressure was easing. Correspondents for *The Observer* and *The Australian* also arrived, reducing the load a little more. It was a good thing. I felt like a pressure cooker about to blow up.

I thought I would finally get a few hours of sleep but, as it turned out, the panic rose to a fever pitch among my friends inside the zone. Although I was supposed to be sleeping, I got calls almost every hour throughout the night. One of the men inside the Peninsula was becoming emotionally unstable. John James was marshalling a group of women and children in the hallway of his building. He said it was at least as noisy as the Tet offensive. The woman from Brooklyn was furious with the American embassy for not getting her out. I felt like an emotional sponge for all of their fears.

In the meantime Joe was having his own problems. In August he had taken a new job as president of a company marketing and managing condominium projects. It pulled him out of the eighteen month doldrums which followed the death of Kiko. Finally, we felt comfortable with him living in the Philippines full time. And he felt enormously fulfilled and challenged by the new job. The real estate boom made the business quite successful—for three months. All of that came to a crashing halt with the coup. He was again desolate and hurt. It was not only a political disaster for him, but a personal disaster as well.

And he was left to sit and brood over the enormity of it all while I worked endless hours. There was barely a minute for me to spare for him even though he was hurting so badly.

With the opening of the airport, at least I could find a few minutes here and there to phone him or give him a hug when he stopped by. We both needed it.

Joe was there in the bureau with me on Monday when a report came through that there was fighting in Santa Mesa. That's a mile from the palace but, more importantly to both of us, it is where Joe was born and where most of his family still lives. Suddenly, my professional detachment vanished. I descended into a raw fear about the possible destruction of people I love. I had somehow been able to divorce myself from my feelings and simply report the story. It was different from the 1986 People Power Revolution beause that was so much more clearly a question of good guys versus bad guys. This time there was no such clarity. But with the news of the fighting in Santa Mesa, the reality of the coup attempt came home to me with a rush.

My relationship with the Philippines is one of love and hate. I felt tremendously disappointed and betrayed by the failure of the Aquino government. I see the things that are wrong and I want to help change them. Joe feels even more passionately about the shortcomings of his government and his people precisely because it is his homeland. The Philippines had been my home for nearly six years. I couldn't imagine what it would be like on a very personal level to live in a Philippines in the hands of a military government that would probably be even more repressive than Marcos.

The mental images of all the killings ran through my head. The tears fell, born of exhaustion and fear, and compassion for Joe's inner torment. I knew that despite all of Cory Aquino's inadequacies as a leader there was no better alternative at the moment.

After the violence of Monday, Tuesday was quiet. There was a ceasefire while an incredibly bold undersecretary for tourism negotiated with the rebels for the evacuation of the civilians in the rebel zone.

The Wednesday morning exodus came without warning. The buses rolled into the hotel driveways; the guests jumped aboard. I called John James to tell him the evacuation had begun and the officials promised they would get to the condominiums within a couple of hours.

"Fuck that. I'm outta here," he shouted as he slammed down the phone that had been his lifeline to the outside world for five days.

When the civilians were safely evacuated, and with the government troops with big guns pointed at the rebels, and the rebels likewise, a few foolhardy journalists, including an ABC crew, sneaked in the back door to the Intercon.

Finally, we got an in-depth look at a leader. Colonel Rafael Galvez, the field commander of the Makati rebels, looked good. He had been well briefed. Galvez talked a good game. He said there was no intent to harm foreigners. Yet Galvez was also caught in an obvious and outrageous lie. He said that the rebels merely accidentally retreated to Makati while they were attempting to go to Fort Bonifacio nearby. A red flag went up in my mind. I knew that was an impossible lie, since many people had reported stockpiles of food and ammunition already in Makati buildings when the takeover began. If Galvez was lying about that, what other lies was he spreading?

After another day of negotiations, the rebels decided to "return to barracks." They insisted they were not giving up. In fact—they had won the day. They had made their point and they had captured the attention of the world for those six days. It took three more days to pry loose the last holdouts from Cebu, but there were strong indications that there would be little, if any, punishment for the rebels from a military that was hopelessly divided. Another coup was inevitable and everyone was betting on a rebel success the next time around.

I had received herograms from Roone Arledge and Peter Jennings for my performance during the coup and I knew it was time to capitalize on my rising star status. Rising stars may plummet very fast in the broadcast industry.

I had become weary of the day-to-day fight of being a free-lancer. I was tired of being a bill collector and a salesman. I was tired of the economic insecurity. I simply wanted to be a journalist and leave the business stuff to somebody else.

So, to make it simple, four days after the December coup ended, I flew off to New York and negotiated a contract with ABC-TV. The plan was for me to stay in Manila for another six months to a year, see how things evolve, get a few good pieces under my belt for ABC and talk again. I had fantasies about being assigned as a staff correspondent in Latin America.

Five years after Mark Litke taught me how to hook up radio clips in the bathroom at the Manila Hotel, I had a contract as a network correspondent. It was a heady thrill. It wasn't a staff job yet, but I knew that with hard work and determination that day was not far off. I was excited as hell and more than a little apprehensive that I couldn't live up to the trust ABC had placed in me.

35 LESSONS FROM AN UNLIKELY TEACHER

I HADN'T SEEN DANTE BUSCAYNO for nearly two years, since the funeral of Lean Alejandro. But stories were filtering back that my old friend Dante was involved in a surprising new venture: organizing a farmer's cooperative. He was working within the system to change the system, nonviolently. And it was working.

It was time to see Dante again. I had missed our long talks and his earthy insights. From what I had heard recently of Dante, it seemed that he was learning something that I once knew and lost. My life was becoming increasingly violent. I have always believed that we attract to us what we really want in life. What was I doing wrong?

The frustrations of everyday life were becoming monotonous. It seemed that I screamed at people ten times a day. I was impatient with secretaries, shopgirls, and workmen, sometimes for a reason but never to any productive end. All I got out of my tirades was elevated blood pressure and more resistance from my victims. It seemed like I was swimming against the tide of an increasingly exasperating culture.

I listened to some journal tapes I had kept when I first left the States in 1984. My voice was soft, my eagerness was contagious. I seemed so young and naive. I looked at my passport photo then. My face looked young; I hardly recognized myself. Two vertical furrows now embellish my brow, born of constant scowling in disbelief. Was the Philippines turning me into a witchy old woman? Or was I turning myself into a witchy old woman?

Over those years I changed. I made myself a success in my profession. I married a wonderful man. I had a beautiful stepdaughter and stepson. Life looked good.

Yet I was not content. I always thought that contentment comes with age, but I found myself on a continuous emotional roller coaster, rising to ecstasy, plumm- eting to depression. It made life full and rich, but I wondered what had happened to the woman I once was. Where was the serene woman who taught yoga and adopted orphaned cats and nursed orphaned mice back to health so they could burrow into her walls? Where was the woman who basked in the sun drinking wine with her best friend under the northern New York summer sky? I had a wonderful, gentle and loving husband, yet I was churning myself into daily furies of which he sometimes was the innocent victim.

I had a strong sense of not belonging anywhere. I have heard that this is a common malady among those of us who live outside our homelands for very long. Joe suffers from the same cultural dislocation because he lived for so many years in Indonesia, Vietnam, and the U.S. I no longer felt comfortable in America. I had become much too intense for most of my old friends, yet the Philippines is not my country or my culture. I don't have a home anymore, except maybe wherever Joe and my laptop computer are (in that order). I found that, by leaving the States, I don't fit anywhere anymore.

I have become harder, more worldly, bolder, said my old friend Christine Burkard-Eggleston after our wedding.

Back in the Philippines, I was becoming distrustful. It pained me to see myself becoming violent in a way I had once abhorred. One night I got off a bus in a seedy neighborhood in Pasay, suburban Manila. I was carrying my computer and all of the disks for this book. My Swiss Army knife was ready in my pocket in case there were any untoward events. I had met a young German tourist on the bus. When he asked for directions to a pension near our house, I offered to drop him off. A cruising taxi picked us up soon enough, but in just a few seconds I realized that the driver wasn't taking the usual route. I asked where he was going.

The surly young many answered, "Shortcut, ma'am."

"That's not a short cut," I snapped as he turned into a dark and flooded street.

"Oh, yes it is, ma'am," he insisted.

"It is not," I replied, seeing the handwriting on the wall. We were about to be robbed if I didn't do something drastic. It was a common scam, but it hadn't happened to me before and I didn't intend for it to happen. Ever.

I calmly pulled my Swiss Army knife out of my pocket, opened the one-and-one-half-inch blade and lightly touched it to the taxi driver's neck.

"Turn around and back out of this street RIGHT NOW," I snarled.

"But ma'am . . ."

I applied a slight pressure with the knife.

"I am honest," he protested.

"I know all of these games. Back up now," I said, at once furious and frightened.

The German tourist's eyes were as big as saucers.

The taxi slowly backed up but I kept the knife against the driver's neck.

"You're a son of a bitch," I raged as I dragged my bag and the stunned young German out of the taxi.

I couldn't believe I had actually pulled a knife on another human being!

What was happening to me? I needed to talk to someone about violence and changing life directions and I looked to the most unlikely source possible, Commander Dante, the founder of the communist New People's Army.

I contacted Dante. One sultry evening I drove up to Tarlac to see him in his placid new place, planted in the midst of verdant rice fields, surrounded by admiring peasants and looking happier than I had ever seen him.

"Kathleen!" he greeted me. His face glowed with pleasure as he introduced me to the office staff as his "forever friend." I realized at that moment it was true. I was his forever friend, as he was mine.

We sat chattering excitedly, drinking beer in the country twilight on a bench outside his office. There was so much to talk about, so much of life lived in the past two years. The cicadas burst into joyous song as the light faded.

"I heard you married Joe," he admonished. There was still something of that old spark there.

I nodded.

"I am glad it was him. He is the best and he has made you more beautiful than ever," Dante said in his gallant and sometimes stilted English.

Dante had irrevocably severed his ties with the communist underground just a few months after he was shot. He said that the movement he fathered had lost touch with political realities. With the new government, it was time for new tactics and new creativity. The NPA had opened its doors to criminals, much the same as his first army, the old Hukbalahaps. When his comrades disagreed, Dante quietly and sadly went his own way.

He had run for office. He had lost. He had made all of the political speeches that were necessary. Finally, Dante knew it was time for him to stop talking and start working. He went home to Tarlac and painstakingly began to form his farmer's cooperative.

"This was what I was always supposed to do, before the circumstances forced me to go underground," he said.

Dante was getting his hands dirty working side by side with the peasants. It sounds corny, but Dante was literally beating swords into plowshares. As a result, the NPA had virtually disappeared from Tarlac, its birthplace and five thousand farmers were earning a decent living.

Dante's conversion from warrior to entrepreneur was causing a media stir.

Later, in the flickering lamplight of a modest country pub, we began to talk of feelings, fears, and futures.

Our paths had been so different. I was the pacifist, the one seeking to stop violence. Dante was born of violence. Again I found myself in awe of his wisdom.

I pressed him on the need for armed struggle in the Philippines. I reminded him of the sugar cane cutter from Negros at Hacienda Luisita who had lost four children to starvation. I reminded him of the years, the blood, the tears he had invested struggling for justice in the mountains. I reminded him of our intertwined and bloody hands after the ambush. Had anything really changed? Was he helping a few only to turn his back on the rest? Would the situation ever warrant the use of force again?

Dante was firm. His eyes were serene in the lamplight as he explained that the time for armed struggle had passed. The time had come for hard work and dedication to the common good. What he was doing was small, but it was working.

"Maybe we have to save the world one human being at a time," he said as he took another sip of cold San Miguel beer.

The rebel army commander was amused to hear my militaristic stance. He knew of my days as an anti–Vietnam War protester and my roots in non-violence.

I told him about the knife and the taxi driver.

"What is happening to me?" I asked him, some of the pain coming to the surface.

"There are so many kinds of violence. Violence is around us all every day. We cannot escape it. What is important is how we make our individual decisions to cope with it," he said gently.

We sat in silence for a moment, looking at the black outlines of the mountains where Dante and his rebel band once retreated at night, relaxing ever so slightly under the cover of darkness and rejoicing that they had escaped death for yet another day.

Could it be that Commander Dante will rekindle my faith in non-violence?

He understands it far better than I.

I have traveled the world searching for the roots of violence. I have wept over the bodies of friends. I have been griped with fear for my own life. I have lived in the heart of violence and survived. But I still don't understand it.

EPILOGUE

IT'S NOT EASY TO WRITE by candlelight, but that's what I spend a lot of time doing lately. We've been without electricity as much as nine hours a day in the past couple of months. Sometimes there is no water. I spend several precious hours each day stuck in monumental traffic jams. Our little backwater street is so filled with garbage that I phone the city's "complaint action line" nearly every day. They don't even bother to answer the phone most of the time now. No one has bothered to rebuild the military headquarters building bombed during the 1987 coup attempt or the Philippine Constabulary headquarters destroyed by the 1989 coup attempt. If the military has lost its self respect, can the country have any heart?

Last week, on the eve of the opening of bases negotiations between the U.S. and the Philippines, another American soldier was murdered, this time at Subic Bay Naval Base. He was the sixth American killed by the NPA in the past year. Last night, two young American airmen were murdered outside Clark Air Base. The NPA is now accused of killing eight Americans in the past thirteen months. Most of my American friends, even the non-governmental employees, are being very cautious about where they go now.

I am cautious. Sometimes, I am scared. In February, I got the shit scared out of me again during a drive north to Pagasinan. It was about ten in the morning when I passed the turnoff to the American Clark Air Base. A battered red Lancer overtook my lovingly cared-for 1978 Mitsubishi like it was standing still. As the Lancer pulled beside me, it paused. The four men inside scrutinized me carefully. Three of them were cradling M-16s and the fourth was resting his M-79 grenade launcher on the window ledge. After they looked me over, they drove on past. I don't have any idea who they were, but it was frightening enough to realize there are several possibilities. They could be military men being macho. They could be members of a private army. They could be NPAs, who had just announced an eighteen-month offensive against Americans.

Life in the Philippines is no longer fun. There is no question that Joe and I will leave the Philippines soon.

If anything, my feelings of disappointment and my pessimism about the future of the Philippines have deepened. It has become abundantly clear that Cory Aquino does not have the ability to lead her country out of the poverty and violence which are swallowing it.

Surprisingly, six months after the bloody December coup, Aquino is still holding on to power by her fingernails. Some people think she will muddle through the last two years of her term while the Philippines sinks slowly to hell.

Election fever grips the Filipinos early and two years is not a long time for presidential campaigns. Could it be possible we will have two years of peace? I doubt it. Most of the senators and congressmen plus a few free-lance politicians are already running in a presidential election which may never happen. Even if Aquino does hang on for two more years, there is such a leadership vacuum here that no one has yet been able to name a candidate who could help this country. I am paralyzed with boredom about election speculation.

Others think the next coup will be a bloodless one because people will be so fed up with the power shortages, the water shortages, the skyrocketing prices and the endless traffic jams that they will gladly support anyone who wants to throw out Aquino's directionless government. The military rebels are far from quiet. It seems inevitable that there will be another effort to throw Aquino out. It could come tomorrow, next month or a year away, but my gut feeling is that the thousands of soldiers holed up in secret camps near Manila are not ready to give up.

Still others think that the Philippines must suffer a bloody revolution which will cleanse it of its pervasive corruption, its selfishness, and its suffocating class system. They think the Filipinos did not pay a high enough price for their freedom.

I honestly don't know what to think anymore. A diplomat friend recently reminded me of something I told her shortly after her arrival.

We were sitting in my living room, sipping San Miguel beers, just three days after she landed in the Philippines. She had that bewildered expression on her face caused by jet lag, the newcomer's inevitable intestinal upsets—and an overload of information.

"I am completely confused," she complained. "I studied all the country data on the Philippines. I know who's who, and what's what, but this place completely defies logic. I don't understand anything."

I took a thoughtful sip of my beer before I answered her. I thought about my years here and my growing fears that the dearth of facts in the Philippines is transforming me into a rumor monger rather than a reporter. I realized that I have stopped considering the Philippines a serious story. That's dangerous. I have become too cynical. It is time to move on. I don't know where, I don't know how. But I am a risk-taker and a survivor.

"Don't worry," I told my new friend. "This place becomes more confusing every day. You understand more about the Philippines now, after only three days, than you will ever understand, even if you stay here for the rest of your life."

Manila, May 14, 1990